STUDY GUIDE
WITH POWER NOTES

FINANCIAL
ACCOUNTING
A Business Process Approach

STUDY GUIDE
WITH POWER NOTES

Study Guide
Nancy P. Lynch & Nancy C. Ruhe
West Virginia University

Power Notes
Jane L. Reimers & Amy Whitaker

FINANCIAL ACCOUNTING
A Business Process Approach

Jane L. Reimers

Pearson
Education

Upper Saddle River, New Jersey 07458

Executive editor: Deborah Hoffman
Managing editor: Alana Bradley
Production editor: Wanda Rockwell
Manufacturer: Courier, (Bookmart Press, Inc.)

ISBN 0-13-035769-3

10 9 8 7 6 5 4 3 2

Contents

Introduction

This Study Guide is intended to supplement, not replace, *Financial Accounting: A Business Process Approach* by Jane L. Reimers. No Study Guide is a substitute for doing your instructor's assignments and regularly attending class.

How to Use the Study Guide

The best way to use this Study Guide is:

- After reading the textbook and completing any assignments from your instructor, you can review the major concepts summarized in the Study Guide's **Chapter Highlights** section.

- Then work the **Featured Exercise**, which applies these major concepts. Check your solution against the solution provided and make a note of any errors you have made. Return to the textbook to review the areas where you had difficulties.

- Once you have mastered the material in the chapter, use the Study Guide's **Review Questions and Exercises** as a self-test. Do not make the mistake of looking at the answers before doing the entire section. Make note of any questions or exercises that you were unable to answer quickly and confidently. Then check your answers, marking any that you missed.

- Before your class test, reread the **Chapter Highlights** and your notes from class. Then go over all your class assignments, paying particular attention to items you missed earlier. Finally, redo the **Featured Exercise** and **Review Questions and Exercises**. Go back to the textbook and study the materials that deal with the items that you were unable to answer quickly and confidently.

Acknowledgments

We appreciate the excellent job that Jane L. Reimers has done in writing a readable, student friendly text that covers the basic material for every student, including those who are not accounting majors. Jane has provided enormous, enthusiastic support for our efforts. We are grateful for the help of Amy Whitaker, Prentice-Hall Project Manager, and Robert H. Bauman, Prentice-Hall accuracy checker. We would also like to thank our Chairperson, Robert S. Maust, for his continuous support and encouragement. Finally, our families deserve some appreciation for putting up with fast-food meals and minimal attention while we worked on this project.

CHAPTER 1
BUSINESS: WHAT'S IT ALL ABOUT?

Chapter Overview

This chapter will help you to understand what a business does and how it is organized. You will be introduced to two major business processes: the acquisition/payment process and sales/collection process. The accounting information from these business processes is summarized and presented in four basic financial statements. You should gain an understanding of who needs the accounting information reflected in these financial statements.

Chapter Highlights

1. A business provides goods or services either to make a profit (**for-profit** organization) or just to help people (**not-for-profit** organization). All businesses carry out the same processes. In the **acquisition/payment process**, a business obtains inputs and pays for them. In the **conversion process**, a business adds value to these inputs and creates outputs. In the **sales/collection process**, a business sells outputs (goods or services) and collects cash.

2. There are four types of businesses:
(a) a **manufacturing** company makes products;
(b) a **merchandising** company buys products (from a manufacturer if it is a **wholesaler** or from a wholesaler if it is a **retailer**), adds value to the products and sells them to its customers;
(c) a **service** company does something of value for its customers such as consulting; and
(d) a **financial services** company adds value for its customers by providing monetary services such as lending, investing, insuring, or advising.

3. All businesses have owners, either individuals, groups of individuals or governments. There are three general forms of ownership:

- A **sole proprietorship** has only one owner. For tax and legal purposes, the owner and the business are considered one and the same. Profits from a sole proprietorship are taxed on the owner's individual income tax return. The owner is responsible for all debts and may have to use personal assets to pay business debts. Even though the law considers the owner and the business to be one, the financial records of the business must be kept separate from the owner's personal financial records. Financial information from a sole proprietorship is not available to the public.

- A **partnership** has two or more owners with the details of their rights and responsibilities specified in the **partnership agreement**. The law considers the partners and the business to be one, just as it does with the sole proprietorship. The partners have unlimited liability for business debts and malpractice. A special form of partnership, called a Limited Liability Partnership (**LLP**), is available in some states and limits an individual partner's malpractice liability.

- A **corporation** has one or more owners, called **stockholders** or **shareholders**. It is considered a separate legal entity that is responsible for its own debts and pays its own taxes. The **Securities and Exchange Commission (SEC)** oversees the activities and financial reporting of corporations whose stock is publicly traded. Advantages of the corporate structure are (a) stockholders can own a small portion of the business allowing them to diversify risk by investing in various other businesses, and (b) owners have limited liability. Disadvantages are (a) separation of management and ownership means that managers may make decisions that are not in an owner's best interest; and (b) corporate profits are taxed twice, once on the corporation's own tax return and a second time on the individual owner's tax return when he or she receives a distribution of corporate profits (called **dividends**).

4. Business events, called **transactions**, should be recorded from the company's point of view. Each of these **exchanges** involves the company getting something by giving up something. **Resources** are the items exchanged, **events** are the actual transactions, and **agents** are the people involved.

- Some transactions in the acquisition/payment process include: (a) getting owner **contributions** in exchange for giving company stock; (b) getting cash now in exchange for giving a promise to pay cash back in the future; (c) getting product for resale (**inventory**) in exchange for giving cash; (d) getting services that the company needs in exchange for giving cash; and (e) when a company repays its loans, getting back the company's previous promise to pay cash (see (b) above) in exchange for giving cash.

- Often the acquisition/payment process begins with a request for an item or service (a **purchase requisition**). The purchasing department sends a **purchase order** to the selected **vendor** (seller). A **receiving report** documents that the goods have been received. After the vendor sends an **invoice** (bill), all of these documents are compared and payment is sent to the vendor.

- A transaction in the sales/collection process includes getting an account receivable or cash in exchange for giving the customer the company's product.

- The sales/collections process begins with a customer order (**sales order**). **Credit sales** require approval since the customer will not be paying until later. A **picking slip** or **stock request** is sent to the warehouse and a **packing slip** is prepared and the goods are sent to the shipping department. Finally, the billing department compares these documents, sends a **sales invoice** to the customer and records the **accounts receivable**, which reflects the amounts owed by customers in the accounting records.

5. The information system provides managers help in making decisions. The financial information, part of this information system, is used by regulatory agencies such as the SEC and the **Internal Revenue Service (IRS)**. The information system also provides the accounting information needed to prepare financial statements that are useful to owners, creditors, and potential investors. To help ensure that these financial statements are accurate and reliable, the statements must be **audited**, examined by **certified public accountants (CPAs)** who give an opinion on the fairness of the financial statements.

6. There are four financial statements: (a) balance sheet; (b) income statement; (c) statement of changes in owners' equity; and (d) statement of cash flows.

- The **balance sheet** shows the financial position at a particular point in time: Assets = Liabilities + Owners' equity. **Assets** are things of value owned by the business. **Liabilities** are amounts owed to others outside of the business. **Owners' equity** represents the owners' claim to the assets after the liabilities have been paid. Owners' equity is made up of **common stock** (owners' contributions) and **retained earnings** (earnings kept by the business).

- The **income statement** (also known as the **statement of operations**, **statement of earnings**, or **profit and loss (P&L) statement**) shows how well the company performed over a period of time. The period of time covered may be a month, quarter or **fiscal year** (a year in the life of a business that may or may not coincide with a calendar year). The income statement summarizes **revenues** (amounts the company has earned by providing goods or services) minus

expenses (costs incurred in earning revenues) which equals **net income** (or **net earnings**). A **single-step income statement** lists revenues first and then groups all expenses together. A **multi-step income statement** starts with sales revenue first, then subtracts cost of goods sold to get a subtotal called **gross profit** (or **gross margin**). Then other operating expenses are deducted.

- The **statement of changes in owners' equity** shows the changes over a period of time in owners' equity. A corporation's statement of changes in stockholders' equity has two separate sections, one for contributed capital and one for retained earnings. Contributed capital increases if additional shares of common stock are sold. Retained earnings increases by the amount of income the company has earned (from the income statement) and decreases by any dividends paid to owners. Ending retained earnings (which will also show up on the balance sheet) equals beginning retained earnings plus net income (from the income statement) minus dividends.

- The **statement of cash flows** summarizes the cash receipts and the cash disbursements during a period of time. The cash activities are classified into one of three sections, either operating activities, investing activities or financing activities. **Operating activities** involve changes in cash from everyday routine activities such as collecting cash from customers and paying suppliers, employees and interest. **Investing activities** involve changes in cash from buying or selling assets the company will own for a long period of time. **Financing activities** involve changes in cash from the company buying or selling its own stock, borrowing or repaying loan principal and paying dividends.

7. All businesses face **risks** (potential injuries or losses) in order to earn rewards. **Controls** are designed to minimize or eliminate these risks.

8. Accountants are no longer mere score keepers but provide a variety of professional services.

Featured Exercise

Part A: Show the effect of each of the following events on the accounting equation.

The following events took place in the month of May, 2005.	Assets =	Liabilities +	Stockholder's equity	
			Contributed capital	Retained earnings
1 Henney Penney started a farm by taking $15,000 from her savings account and depositing it in a business checking account. The business, which is a corporation, HP Farms, Inc., gives her shares of stock.				
2 On May 1, the business borrowed $5,000 on a two-year, 12% note. One month's interest will be paid in cash on the last day of each month.				
3 The company paid Old McDonald $1,000 for one month's rent on a farm.				
4 The company paid $6,000 cash for chickens to be held in inventory.				
5 Sold 2/3 of the chickens to Pop Weasel for $9,000. a. Record the sale. b. Record the cost of goods sold.				
6 Paid Tom Piper $100 for cleaning the chicken coop.				
7 The company declared and paid a $1,000 dividend to Henney Penney, its owner.				
8 On May 31, paid $50 interest on the loan.				
Totals				

Part B: Using the information from Part A, prepare the four financial statements for HP Farms, Inc.

Part C: Answer the following questions using Parts A and B.

1. In Part A, item 4, the company paid $6,000 cash for chickens to be held in inventory. Fill in the boxes in the REA model below:

"Get"

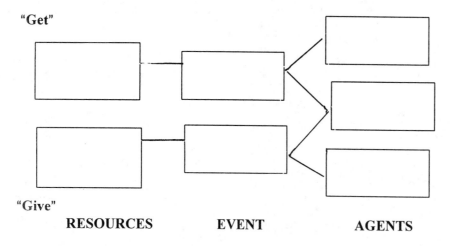

"Give"

| RESOURCES | EVENT | AGENTS |

2. For each question below, fill in the correct dollar amount and circle the correct financial statement on which it appears using the following code:

        IS for the income statement for the month ended May 31, 2005
        BS for the balance sheet at May 31, 2005
        SOCF for the statement of cash flows for the month ended May 31, 2005

a. Cash paid to suppliers for inventory of $_____ appears on the: **IS**   **BS**   **SOCF**

b. Inventory of $_____ appears on the: **IS**   **BS**   **SOCF**

c. Cost of goods sold of $_____ appears on the: **IS**   **BS**   **SOCF**

d. Total liabilities of $_____ appears on the: **IS**   **BS**   **SOCF**

e. Common stock of $_____ appears on the: **IS**   **BS**   **SOCF**

f. Net income of $_____ appears on the: **IS**   **BS**   **SOCF**

g. Retained earnings of $_____ appears on the: **IS**   **BS**   **SOCF**

h. Cash collected from customers of $_____ appears on the: **IS**   **BS**   **SOCF**

i. Sales of $_____ appears on the: **IS**   **BS**   **SOCF**

Solution

		Assets =	Liabilities +	Stockholder's equity	
	The following events took place in the month of May, 2005.			**Contributed capital**	**Retained earnings**
1	Henney Penney started a farm by taking $15,000 from her savings account and depositing it in a business checking account. The business, which is a corporation, HP Farms, Inc., gives her shares of stock.	$15,000 Cash		$15,000 Common stock	
2	On May 1, the business borrowed $5,000 on a two-year, 12% note. One month's interest will be paid in cash on the last day of each month.	5,000 Cash	$5,000 Notes payable		
3	The company paid Old McDonald $1,000 for one month's rent on a farm.	(1,000) Cash			$(1,000) Rent expense
4	The company paid $6,000 cash for chickens to be held in inventory.	6,000 Inventory (6,000) Cash			
5	Sold 2/3 of the chickens to Pop Weasel for $9,000. a. Record the sale. b. Record the cost of goods sold.	9,000 Cash (4,000) Inventory			9,000 Sales (4,000) Cost of goods sold
6	Paid Tom Piper $100 for cleaning the chicken coop.	(100) Cash			(100) Cleaning expense
7	The company declared and paid a $1,000 dividend to Henney Penney, its owner.	(1,000) Cash			(1,000) Dividends
8	On May 31, paid $50 interest on the loan.	(50) Cash			(50) Interest expense
	Totals	$22,850	$5,000	$15,000	$2,850

Part B:

HP Farms, Inc
Income Statement
For the Month Ended May 31, 2005

Revenue
    Sales $9,000
Expenses
    Cost of sales $4,000
    Rent   1,000
    Cleaning   100
    Interest   50
Total expenses   5,150
Net income $3,850

HP Farms, Inc.
Statement of Changes in Shareholder's Equity
For the Month Ended May 31, 2005

Beginning contributed capital	$ 0	
Stock issued during the month	15,000	
Ending contributed capital		$15,000
Beginning retained earnings	0	
Net income for the month	3,850	
Dividends	(1,000)	
Ending retained earnings		2,850
Total shareholder's equity		$17,850

HP Farms, Inc.
Statement of Cash Flows
For the Month Ended May 31, 2005

Cash from operating activities		
Cash collected from customers	$ 9,000	
Cash paid to vendors for chickens	(6,000)	
Cash paid for rent	(1,000)	
Cash paid for cleaning	(100)	
Cash paid for interest	(50)	
Total cash from operations		$ 1,850
Cash from investing activities		0
Cash from financing activities		
Issue of stock	15,000	
Proceeds from loan	5,000	
Dividends paid	(1,000)	
Total cash from financing activities		19,000
Net increase in cash		$20,850

8

HP Farms, Inc.
Balance Sheet
At May 31, 2005

Assets		Liabilities + Shareholder's equity	
Cash	$20,850	Note payable	$ 5,000
Inventory	2,000		
		Common stock	15,000
		Retained earnings	2,850
Total assets	$22,850	Total liabilities & shareholder's equity	$22,850

Part C:

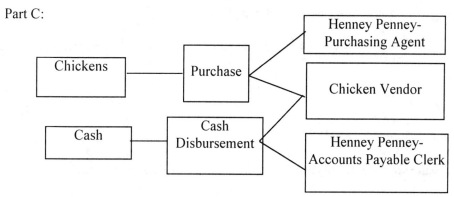

2.
a. Cash paid to suppliers for inventory of **$6,000** appears on the **SOCF**.
b. Inventory of **$2,000** appears on the **BS**.
c. Cost of goods sold of **$4,00**0 appears on the **IS**.
d. Total liabilities of **$5,000** appears on the **BS**.
e. Common stock of **$15,000** appears on the **BS**.
f. Net income of **$3,850** appears on the **IS**.
g. Retained earnings of **$2,850** appears on the **BS**.
h. Cash collected from customers of **$9,000** appears on the **SOCF**.
i. Sales of **$9,000** appears on the **IS**.

Review Questions and Exercises

Completion Statements

Fill in the blank(s) to complete each statement.

1. In the _____ process, a business obtains inputs and pays for them.

2. In the _____ process, a business adds value to these inputs.

3. In the _____ process, a business sells outputs (goods or services) and collects cash.

4. A _____ company buys products and resells them to its customers.

9

5. The _____ oversees the activities and financial reporting of corporations whose stock is publicly traded.

6. All businesses face risks in order to earn rewards. _____ are designed to minimize or eliminate these risks.

7. Financial statements must be _____ (i.e., examined) by _____ who give an opinion on the fairness of the financial statements to ensure that they are accurate and reliable.

8. The _____shows the financial position of a company at a particular point in time.

9. The _____shows revenues minus expenses.

10. The_____ shows changes in contributed capital and retained earnings over a period of time.

True/False

Indicate whether each statement is true (T) or false (F).

_____1. The income statement shows the results of operations for a specific period of time.

_____2. A picking slip or stock request is sent to the customer who then sends payment for the goods.

_____3. An asset is something of value that the company owns.

_____4. Retained earnings represents the amount owners have contributed to the business.

_____5. Dividends are a type of expense shown on the income statement.

_____6. Acquisition/payment and sales/collection are sections in the statement of cash flows.

_____7. Net income appears on both the income statement and the statement of changes in owners' equity.

_____8. There are four financial statements a company uses to report its financial condition.

Multiple Choice

Select the best answer for each question.

_____1. Which of the following groups uses accounting information about a business organization?
A. Investors
B. Managers
C. Internal Revenue Service
D. Securities and Exchange Commission
E. All of these

_____2. Which of these businesses pays taxes on its income?
A. Corporation
B. Sole proprietorship
C. Partnership
D. Two of these
E. All of these

_____3. How many of a company's four financial statements report information about the company over a specific period of time?
A. One
B. Two
C. Three
D. Four
E. None

_____4. Dividends are
A. the same as revenues.
B. distributions to owners of a corporation.
C. owners' contributions to the firm.
D. another term for each partner's share of partnership income.
E. shown on the income statement.

_____5. Which of the following is legally a separate entity from its owner?
A. Sole proprietorship
B. Partnership
C. Corporation
D. Two of these
E. All three of these

_____6. What piece of information flows from the income statement to the statement of changes in owners' equity?
A. Revenues
B. Total expenses
C. Cash
D. Net income
E. Gross margin

_____7. In which of the following businesses are the owners' or owner's personal assets at risk when the business is unable pay its debts?
A. Sole proprietorship
B. Partnership
C. Corporation
D. Two of these
E. All three of these

_____8. Which financial statement shows cash collected from customers?
   A. Balance sheet
   B. Income statement
   C. Statement of changes in owners' equity
   D. Statement of cash flows
   E. Two or more of the above.

_____9. What is the proper order of documents in the sales/collection process?
   A. Customer order, picking slip, packing slip, shipping notice, sales invoice.
   B. Purchase requisition, purchase order, receiving report, payment requisition, check.
   C. Customer order, sales invoice, slipping notice, check.
   D. Balance sheet, income statement, statement of changes owners' equity, statement of cash flows.
   E. Purchase requisition, packing slip, shipping notice, collection requisition, check.

_____10. Which of the following events increases retained earnings?
   A. Owners' contributions
   B. Purchase of inventory
   C. Sale of inventory
   D. Payment of rent
   E. Payment of interest on a loan

Exercises

1. Identify each of the following as an asset, liability, or equity account by putting an "X" in the appropriate box. Only one box should be checked for each account.

Account Title	Asset	Liability	Equity
a. Notes payable			
b. Interest expense			
c. Sales revenue			
d. Cash			
e. Dividends			
f. Cost of goods sold			
g. Inventory			
h. Common stock			
i. Rent expense			

12

2. Put an "X" in the appropriate box to indicate the financial statement that is being described. Only one box should be checked for each item.

	Balance Sheet	Income Statement	Statement of Changes in Owners' Equity	Statement of Cash Flows
a. Reports the results of operations.				
b. Reports the inflows and outflows of cash.				
c. Reports assets, liabilities and owners' equity.				
d. Reports amounts as of a specific point in time.				
e. Reports the company's financial position.				
f. Reports the economic resources owned and the claims to those resources.				
g. Summarizes revenues and expenses.				
h. Reports the activity in contributed capital and retained earnings for the period.				

3. Use the following information to fill in the missing amounts A, B, C and D in the balance sheet below.

Tim's Wares, Inc. began its first year of operations by selling common stock for $6,000. During this first year, Tim's Wares earned revenues of $10,000. Expenses were $8,000. A cash dividend of $1,000 was paid to stockholders. At the end of the year, Tim's Wares' balance sheet looked like this:

Assets			Liabilities	
Cash	$ 1,000		Notes payable	$20,000
Accounts receivable	3,000		**Owners' equity**	
Inventory	2,000		Common stock	B
Land	A		Retained earnings	C
Total assets	$ 27,000		Total liabilities & stockholders' equity	D

4. For each of the transactions below, show the effect on the accounting equation by circling one item in each column.

a. Paid $50 for a newspaper advertisement announcing an upcoming sale.

Total assets	Total liabilities	Total shareholders' equity	
		Contributed capital	Retained earnings
Increase	Increase	Increase	Increase
Decrease	Decrease	Decrease	Decrease
No effect	No effect	No effect	No effect

b. Paid $10,000 for merchandise (inventory).

Total assets	Total liabilities	Total shareholders' equity	
		Contributed capital	Retained earnings
Increase	Increase	Increase	Increase
Decrease	Decrease	Decrease	Decrease
No effect	No effect	No effect	No effect

c. Sold $5,000 of merchandise to a customer. Record the sale.

Total assets	Total liabilities	Total shareholders' equity	
		Contributed capital	Retained earnings
Increase	Increase	Increase	Increase
Decrease	Decrease	Decrease	Decrease
No effect	No effect	No effect	No effect

d. The merchandise sold in c. above originally cost the company $3,000. Record the cost of goods sold.

Total assets	Total liabilities	Total shareholders' equity	
		Contributed capital	Retained earnings
Increase	Increase	Increase	Increase
Decrease	Decrease	Decrease	Decrease
No effect	No effect	No effect	No effect

5. Tim's Wares, Inc., had the following assets and liabilities at the beginning and end of 2005:

	Assets	Liabilities	Equity
January 1, 2005	$300,000	$100,000	?
December 31, 2005	500,000	200,000	?

Compute net income for 2005 assuming no additional stock was issued and no dividends were paid.

Completion Statements

1. acquisition/payment
2. conversion
3. sales/collection
4. merchandising
5. Securities and Exchange Commission (SEC)
6. Controls
7. audited, certified public accountants (CPAs)
8. balance sheet
9. income statement
10. statement of changes in owners' (or shareholders' or stockholders') equity

True/False

1. True
2. False   A picking slip notifies the warehouse of the goods to send to the shipping department. An invoice (bill) is sent to the customer to request payment.
3. True
4. False   Contributed capital (or common stock) represents the amount owners have contributed to the business. Retained earnings represents the amounts earned and kept by the business.
5. False   Dividends are distributions of companies' profits to owners and are not expenses. Expenses are incurred to generate revenues; dividends do not generate revenues.
6. False   Acquisition/payment and sales/collection are two major business processes. Operating activities, investing activities, and financing activities are the sections in the statement of cash flows.
7. True
8. True

Multiple Choice

1. E   All of these groups and many others use accounting information.
2. A   A corporation is considered a separate legal entity and thus must pay corporate income taxes on its profits. The stockholders must then pay individual income taxes on the dividends (or distributions of these profits). The law does not recognize sole proprietors or partners as separate from the business, so the owners pay taxes only on the profits of the business and not on the distributions of these profits.
3. C   The income statement, statement of changes in owners' equity, and the statement of cash flows report business activities during the accounting period covered by these statements. The balance sheet shows the financial position of the company at a specific point in time; it does not show the activity during the period.
4. B   Dividends are distributions (not contributions) of a corporation's (not partnership's) profit that are shown on the statement of changes of stockholders' equity and the statement of cash flows.
5. C   A corporation is considered a separate legal entity. The law does not recognize sole proprietors or partners as separate from the business.
6. D   The income statement shows net income (revenues minus expenses) for the period. Net income from the income statement is needed to determine the ending retained earnings balance (beginning retained earnings plus net income minus dividends) on the statement of changes in owners' equity.
7. D   The owners of sole proprietorships and partnerships are responsible for all business debts and may have to use personal assets to pay the debts.
8. D   Cash collected from customers is in the operating activities section of the statement of cash flows.
9. A   Note that B. is the proper order for the acquisition/payment cycle and that D. lists the four audited financial statements.
10. C   Retained earnings is increased by net income. A sale increases net income and thus increases retained earnings. Although owners' contributions increase owners' equity, they increase contributed capital, not retained earnings.

Exercises

1. Account Title	Asset	Liability	Equity
a. Notes payable		X	
b. Interest expense			X
c. Sales revenue			X
d. Cash	X		
e. Dividends			X
f. Cost of goods sold			X
g. Inventory	X		
h. Common stock			X
i. Rent expense			X

2.	Balance Sheet	Income Statement	Statement of Changes in Owners' Equity	Statement of Cash Flows
a. Reports the results of operations.		X		
b. Reports the inflows and outflows of cash.				X
c. Reports assets, liabilities, and owners' equity.	X			
d. Reports amounts as of a specific point in time.	X			
e. Reports the company's financial position.	X			
f. Reports the economic resources owned and the claims to those resources.	X			
g. Summarizes revenues and expenses.		X		
h. Reports the activity in contributed capital and retained earnings for the period.			X	

3. First find the missing value for Land (A) which is $21,000 (=$27,000 - 1,000 - 3,000 - 2,000). Next find the missing value for total liabilities & stockholders' equity (D) which is $27,000 (=total assets of $27,000). Common stock (B) is equal to the $6,000 for which common stock was sold. Finally, retained earnings (C) is equal to $1,000 [=beginning retained earnings ($0 since it is the first year of business) plus net income ($2,000 = $10,000 - 8,000) minus dividends ($1,000)].

4. Total assets	Total liabilities	Total shareholders' equity	
		Contributed capital	Retained earnings
a. Decrease $(50) Cash	No effect	No effect	Decrease $(50) Advertising expense
b. No effect 10,000 Inventory (10,000) Cash	No effect	No effect	No effect
c. Increase 5,000 Cash	No effect	No effect	Increase 5,000 Sales revenue
d. Decrease (3,000) Inventory	No effect	No effect	Decrease (3,000) Cost of goods sold

5.	Assets	Liabilities	Equity
January 1, 2005	$300,000	$100,000	**$200,000**
December 31, 2005	500,000	200,000	**300,000**

Equity has increased by $100,000. Since there has been no change in contributed capital (no additional stock was issued) and there were no dividends during the year, the increase in retained earnings is due to net income equaling $100,000.

CHAPTER 2
QUALITIES OF ACCOUNTING INFORMATION

Chapter Overview

In Chapter 1, you were introduced to the four basic financial statements: the income statement; the balance sheet; the statement of changes in shareholders' equity; and the statement of cash flows. For these financial statements to be useful, the statements must be prepared in a consistent way so that a user can compare the financial statements of one accounting period to other accounting periods, as well as compare one company's financial statements with other companies'. A set of rules called **generally accepted accounting principles** (GAAP) must be followed to help ensure the financial statements are useful. In Chapter 2, you will learn how these rules are applied and the importance of accrual accounting in preparing financial statements that are useful to decision-makers.

Chapter Highlights

1. GAAP are the rules currently set by the **Financial Accounting Standards Board** (FASB). Business events and transactions have become more and more complex. In the 1970's, the **Statements of Financial Accounting Concepts** (SFAC) were issued to help provide guidance in setting new accounting rules necessary to address these complexities.

- A first step in providing financial information is to do a **cost-benefit analysis**, to determine that the cost of providing specific information is less than the benefit provided by this information. The **materiality** principle helps companies reduce the cost of financial reporting by allowing companies to report insignificant items in the most cost-effective manner, even if it means a departure from GAAP. GAAP must be followed when an amount is considered material, that is, large enough to affect someone's interpretation or decision.

- Professional judgment and approximations are required in providing financial information to the public. Determining whether something is material, determining how items should be reported and summarized, and having to estimate amounts that are not easily measured all require judgment.

- SFAC's primary objective is to ensure that financial statements, prepared in accordance with GAAP, provide useful information for making decisions. The rules should help ensure **consistency** and **comparability**. The quality of consistency is needed so that decision-makers can compare the financial statements of one accounting period to other accounting periods. Comparability is needed to compare one company's financial statements with other companies'.

- Two more characteristics of useful information are relevance and reliability. **Relevance** means the information must be reported in a timely manner so that it is not stale or outdated. **Reliability** means the information must be accurate and truthful, *i.e.*, must have **representational faithfulness**.

- SFAC require companies to keep the owners' personal financial records separate from the businesses'. This is called the **separate-entity** assumption.

2. A complete set of financial statements includes (a) the income statement (also called the statement of operations), (b) the balance sheet (also called the statement of financial position), (c) the statement of changes in shareholders' (or owners') equity, (d) the statement of cash flows, and (e) notes to the financial statements (sometimes called footnotes). Before financial statements are prepared, the company must be

sure to adjust all account balances to reflect accurate amounts. This process is called **adjusting the books**.

3. The income statement is prepared first. It lists the revenues earned minus all the expenses incurred in generating revenue during the accounting period covered by the statement. The revenues and expenses can be found in the retained earnings column of the worksheet under shareholders' equity:

Assets	Liabilities	Shareholders' equity	
		Contributed capital	Retained earnings
			+ Revenues
			- Expenses

Net income (or net earnings) is the difference between the revenues (or sales) and the expenses (such as cost of goods sold, advertising expense, etc.). See Exhibit 2-4 in the text for an example of an income statement.

- Revenue equals the dollar amounts of goods or services delivered during the period; it does not reflect the amount of cash received during the period. Some sales may have been made **on account**. **Accounts receivable**, an asset on the balance sheet, will show the amount that has not yet been collected from customers. The statement of cash flows will show the amount of cash collected from customers during the period. Thus, the three statements tell three important pieces of information about the sales/collection process: 1) the income statement shows the dollar amount of goods or services delivered (revenue), 2) the statement of cash flows shows the amount of cash received, and 3) the balance sheet links the two and shows the amount of revenue not yet collected (accounts receivable).

- Expenses equal the dollar amount of goods or services consumed (used) during the period; they do not reflect the amount of cash paid during the period. Some expenses may have been paid for in advance (*i.e.*, in a previous accounting period). **Prepaids**, an asset on the balance sheet, will show the amount that has been paid for in advance but not yet used. Some expenses may not be paid for until a later accounting period. **Payables**, which are liabilities on the balance sheet, show the amounts still owed on items that may have been consumed (used) during the period. The statement of cash flows will show the amount paid during the period. Thus, the three statements tell three important pieces of information about the purchase/acquisition process: 1) the income statement shows the dollar amount of goods or services consumed (expenses), 2) the statement of cash flows shows the amount of cash paid, and 3) the balance sheet links the two and shows the amount of expenses not yet paid (payables) or the amount paid for in advance (prepaids).

4. Net income from the income statement is needed to prepare the statement of changes in shareholders' equity. This statement shows the changes over a period of time in owners' equity caused by the following:

Assets	Liabilities	Shareholders' equity	
		Contributed capital	Retained earnings
		+ Common stock	
			+Net income
			- Dividends

See Exhibit 2-5 in the text for an example of a statement of changes in shareholders' equity.

5. The balance sheet is prepared by calculating and summarizing the balance of each asset,

20

liability, and owners' equity account as of the balance sheet date. The balance sheet balances because Assets = Liabilities + Owners' equity. The balance for each account is calculated by adding the changes in the account during the period to its beginning balance (*i.e.*, its balance at the end of the previous accounting period).

6. The assets, items of value that will provide future benefit, are listed in order of liquidity (the relative quickness with which each asset is to be turned into cash or used). A **classified balance sheet** categorizes assets (and liabilities) as either current or noncurrent. **Current assets**, which will be turned into cash or used up within the year, are listed first, typically in this order:

*   Cash, the most liquid asset.

*   **Accounts receivable**, often listed next, represents the amounts owed by customers from credit sales.

*   **Inventory** is merchandise the company has available to sell.

*   **Prepaids** represent payments made in advance for items that will provide future benefit - for example, prepaid insurance.

Noncurrent (or **long-term**) **assets** will last for more than one year and are listed below current assets.

7. Liabilities are obligations a company owes and, like assets, are separated into current and noncurrent sections on a formal classified balance sheet. **Current liabilities** will be settled (or paid off) within the year.

*   An example of a current liability is **Accounts payable**, which is amounts owed to vendors for the purchase of inventory on account.

*   Other payables are amounts owed to others for services or goods other than inventory.

Noncurrent (or **long-term**) **liabilities** are the obligations that will not be satisfied within the year and are listed below current liabilities.

Equity is the last section of the balance sheet and represents the owners' claims to the assets. Shareholders' equity for a corporation is separated into **contributed capital** (also known as **paid-in capital** or **investments** by owners) and **retained earnings** (capital earned and kept by the company). The balance sheet of a sole proprietorship or partnership shows the two sections, investments by owners and earned capital, combined as one, called **capital**.

8. As mentioned earlier, the SFAC and GAAP provide guidance in measuring and reporting the elements of the financial statements. The **unit of measure assumption** requires the elements to be measured in monetary units. The items on the financial statements are to be recorded at cost, referred to as the **historical cost principle** or **cost principle**. The justification for reporting items at cost rather than their current values is based on the **going-concern assumption**. The assumption is that a company is not going to go out of business and sell off all of its assets. Thus, it is not relevant to know what items are worth today if they are not going to be sold today. Asset values are more reliable and objective if they are reported at cost and **not revalued** to what the company *thinks* they may be worth. Certain assets are, however, revalued using an objective method of revaluing (more on that in later chapters).

9. For financial statements to be relevant to users, GAAP requires them to reflect the economic substance of the company's transactions and not just the exchange of cash. **Accrual-basis accounting** requires revenue and expense be recorded when in substance the revenue is earned and the expense is incurred, regardless of whether cash has changed hands. Often revenues and expenses are reported in a different accounting period than when the cash is received or paid. **Accruals** exist when the action (revenue or expense) comes before the cash (receipt or

payment). **Deferrals** exist when the cash comes before the action.

- The rule for recording revenue is the **revenue recognition principle**. Revenue is **recognized** (*i.e.*, reported) on the income statement in the period it is **earned** even if cash has not been received or was received in advance. For example, when a company delivers a product to a customer on account, the revenue should be recorded when the product is delivered. In substance the company has completed its side of the bargain and should be able to reflect this transaction on its financial statements. The company should not have to wait until later when the cash is finally received.

- The rule for recording expenses is the **matching principle**. Expenses are to be recorded (matched) on the income statement in the same period as the revenue they helped to generate even if cash has not been paid or was paid in advance. For example, when a product is delivered to a customer, the expense of the product (cost of goods sold) should be matched with the related revenue (sales) regardless of whether the company has paid for the inventory in advance or still owes for the inventory.

10. In contrast to accrual-basis accounting, **cash-basis accounting** records revenue only when cash is received and expenses only when cash is paid. It often ignores the substance of the transaction and can result in manipulation and inconsistencies in the timing of revenues and expenses. It is not an acceptable method of accounting under GAAP.

11. Financial statements provide information about the risk of investing in a company. **Risk** is the uncertainty associated with the amount and timing of future returns. If the risk is considered high, then the investor expects a higher return. Investing as an owner is riskier than investing as a creditor because a company has a legal obligation to pay its creditors before its owners. Thus, an owner expects a higher return than a creditor via dividends and an increase in the stock price. A creditor can only expect to receive the agreed upon interest and repayment of the principal.

12. The **current ratio** equals current assets divided by current liabilities. It is a measure of a company's **liquidity**, or ability to meet its short-term obligations.

13. **Internal controls** are policies and procedures used within a company to help ensure the assets are safe. They also ensure the information system's **inputs** (or transaction data) are **processed** (reorganized and manipulated) and **outputs** (reports such as financial statements) are provided that are accurate and reliable. Internal controls include limiting access to assets and having written detailed policies and procedures. **Input controls** include authorization and adequate documentation. **Processing controls** include segregating duties so those employees who have access to assets do not also have access to the records related to these assets; otherwise an employee could manipulate the records to conceal the theft of assets. Written guidelines (documentation controls) should be provided that require reconciling and crosschecking processed data. Internal controls such as passwords and restrictions on type and size of data can be programmed into computerized systems. **Output controls** include periodic reviews, internal audits and external audits (performed by independent auditors from outside the company).

Featured Exercise

Part A: Show the effect of the following events on the accounting equations for each of the childcare companies, Tom's Tots, Inc. and Tiny Tim's, Inc.

Tom's Tots, Inc.		Assets =	Liabilities +	Owner's equity
	Balances at May 1, 2005	$900 Cash 600 Prepaid insurance 200 Supplies	$400 Note payable	$700 Common stock 600 Retained earnings
1	Cares for 5 children for a fee of $300 per month for each child. Collects cash.			
2	Pays off the entire loan plus $4 interest.			
3	Pays $500 for May's rent.			
4	Determines that 1/3 of the insurance is used up.			
5	On May 31, only $50 of supplies are left.			

Tiny Tim's, Inc.		Assets =	Liabilities +	Owner's equity
	Balances at May 1, 2005	$900 Cash 600 Prepaid insurance 200 Supplies	$400 Note payable	$700 Common stock 600 Retained earnings
1	Cares for 5 children for a fee of $300 per month for each child, to be collected in June.			
2	Pays $4 interest on the loan.			
3	Pays $500 for May's rent.			
4	Determines that 1/3 of the insurance is used up.			
5	On May 31, only $50 of supplies are left.			

23

Part B: Using the information from Part A, prepare the four financial statements for both companies.

Tom's Tots, Inc.
Income Statement
For the Month Ended May 31, 2005

Tiny Tim's, Inc.
Income Statement
For the Month Ended May 31, 2005

Tom's Tots, Inc.
Statement of Changes in Shareholder's Equity
For the Month Ended May 31, 2005

Tiny Tim's, Inc.
Statement of Changes in Shareholder's Equity
For the Month Ended May 31, 2005

Tom's Tots, Inc.
Balance Sheet
May 31, 2005

Tiny Tim's, Inc.
Balance Sheet
May 31, 2005

Tom's Tots, Inc.
Statement of Cash Flows
For the Month Ended May 31, 2005

Tiny Tim's, Inc.
Statement of Cash Flows
For the Month Ended May 31, 2005

Part C: Answer the following questions using Parts A and B.

1. Are Tom's Tots and Tiny Tim's sole proprietorships, partnerships or corporations? How can you tell?

2. Who should expect a higher return, the creditor who lent Tiny Tim's $400 or Tim, the owner of Tiny Tim's? Why?

3. Is Tom allowed to include his personal rent expense in Tom's Tots' income statement? Why or why not?

4. Which assumption requires that the items in the financial statements be measured in money, not inches or number of kids?

5. Tom's Tots' supplies on hand, which were bought at deeply discounted prices, would cost $75 to replace as of May 31, 2005. Should Tom's Tots revalue the supplies to $75 on its financial statements? Why or why not?

6. Describe and explain the revenue recognition principle using the transactions from Tiny Tim's during the month ended May 31, 2005.

7. Describe and explain the matching principle using the adjusting entry for supplies during the month ended May 31, 2005.

8. Which company is more profitable for the month ended May 31, 2005? Would your answer be different if cash-basis accounting was used instead of accrual-basis accounting? Explain.

9. Identify some internal controls that Tom's Tots may use to help ensure the cash balance is accurate and complete.

Solution

Tom's Tots		Assets =	Liabilities +	Owner's equity
	Balances at May 1, 2005	$900 Cash 600 Prepaid insurance 200 Supplies	$400 Note payable	$700 Common stock 600 Retained earnings
1	Cares for 5 children for a fee of $300 per month for each child. Collects cash.	1,500 Cash		1,500 Revenue
2	Pays off the entire loan plus $4 interest.	(404) Cash	(400) Note payable	(4) Interest expense
3	Pays $500 for May's rent.	(500) Cash		(500) Rent expense
4	Determines that 1/3 of the insurance is used up.	(200) Prepaid insurance		(200) Insurance expense
5	On May 31, only $50 of supplies are left.	(150) Supplies		(150) Supplies expense
	Balances at May 31, 2005	$1,496 Cash 400 Prepaid insurance 50 Supplies		$ 700 Common stock 1,246 Retained earnings

Tiny Tim's		Assets =	Liabilities +	Owner's equity
	Balances at May 1, 2005	$900 Cash 600 Prepaid insurance 200 Supplies	$400 Note payable	$700 Common stock 600 Retained earnings
1	Cares for 5 children for a fee of $300 per month for each child, to be collected in June.	1,500 Accounts receivable		1,500 Revenue
2	Pays $4 interest on the loan.	(4) Cash		(4) Interest expense
3	Pays $500 for May's rent.	(500) Cash		(500) Rent expense
4	Determines that 1/3 of the insurance is used up.	(200) Prepaid insurance		(200) Insurance expense
5	On May 31, only $50 of supplies are left.	(150) Supplies		(150) Supplies expense
	Balances at May 31, 2005	$ 396 Cash 1,500 Accounts receivable 400 Prepaid insurance 50 Supplies	$400 Note payable	$700 Common stock 1,246 Retained earnings

Part B:

<table>
<tr><td colspan="3">Tom's Tots, Inc.
Income Statement
For the Month Ended May 31, 2005</td><td colspan="3">Tiny Tim's, Inc.
Income Statement
For the Month Ended May 31, 2005</td></tr>
<tr><td>Revenue</td><td></td><td></td><td>Revenue</td><td></td><td></td></tr>
<tr><td>Service fees earned</td><td></td><td>$1,500</td><td>Service fees earned</td><td></td><td>$1,500</td></tr>
<tr><td>Expenses</td><td></td><td></td><td>Expenses</td><td></td><td></td></tr>
<tr><td>Rent</td><td>$500</td><td></td><td>Rent</td><td>$500</td><td></td></tr>
<tr><td>Supplies</td><td>150</td><td></td><td>Supplies</td><td>150</td><td></td></tr>
<tr><td>Insurance</td><td>200</td><td></td><td>Insurance</td><td>200</td><td></td></tr>
<tr><td>Interest</td><td>4</td><td></td><td>Interest</td><td>4</td><td></td></tr>
<tr><td>Total expenses</td><td></td><td>854</td><td>Total expenses</td><td></td><td>854</td></tr>
<tr><td>Net income</td><td></td><td>$ 646</td><td>Net income</td><td></td><td>$ 646</td></tr>
</table>

<table>
<tr><td colspan="3">Tom's Tots, Inc.
Statement of Changes in Shareholder's Equity
For the Month Ended May 31, 2005</td><td colspan="3">Tiny Tim's, Inc.
Statement of Changes in Shareholder's Equity
For the Month Ended May 31, 2005</td></tr>
<tr><td>Common stock</td><td></td><td>$ 700</td><td>Common stock</td><td></td><td>$ 700</td></tr>
<tr><td>Beginning retained earnings</td><td>$600</td><td></td><td>Beginning retained earnings</td><td>$600</td><td></td></tr>
<tr><td>Plus net income</td><td>646</td><td></td><td>Plus net income</td><td>646</td><td></td></tr>
<tr><td>Less distributions to owners</td><td>0</td><td></td><td>Less distributions to owners</td><td>0</td><td></td></tr>
<tr><td>Ending retained earnings</td><td></td><td>1,246</td><td>Ending retained earnings</td><td></td><td>1,246</td></tr>
<tr><td>Total shareholder's equity</td><td></td><td>$1,946</td><td>Total shareholder's equity</td><td></td><td>$1,946</td></tr>
</table>

<table>
<tr><td colspan="4">Tom's Tots, Inc.
Balance Sheet
May 31, 2005</td><td colspan="4">Tiny Tim's, Inc.
Balance Sheet
May 31, 2005</td></tr>
<tr><td>Assets</td><td></td><td>Liabilities</td><td>$ 0</td><td>Assets</td><td></td><td>Liabilities</td><td></td></tr>
<tr><td>Cash</td><td>$1,496</td><td>Owner's equity:</td><td></td><td>Cash</td><td>$ 396</td><td>Note payable</td><td>$ 400</td></tr>
<tr><td>Prepaid insurance</td><td>400</td><td>Common stock</td><td>700</td><td>Accounts</td><td></td><td>Owner's equity:</td><td></td></tr>
<tr><td>Supplies</td><td>50</td><td>Retained earning</td><td>1,246</td><td>receivable</td><td>1,500</td><td>Common stock</td><td>700</td></tr>
<tr><td></td><td></td><td>Total liabilities</td><td></td><td>Prepaid</td><td></td><td>Retained earnings</td><td></td></tr>
<tr><td>Total assets</td><td>$1,946</td><td>and equity</td><td>$1,946</td><td>1,246</td><td></td><td></td><td></td></tr>
<tr><td></td><td></td><td></td><td></td><td>insurance</td><td>400</td><td></td><td></td></tr>
<tr><td></td><td></td><td></td><td></td><td>Supplies</td><td>50</td><td>Total liabilities</td><td></td></tr>
<tr><td></td><td></td><td></td><td></td><td>Total assets</td><td>$2,346</td><td>and equity</td><td>$2,346</td></tr>
</table>

<table>
<tr><td colspan="3">Tom's Tots, Inc.
Statement of Cash Flows
For the Month Ended May 31, 2005</td></tr>
<tr><td>Cash from operating activities</td><td></td><td></td></tr>
<tr><td>Cash collected from customers</td><td>$1,500</td><td></td></tr>
<tr><td>Cash paid for rent</td><td>(500)</td><td></td></tr>
<tr><td>Cash paid for interest</td><td>(4)</td><td></td></tr>
<tr><td>Total cash from operations</td><td></td><td>$996</td></tr>
<tr><td>Cash from investing activities</td><td></td><td>0</td></tr>
<tr><td>Cash from financing activities</td><td></td><td></td></tr>
<tr><td>Repayment of loan</td><td>(400)</td><td></td></tr>
<tr><td>Total cash from financing activities</td><td></td><td>(400)</td></tr>
<tr><td>Net change in cash</td><td></td><td>$596</td></tr>
</table>

<table>
<tr><td colspan="3">Tiny Tim's, Inc.
Statement of Cash Flows
For the Month Ended May 31, 2005</td></tr>
<tr><td>Cash from operating activities</td><td></td><td></td></tr>
<tr><td>Cash paid for rent</td><td>$(500)</td><td></td></tr>
<tr><td>Cash paid for interest</td><td>(4)</td><td></td></tr>
<tr><td>Total cash from operations</td><td></td><td>$(504)</td></tr>
<tr><td>Cash from investing activities</td><td></td><td>0</td></tr>
<tr><td>Cash from financing activities</td><td></td><td>0</td></tr>
<tr><td>Net change in cash</td><td></td><td>$(504)</td></tr>
</table>

Part C: Answer the following questions using Parts A and B.

1. Tom's Tots, Inc. and Tiny Tim's, Inc. are both corporations as indicated by the Inc. designation. Also, the owner's equity is separated into common stock and retained earnings. Sole proprietorships or partnerships combine contributed and earned capital into one amount called "capital."

2. Investing in a company as an owner is riskier than as a creditor. There is a legal obligation for a company to pay both interest and principal to its creditors. There is no legal obligation for a company to make any distributions to owners. There is a positive correlation between risk and return, thus an owner should expect a higher return.

3. The separate-entity assumption states that the owner's personal financial records and transactions should not be part of the company's. Only the company's rent expense should be on Tom's Tots' income statement.

4. The unit of measure assumption requires financial statement items to be measured in monetary units.

5. The historical cost principle (or cost principle) requires Tom's Tots' supplies on hand to be reported at the cost of $50 and not revalued at their current market value of $75.

6. The revenue recognition principle requires revenue to be recorded (recognized) when it is earned (*i.e.*, when goods or services have been delivered) without regard to when the cash is collected from customers. Tiny Tim's reported revenue ($1,500) on the income statement even though no cash has been received from its customers. Accounts receivable, an asset on the balance sheet, will show the amount that has not yet been collected from customers ($1,500). The statement of cash flows will show the amount of cash collected from customers during the period ($0). Thus, the three statements tell three important pieces of information about the sales/collection process: 1) the income statement shows the amount of goods or services delivered (revenue); 2) the statement of cash flows shows the amount of cash received; and 3) the balance sheet links the two and shows the amount of revenue not yet collected (accounts receivable).

7. The matching principle requires expenses to be matched on the income statement with the revenue they helped generate. Only the supplies that are used to earn revenue during the period should be expensed. The unused supplies stay on the balance sheet until they are used.

8. Net income is a measure of profitability. Since both have the same net income both are equally profitable. If cash-basis accounting were used instead of accrual-basis accounting, Tom's Tots would be considered more profitable which is misleading since both companies, in substance, performed equally well. The only difference is that Tiny Tim's did not collect cash from its customers. Accrual-basis accounting better reflects the economic substance of the companies' activities during the month.

9. Internal controls that may help ensure the cash balance is accurate and complete include: limiting access to the cash; reconciling (comparing) the cash balance on the company's books to the bank statement; and separating the responsibility of recording cash transactions from those who have access to cash.

Review Questions and Exercises

Completion Statements

Fill in the blank(s) to complete each statement.

1. A set of rules called _____ must be followed to help ensure the financial statements are useful.

2. GAAP must be followed when an amount is considered _____, *i.e.*, if it would affect someone's interpretation or decision.

3. _____ and _____ are needed so that decision-makers can compare the financial statements of one accounting period to other accounting periods and compare one company's financial statements with other companies'.

4. _____ means the information must be reported in a timely manner and _____ means the information must be accurate and truthful.

5. Before financial statements are prepared, the company must be sure to adjust all account balances to reflect accurate amounts. This process is called _____.

6. A _____ categorizes and lists assets as _____ if the assets will be turned into cash or used up within the year and _____ if the assets will be used for more than one year. It also lists _____ for the liabilities that will be satisfied during the year and _____ if the liabilities will not be satisfied within the year.

7. _____ is the uncertainty associated with the amount and timing of future returns. The higher the _____ the higher the _____.

8. _____ controls include periodic reviews, internal audits (performed by the company's employees) and external audits (performed by independent auditors from outside the company).

True/False

Indicate whether each statement is true (T) or false (F).

_____1. Financial statements prepared using cash-basis accounting will never have Accounts receivable or Accounts payable on the balance sheet.

_____2. Accrual-basis accounting is GAAP; cash-basis accounting is not GAAP.

_____3. An owner of a corporation has the legal right to receive interest and dividends.

_____4. Investing as a creditor is riskier than investing as an owner and thus requires a higher return.

_____5. An accrual is recorded when the event occurs before the cash changes hands and a deferral is recorded when the cash changes hands before the event.

_____6. The going concern assumption assumes a business is going to close in the near future and thus all its assets must be revalued to their current market values.

_____7. It is important to have the same person who has access to cash be the one who maintains the cash records in order to ensure accuracy.

_____8. Company A paid off its $400 note payable, as well as the related interest of $4, on the last day of the accounting period. Company B only pays the interest expense of $4 during the accounting period. As a result, Company A will show a lower net income during this accounting period than it would have had it not paid off the note.

Multiple Choice

Select the best answer for each question.

_____1. Rite-it-up, Inc. purchased land for $20,000 on May 1, 2005. On December 31, 2005, similar land sells for $25,000. The land should be shown:
  A. on the balance sheet as a $25,000 asset.
  B. on the income statement as revenue of $5,000.
  C. on the balance sheet as a $20,000 asset.
  D. on the income statement as an expense of $20,000.

_____2. Ivan Rich is considering lending money to Kneady, Inc. As a potential creditor of Kneady, Inc., Ivan computed Kneady's current ratio in order to measure:
  A. Kneady's ability to replace current assets as they are used.
  B. Kneady's liquidity, _i.e._, its ability to pay its current debts as they come due.
  C. Kneady's ability to convert its noncurrent assets into current assets.
  D. Kneady's profitability.
  E. The current ratio measures all of the above.

_____3. Materiality refers to:
  A. the recording of all expenditures as assets when they are significant in amount.
  B. the use of dollars instead of some other unit in preparing financial statements.
  C. the exception where companies are allowed to ignore recording small dollar items in the accounting records.
  D. the recording of insignificant items in the most convenient way even if it is not in accordance with GAAP.

_____4. Retained earnings can be found on:
  A. the income statement and statement of cash flows.
  B. the statement of changes in shareholders' equity only.
  C. the statement of changes in shareholders' equity and the balance sheet.
  D. the balance sheet only.
  E. the income statement only.

_____5. The owner of Shady Groove Company has the bookkeeper write company checks to pay for his personal items. This violates:
   A. the matching principle.
   B. the monetary assumption.
   C. the materiality concept.
   D. the separate entity assumption.

_____6. If you were told a company's net income was $100,000, what other information would be helpful in making this more meaningful?
   A. The time period covered.
   B. The method used: accrual-basis or cash-basis accounting.
   C. The amount of net income retained versus paid out in dividends.
   D. All of the above.

_____7. A company in its first year of business earned revenues of $100,000 but collected only $80,000 in cash from its customers. Which of the following is correct?
   A. The income statement will show Revenues of $100,000, the balance sheet will show Accounts receivable of $20,000, and the statement of cash flows will show Cash collected from customers of $80,000.
   B. The income statement will show Revenues of $80,000, the balance sheet will show Accounts receivable of $100,000, and the statement of cash flows will show Cash collected from customers of $80,000.
   C. The income statement will show Revenues of $100,000, the balance sheet will show Accounts receivable of $20,000, and the statement of cash flows will show Cash collected from customers of $100,000.
   D. The income statement will show Revenues of $180,000, the balance sheet will show Accounts receivable of $100,000, and the statement of cash flows will show Cash collected from customers of $80,000.

_____8. During the year, ABC Company had revenues of $100,000 of which $90,000 has been collected from customers. It also had expenses of $60,000 of which $40,000 has been paid. The owners were paid $20,000 in dividends. Net income for the year equals:
   A. $50,000.   D. $20,000.
   B. $40,000.   E. $10,000.
   C. $30,000.

_____9. Which of the following statements about cash is true?
   A. Cash is part of owners' equity.
   B. Increases in cash and net income will be the same during an accounting period.
   C. Revenue is earned only when cash is collected.
   D. Expenses are recorded only when cash is paid.
   E. None of the above is true.

_____10. Which of the following is not part of an internal control system?
   A. External audits
   B. Internal audits
   C. Consolidation of duties
   D. Limited access to assets

Matching

From the list of concepts, principles, and assumptions, write the appropriate letter which best matches each item below.

A. Accrual accounting	G. Materiality
B. Cost principle	H. Relevance
C. Consistency	I. Reliability
D. Comparability	J. Revenue recognition principle
E. Going-concern assumption	K. Separate-entity assumption
F. Matching principle	L. Unit of measure assumption

1. Which principle is violated when an owner of a company includes his personal expenses in the company's financial records?	
2. ABC Company records revenues when the goods are delivered even though the cash will not be collected until a later accounting period.	
3. Inventory is presented in dollars, not units, on the balance sheet.	
4. Assumes companies are not going to liquidate in the near future and thus helps justify the use of historical cost rather than current cost in valuing assets.	
5. The accounting information is provided in a timely fashion so that the information is still useful.	
6. Assets are typically recorded at the amount paid for them.	
7. Supplies are recorded as an asset and then expensed in the period they are used in helping generate revenue.	
8. It is important for companies to use the same methods of measuring items on the financial statement each accounting period.	
9. Comparing financial statements of different companies is more meaningful when the statements are prepared in accordance with GAAP.	
10. The items on the financial statements should be accurate and truthful.	
11. Revenues are recorded when earned and expenses are recorded when incurred regardless of when the related cash changes hands.	
12. Items that are too small to affect anyone's decision making can be recorded in a manner that is not necessarily in accordance with GAAP.	

Exercises

1. Fill in the accounting equation below for Tim's Ware, Inc.'s events that occurred during 2005, its first year of business:

Tim's Ware, Inc.		Assets =	Liabilities +	Owners' equity
a.	Tim's Ware began operations by issuing $6,000 of common stock to its owners.			
b.	Tim's Ware purchased $3,000 of inventory and paid cash.			
c.	Tim's Ware purchased $400 of supplies and paid cash.			
d.	Tim's Ware made sales of $3,300 on account. The cost of the sales was $2,500.			
e.	Tim's Ware collected $2,700 of receivables during the year.			
f.	On July 1, 2005 Tim's Ware paid $2,400 in advance for an insurance policy that covers two years beginning July 1.			
g.	As of December 31, 2005, six months of insurance coverage has expired.			
h.	Supplies on hand as of December 31, 2005 amounted to $100.			

2. Tim's Ware's account titles:		Fill in the correct dollar amount: Amount as of or for the year ended December 31	Put an "X" in the column of the statement where the item will most likely appear:		
			Income Statement	Balance Sheet	Statement of Cash Flows
a.	Stock issued for cash				
b.	Supplies expense				
c.	Supplies				
d.	Insurance expense				
e.	Prepaid insurance				
f.	Cash paid for insurance				
g.	Cash received from customers				
h.	Accounts receivable				
i.	Sales				
j.	Cost of goods sold				
k.	Inventory				

Completion Statements

1. GAAP
2. material
3. Consistency; comparability
4. Relevance; reliability
5. adjusting the books
6. Classified balance sheet; current assets; noncurrent assets; current liabilities; noncurrent liabilities
7. Risk; risk; return
8. Internal

True/False

1. True   Revenues and expenses are recorded only when cash changes hands under the cash-basis accounting, which is not GAAP. Accounts receivable and Accounts payable reflect the timing differences between when revenues and expenses are earned and incurred and when the cash later changes hands. These timing differences exist only under accrual-basis accounting which is required under GAAP.

2. True   See 1. above.

3. False   Creditors have the legal right to receive interest and repayment of principal. Owners have no legal rights to receive dividends.

4. False   See 3. above. In the event of liquidation, creditor obligations must be paid before the owners can receive anything. Since owners are taking more risk, they expect to receive a higher return.

5. True   An example of an accrual is recording an account receivable when revenue is earned before cash is received. An example of a deferral is recording prepaid insurance as an asset when the cash changes hands and later recording the expense when the insurance is used.

6. False   The going-concern assumption assumes companies are not going to liquidate in the near future and thus helps justify valuing assets at their historical cost and not their current market values.

7. False   The separation of duties includes separating those who have access to cash from those who do the record keeping. This will help ensure that an employee does not pocket cash and then alter the books to conceal the theft.

8. False   The $400 payment of principal reduces assets (cash) and liabilities (notes payable); it does not decrease owners' equity. Both will have net income lowered by the same amount, the $4 interest expense.

Multiple Choice

1. C   GAAP require assets to be recorded at historical cost. (There are some exceptions that you will learn about later on in the text.)

2. B   The current ratio is a measure of liquidity and is calculated by dividing current assets by current liabilities.

3. D   Materiality allows companies to record items in a way that does not conform to GAAP as long as it does not have an effect on users' decisions. It doesn't mean a company is allowed not to record small dollar items (C.).

4. C   The statement of changes in shareholders' equity shows beginning retained earnings plus net income minus dividends to arrive at retained earnings at the end of the accounting period, which also is shown on the balance sheet.

5. D   The owner's personal transactions and records must be kept separate from the company's transactions and records.

6. D   Financial statements must state the time period covered, which could be a month, quarter or year (A). GAAP require companies to use accrual-basis accounting which typically results in a better measure of net income than cash-basis accounting (which is not GAAP) (B). It is useful to know how much of net income is retained and reinvested into the company versus paid out in dividends to owners; the statement of changes in shareholders' equity shows this amount.

7. A   The activity can be summarized as follows:

Assets	Liabilities	Owners' equity
$100,000 Accounts receivable (1)		$100,000 Revenue (2)
80,000 Cash (3) (80,000) Accounts receivable (4)		

The balance sheet will show Accounts receivable as $20,000 or (1) + (4), the income statement will show Revenues as $100,000 (2), and the statement of cash flows will show Cash collected from customers as $80,000 (3) in the cash from operating activities section.

8. B   Revenues ($100,000) minus expenses ($60,000) equals net income ($40,000). Accrual-basis accounting requires revenues and expenses to be recorded when earned and incurred regardless of when the cash changes hands. Also, a dividend (which is shown on the statement of changes in shareholders' equity) is not an expense since it does not help generate revenues.

9. E   Cash is an asset, not owners' equity. Net income and changes in Cash are typically different. Net income often includes revenues that may not have been collected and expenses that may not have been paid in the same accounting period as when the revenues were earned and the expenses incurred.

10. C   Separation of duties, not consolidation of duties, is an important internal control.

Matching

1. K
2. J
3. L
4. E
5. H
6. B
7. F
8. C
9. D
10. I
11. A
12. G

Exercises

1. Tim's Ware, Inc.		Assets	Liabilities	Owners' equity
a.	Tim's Ware began operations by issuing $6,000 of common stock to its owners.	6,000 Cash		6,00 Common stock
b.	Tim's Ware purchased $3,000 of inventory and paid cash.	3,000 Inventory (3,000) Cash		
c.	Tim's Ware purchased $400 of supplies and paid cash.	400 Supplies (400) Cash		
d.	Tim' s Ware made sales of $3,300 on account. The cost of the sales was $2,500.	3,300 Accounts receivable (2,500) Inventory		3,300 Sales (2,500) Cost of goods sold
e.	Tim's Ware collected $2,700 of receivables during the year.	2,700 Cash (2,700) Accounts receivable		
f.	On July 1, 2005 Tim's Ware paid $2,400 in advance for an insurance policy which covers two years beginning July 1.	2,400 Prepaid insurance (2,400) Cash		
g.	As of December 31, 2005, six months of insurance coverage has expired.	(600) Prepaid insurance		(600) Insurance expense
h.	Supplies on hand as of December 31, 2005 amounted to $100.	(300) Supplies		(300) Supplies expense

2. Tim's Ware's account titles:		Amount as of or for the year ended December 31	Select one for each line item:		
			Income Statement	Balance Sheet	Statement of Cash Flows
a.	Stock issued for cash	$6,000			X
b.	Supplies expense	$300	X		
c.	Supplies	$100		X	
d.	Insurance expense	$600	X		
e.	Prepaid insurance	$1,800		X	
f.	Cash paid for insurance	$2,400			X
g.	Cash received from customers	$2,700			X
h.	Accounts receivable	$600		X	
i.	Sales	$3,300	X		
j.	Cost of goods sold	$2,500	X		
k.	Inventory	$500		X	

CHAPTER 3
ACCRUALS AND DEFERRALS: TIMING IS EVERYTHING IN ACCOUNTING

Chapter Overview

In Chapter 2, you learned about the difference between cash-basis and accrual-basis accounting. Often there is a difference in timing between a business event and the collection or payment of cash. Chapter 3 deals with accounting for the most common types of business events that involve these timing differences.

Chapter Highlights

1. **Net income** (or **net profit** or **net earnings**) is equal to **revenues** minus **expenses.** The life of a business is continuous, but we must be able to measure income for a shorter period of time, usually a year, quarter, or month. The **income statement**, also called the **statement of operations** or the **profit and loss statement**, reports income earned over a period of time. All revenues earned during the period and all expenses for the period must be included on the income statement. **Timing differences**, the differences between the time when business events take place and the time when cash changes hands, can make it difficult to measure income for a particular accounting period. Companies must make **adjustments** for these timing differences before financial statements can be prepared.

2. **Accruals**, business transactions in which the action takes place before the exchange of cash, can be either revenues or expenses. Making the necessary adjusting entries is called **accruing** revenues or expenses. Accruals affect both the income statement and the balance sheet.

	Revenue	Expenses
Action first	Revenue must be on the income statement even though cash has not yet been collected.	Expenses must be on the income statement even though cash has not yet been paid.

- Interest expense, and the related liability Interest payable, must be accrued for all outstanding notes payable. Interest expense is the cost of using someone else's money for a period of time, and it must be shown as an expense on the income statement even though interest has not yet been paid in cash.

Assets	Liabilities	Owners' equity
	+ Interest payable	- Interest expense

Interest = Principal *times* Rate *times* Time. Keep in mind that interest rates are usually stated as percentages that apply to a full twelve months of borrowing, and be careful to use the correct fraction of a year in calculating interest expense for shorter amounts of time. If cash for this period's accrued interest expense is paid in the following accounting period, the interest expense will not be recorded again. Instead, the payment will reduce both Cash and Interest payable.

Assets	Liabilities	Owners' equity
- Cash	- Interest payable	

- Interest revenue, and the related asset Interest receivable, must be accrued on loans the company has made to others. The company has earned interest revenue and must show this revenue on the current period's income statement, even though it has not yet been received in cash.

- At the end of an accounting period, a company must look over its records to make sure that all revenues for services performed or goods delivered to customers are properly recorded. Revenue earned very late in the period may not even have been billed to the customers yet, but it still must be included as revenue on the income statement, and the related Accounts receivable must be shown as a current asset on the balance sheet.

Assets	Liab.	Owners' equity
+ Accounts receivable		+ Sales

When cash is finally collected from these customers in the following accounting period, the company will not record revenue again. Instead, the company will record an increase in Cash and a decrease in Accounts receivable.

Assets	Liab.	Owners' equity
+ Cash - Accounts receivable		

- Expenses must be accrued at the end of each accounting period, too. A company must examine all of its business transactions to make sure that no expenses (and related liabilities) have been forgotten because the bills have not yet been received or paid.

- Salary expense is normally recorded when employees are paid. However, the last payday of the accounting period may not be the same as the last day of the accounting period. A company must accrue salary expense for work done by employees between the last payday and the financial statement date. Then the income statement will show the correct Salary expense for all work done by employees during the accounting period, and the balance sheet will show the related Salaries payable for amounts still owed to employees.

Assets	Liabilities	Owners' equity
	+ Salaries payable	- Salary expense

On the first payday of the following accounting period, the company must decrease Salaries payable for the amount of salary that was reported as a liability in the previous accounting period. It must also decrease Retained earnings for any additional salary expense incurred since the beginning of the new accounting period, and decrease Cash for the total amount paid to employees.

3. **Deferrals**, business transactions in which the dollars are exchanged before the business activity has occurred, can also be either revenues or expenses.

	Revenue	Expenses
Dollars first	Cash has been received from customers, but the company hasn't done its part to earn it.	Cash has been paid for services or goods not yet used.

- Sometimes a company collects cash from its customers before shipping merchandise to them or performing services for them. The company **defers revenue** when it receives these advance payments. It cannot record revenue yet because it has not done anything to earn the revenue. Instead, the company records the increase in Cash, and an increase in **Unearned revenue**, a liability.

Assets	Liabilities	Owners' equity
+ Cash	+ Unearned revenue	

When the company finally ships the merchandise or performs the service for its customer, it decreases the liability, Unearned revenue, and records Sales revenue as an increase in Retained earnings.

Assets	Liabilities	Owners' equity
	- Unearned revenue	+ Sales

- Four kinds of **expenses** are **deferred**, or paid for in advance. A company normally pays for many months of insurance in advance. When insurance coverage is paid for, no Insurance expense is recorded. Instead, the company decreases Cash and increases **Prepaid insurance**, an asset.

Assets	Liab.	Owners' equity
+ Prepaid insurance - Cash		

When financial statements are prepared, the company makes an adjusting entry to show the expired (used up) part of the insurance coverage as an expense. This adjustment decreases the asset, Prepaid insurance, and records Insurance expense, which decreases Retained earnings.

Assets	Liab.	Owners' equity
- Prepaid insurance		- Insurance expense

After this adjusting entry is made, the asset, prepaid insurance, will show the amount of insurance coverage still remaining for future months.

- Like insurance, rent is usually paid in advance. When a company pays cash for rent in advance, it records an increase in an asset, **Prepaid rent,** along with a decrease in Cash. When financial statements are prepared, an adjusting entry is made to decrease the asset Prepaid rent for the amount of rent that has been used up. This adjustment also records Rent expense, which decreases Retained earnings.

- **Supplies** are miscellaneous items used in a business, and are not the same as **inventory**, which is merchandise purchased for resale. A company will usually buy and pay for supplies in advance. This purchase is recorded as a decrease in Cash and an increase in the asset, Supplies. As these supplies are used up day by day, no record is made of Supplies expense. Instead, at the end of an accounting period, the company counts the supplies that remain. An adjusting entry is made to decrease the asset account, Supplies, so that it equals the amount of supplies remaining. The amount of this decrease represents Supplies expense, the portion of supplies that have been used up. After this adjusting entry is made, the asset account on the balance sheet properly represents the amount of supplies left for future use. The income statement shows the expense of the supplies that have been used up.

- Often a company will buy an asset like equipment that benefits more than one future accounting period. The whole cost of the equipment is not treated as an expense in the period it is purchased. Instead, the matching principle requires that the cost be spread out over all of the accounting periods that benefit from using the equipment to earn revenue. This is called **depreciating** the asset and the expense reported in each accounting period is known as **Depreciation expense**.

When equipment is first purchased, the company decreases Cash and increases the asset, Equipment.

Assets	Liab.	Owners' equity
- Cash + Equipment		

At the end of the accounting period, the company calculates Depreciation expense by dividing the cost of the equipment by the number of accounting periods it will be used. The adjusting entry records Depreciation expense, which decreases Retained earnings, and **Accumulated depreciation**, a **contra-asset**.

Assets	Liab.	Owners' equity
- Accumulated depreciation		- Depreciation expense

Accumulated depreciation is considered to be an asset account, but it is subtracted from Equipment in the calculation of total assets on the balance sheet. The company's balance sheet will continue to show the cost of the equipment, but along with this cost the company will report Accumulated depreciation, the total depreciation that has been recorded for the equipment so far. Cost minus accumulated depreciation is the **book value** or **carrying value** of the equipment.

4. **Working capital** is equal to **current assets** minus **current liabilities**. It measures a company's ability to finance operations.

5. Business owners and managers must analyze risks and plan to minimize these risks. Larger companies have more risk and need more controls. However, small companies face risks as well, and need controls too. A small business like Tom's Wear needs to implement the five components of an internal control system: 1) The control environment: management needs to establish the tone at the top. It must make it clear that it will not tolerate dishonesty from vendors, creditors, customers, or employees. 2)

Risk assessment: management must evaluate the risks involved in the business, such as buying and storing inventory, selling to customers on credit, and handling cash. 3) Control activities: the company must try to minimize the risks it has identified, by such activities as storing inventory in a locked warehouse, checking the credit records of customers, and keeping cash in a bank account. 4) The information system: Tom's Wear needs a system that records financial transactions and also stores additional information about customers, suppliers, and employees. 5) Monitoring: management needs to make sure that the controls are working properly.

Featured Exercise

For each question below, fill in the correct dollar amount and circle the correct financial statement on which it appears, using the following code:

IS for the income statement for the year ended December 31, 2005
BS for the balance sheet at December 31, 2005
SOCF for the statement of cash flows for the year ended December 31, 2005

1. On September 1, 2005, Acme Enterprises borrowed $10,000 from the bank on a two-year, 9% note payable. All interest will be paid when the loan is repaid. On December 31, 2005, the correct adjusting entry was made for interest.

   a. Cash received from borrowing of $_____ appears on the: **IS   BS   SOCF**

   b. Interest payable of $_____ appears on the: **IS   BS   SOCF**

   c. Notes payable of $_____ appears on the: **IS   BS   SOCF**

   d. Interest expense of $_____ appears on the: **IS   BS   SOCF**

   e. Cash paid for interest of $_____ appears on the: **IS   BS   SOCF**

2. On October 1, 2005, Acme Enterprises loaned $100,000 to its CEO on a one-year, 12% note receivable. All interest will be received when the loan is collected. On December 31, 2005, the correct adjusting entry was made for interest.

   a. Notes receivable of $_____ appears on the: **IS   BS   SOCF**

   b. Interest receivable of $_____ appears on the: **IS   BS   SOCF**

   c. Interest revenue of $_____ appears on the: **IS   BS   SOCF**

   d. Cash received for interest of $_____ appears on the: **IS   BS   SOCF**

3. On December 30, 2005, Acme Enterprises completed a $2,000 consulting job for a client. Because most of the company employees are celebrating the New Year a little early, no one billed the customer when the job was finished. However, on December 31, 2005, the correct adjusting entry was made.

   a. Cash received from customers of $_____ appears on the: **IS   BS   SOCF**

   b. Accounts receivable of $_____ appears on the: **IS   BS   SOCF**

   c. Revenue of $_____ appears on the: **IS   BS   SOCF**

4. Acme Enterprises pays its employees every other Friday. The last payday was Friday, December 23, 2005, and the next payday will be Friday, January 6, 2006. Employees earned $3,500 in the last week of December, 2005. The correct adjusting entry was made on December 31.

   a. $_____ of this $3,500 appears as cash paid to employees on the: **IS   BS   SOCF**

   b. $_____ of this $3,500 appears as salary expense on the: **IS   BS   SOCF**

   c. Salaries payable of $_____ appears on the: **IS   BS   SOCF**

5. On August 1, 2005, Acme Enterprises received $6,000 in advance from a customer for services that Acme expected to perform over the next twelve months. The entire $6,000 was properly recorded as unearned revenue. On December 31, 2005, the correct adjusting entry was made.

   a. Revenue of $_____ appears on the: **IS   BS   SOCF**

   b. Unearned revenue of $_____ appears on the: **IS   BS   SOCF**

   c. Cash received from customers of $_____ appears on the: **IS   BS   SOCF**

6. On April 1, 2005, Acme Enterprises paid $1,200 for a 24-month insurance policy that went into effect the same day. On December 31, 2005, the correct adjusting entry was made.

   a. Cash paid for insurance of $_____ appears on the: **IS   BS   SOCF**

   b. Prepaid insurance of $_____ appears on the: **IS   BS   SOCF**

   c. Insurance expense of $_____ appears on the: **IS   BS   SOCF**

7. On January 1, 2005, Acme Enterprises had $1,000 of supplies in its supply room. During 2005, Acme paid $5,000 cash for more supplies. On December 31, 2005, Acme counted the supplies and found that only $800 of supplies remained. On December 31, 2005, the correct adjusting entry was made.

   a. Supplies of $_____ appears on the: **IS   BS   SOCF**

   b. Supplies expense of $_____ appears on the: **IS   BS   SOCF**

   c. Cash paid for supplies of $_____ appears on the: **IS   BS   SOCF**

8. On January 1, 2005, Acme Enterprises bought a delivery truck for $30,000 cash. The truck is expected to be used for six years. On December 31, 2005, the correct adjusting entry was made.

   a. Equipment of $_____ appears on the: **IS**   **BS**   **SOCF**

   b. Depreciation expense of $_____ appears on the: **IS**   **BS**   **SOCF**

   c. Cash paid for depreciation of $_____ appears on the: **IS**   **BS**   **SOCF**

   d. Accumulated depreciation of $_____ appears on the: **IS**   **BS**   **SOCF**

   e. Cash paid for equipment of $_____ appears on the: **IS**   **BS**   **SOCF**

Solution

1. a. Cash received from borrowing of **$10,000** appears on the **SOCF**.
   b. Interest payable of **$300** appears on the **BS**.
   c. Notes payable of **$10,000** appears on the **BS**.
   d. Interest expense of **$300** appears on the **IS**.
   e. Cash paid for interest of **$0** appears on the **SOCF**.

2. a. Notes receivable of **$100,000** appears on the **BS**.
   b. Interest receivable of **$3,000** appears on the **BS**.
   c. Interest revenue of **$3,000** appears on the **IS**.
   d. Cash received for interest of **$0** appears on the **SOCF**.

3. a. Cash received from customers of **$0** appears on the **SOCF**.
   b. Accounts receivable of **$2,000** appears on the **BS**.
   c. Revenue of **$2,000** appears on the **IS**.

4. a. **$0** of this $3,500 appears as cash paid to employees on the **SOCF**.
   b. **$3,500** of this $3,500 appears as salary expense on the **IS**.
   c. Salaries payable of **$3,500** appears on the **BS**.

5. a. Revenue of **$2,500** appears on the **IS**.
   b. Unearned revenue of **$3,500** appears on the **BS**.
   c. Cash received from customers of **$6,000** appears on the **SOCF**.

6. a. Cash paid for insurance of **$1,200** appears on the **SOCF**.
   b. Prepaid insurance of **$750** appears on the **BS**.
   c. Insurance expense of **$450** appears on the **IS**.

7. a. Supplies of **$800** appears on the **BS**.
   b. Supplies expense of **$5,200** appears on the **IS**.
   c. Cash paid for supplies of **$5,000** appears on the **SOCF**.

8. a. Equipment of **$30,000** appears on the **BS**.
   b. Depreciation expense of **$5,000** appears on the **IS**.
   c. Cash paid for depreciation of **$0** appears on the **SOCF**.
   d. Accumulated depreciation of **$5,000** appears on the **BS**,
   e. Cash paid for equipment of **$30,000** appears on the **SOCF**.

Review Questions and Exercises

Completion Statements

Fill in the blank(s) to complete each statement.

1. Working capital is _____ minus _____.

2. The book value of equipment is _____ minus _____.

3. An asset that is subtracted from other assets to calculate total assets is called a _____.

4. The _____ principle requires that the cost of equipment be treated as an expense over all of the accounting periods the equipment is used.

5. Two financial statements, the _____ and the _____ are affected by adjusting entries.

6. Interest equals _____ times _____ times _____.

7. When a company receives payment in advance, it records _____, a liability.

8. Before financial statements can be prepared, _____ entries must be recorded for accruals.

True/False

Indicate whether each statement is true (T) or false (F).

_____ 1. The income statement is also known as a profit and loss statement.

_____ 2. Interest expense is recorded only after it is paid in cash.

_____ 3. Accruals involve business events that take place before cash is received or paid.

_____ 4. Supplies are part of a company's inventory.

_____ 5. Interest receivable must be accrued on notes payable.

_____ 6. Deferrals involve cash collected or paid before a business event takes place.

_____ 7. The cost of equipment is an expense of the period when it is purchased.

_____ 8. Most companies pay for insurance coverage in advance.

_____ 9. Large businesses face more risks than small businesses.

_____ 10. Depreciation expense is always the same as Accumulated depreciation.

Multiple Choice

Select the best answer for each question.

_____ 1. The adjusting entry to record an accrued expense also involves recording:
A. a revenue.
B. an asset.
C. a liability.
D. a decrease in Cash.

_____ 2. The adjusting entry to record an accrued revenue also involves recording:
A. an expense.
B. an asset.
C. a liability.
D. an increase in Cash.

_____ 3. When a company pays for six months insurance in advance, it records:
A. prepaid insurance, an asset.
B. insurance expense, a liability.
C. prepaid insurance, an expense.
D. insurance expense, a decrease in Retained earnings.

_____ 4. When a company receives cash in advance for services it has not yet performed, it records:
A. Revenue earned.
B. Unearned service revenue, a liability.
C. Unearned service revenue, an asset.
D. This is a trick question. Nothing is recorded until services are performed.

_____ 5. ABC, Inc., shows $300 of Supplies expense on its income statement. ABC must have:
A. purchased $300 of supplies during the period.
B. paid cash for $300 of supplies during the period.
C. used $300 of supplies during the period.
D. The answer cannot be determined from the information given.

_____ 6. During June, Busy Beaver bought $5,000 of office supplies on account, and promised to pay the vendor the full amount in July. At the end of June, Busy Beaver estimated that there were $2,000 of office supplies left unused. How much Supplies expense should Busy Beaver report for June?
A. $5,000
B. $2,000
C. $3,000
D. $ 0

_____ 7. During June, Busy Beaver performed $3,500 of services for clients on account. In June, $500 of this amount was collected in cash. The remaining $3,000 was collected in July. How much Service revenue should Busy Beaver report for June?
A. $ 0
B. $500
C. $3,000
D. $3,500

_____ 8. Salaries payable on a company's balance sheet indicates that:
   A. the company is in serious financial difficulty. It doesn't even have enough cash to pay its employees.
   B. the company's accountants are seriously confused. Salaries appear on the income statement, not the balance sheet.
   C. employees had not received payment for the last few days of work because the last day of the accounting period was not a payday.
   D. employees were overpaid and now owe the company money.

_____ 9. Accounts receivable appear on a company's balance sheet because:
   A. the company collected cash when it sold merchandise to customers.
   B. the company sold merchandise to customers but has not received payment yet.
   C. the company bought merchandise on account.
   D. the company paid for merchandise previously purchased on account.

_____ 10. The accountant for Ace Electronics forgot to make the adjusting entry for depreciation on the company's equipment. As a result of this mistake:
   A. net income is too high.
   B. total liabilities are too low.
   C. net income is too low.
   D. stockholders' equity is too low.

Matching

Adjusting entries affect both the income statement and the balance sheet. The left-hand column below lists revenue and expense accounts commonly used in adjusting entries. Match each of these income statement accounts with a related balance sheet account that would appear in an adjusting entry with the revenue or expense.

	Income statement		**Balance sheet**
_____ 1.	Subscription revenue	A.	Accumulated depreciation
_____ 2.	Interest revenue	B.	Supplies
_____ 3.	Interest expense	C.	Prepaid rent
_____ 4.	Depreciation expense	D.	Interest payable
_____ 5.	Supplies expense	E.	Salaries payable
_____ 6.	Insurance expense	F.	Interest receivable
_____ 7.	Salary expense	G.	Prepaid insurance
_____ 8.	Rent expense	H.	Unearned revenue

Exercises

Show the effect on the accounting equation of each of the events described. This company has a fiscal year that ends on December 31.

1		Assets =	Liabilities +	Owners' Equity
a	On December 31, made an adjusting entry to accrue $3,000 of sales revenue earned that has not yet been billed to a customer.			
b	On January 2, billed the customer for $3,000.			
c	On January 15, collected all $3,000 in cash.			

2		Assets =	Liabilities +	Owners' Equity
a	On October 31, paid $2,400 for six months' rent in advance.			
b	Made the adjusting entry required on December 31.			

3		Assets =	Liabilities +	Owners' Equity
a	On June 1, borrowed $10,000 for two years at 9% interest. Interest will be paid when the loan is repaid.			
b	Made the adjusting entry required on December 31.			

4		Assets =	Liabilities +	Owners' Equity
a	On August 1, loaned $20,000 for two years at 12% interest. Interest will be collected when the loan is repaid.			
b	Made the adjusting entry required on December 31.			

5		Assets =	Liabilities +	Owners' Equity
a	On December 30, the last working day of the year, employees have earned $1,800. They will not be paid for another week. Make the adjusting entry required on December 31.			
b	Paid employees $4,000 for work done in December and January.			

6		Assets =	Liabilities +	Owners' Equity
a	Noticed that only $100 of office supplies remain in the back room. Bought $700 more office supplies on account.			
b	Paid the vendor for the office supplies purchased in (6a) above.			
c	On December 31, $200 of office supplies are left in the back room. Made the adjusting entry required on December 31.			

7		Assets =	Liabilities +	Owners' Equity
a	On June 21, paid $9,000 for rent for the six months beginning August 1.			
b	Made the adjusting entry required on December 31.			
c	On December 21, paid $10,000 for rent for the six months beginning February 1 of next year.			
d	Made the adjusting entry required on December 31.			

8		Assets =	Liabilities +	Owners' Equity
a	On December 28, received a $75 bill for electric service used between November 25 and December 25. Payment is not due until January 10.			
b	On January 10, paid December's $75 electric bill.			
c	On December 31, the company still had not received the December bill from the gas company. This bill usually runs about $225 for winter months.			
d	December's gas bill for $230 arrived on January 3. The bill was paid on January 15.			

9		Assets =	Liabilities +	Owners' Equity
a	On January 1, bought a $3,600 copy machine, which is expected to last for three years.			
b	Made the adjusting entry required on December 31.			

Completion Statements

1. current assets, current liabilities
2. cost, accumulated depreciation
3. contra-asset
4. matching
5. income statement, balance sheet
6. principal, rate, time
7. unearned revenue
8. adjusting

True/False

1. True
2. False: Interest expense must be accrued for notes payable.
3. True
4. False: Supplies are miscellaneous items used in a business. Inventory is merchandise purchased for resale.
5. False: Interest expense and Interest **payable** must be accrued on notes payable.
6. True
7. False: The matching principle requires that the cost of equipment be treated as an expense over all of the accounting periods when the equipment is used, not just the period when it is purchased.
8. True
9. True
10. False: Depreciation expense is just the current period's depreciation. Accumulated depreciation is all of the depreciation expense that has ever been recorded for a particular asset. In the first accounting period an asset is used, Accumulated depreciation will be the same as Depreciation expense. In later accounting periods, Accumulated depreciation will be more than Depreciation expense for the period.

Multiple Choice

1. C   Expenses are accrued because something has been used up to earn revenue, but cash has not been paid yet. The liability to make future payment for something already used up must be recorded as well.
2. B   Revenues are accrued because they have been earned and should appear on the income statement. However, cash has not yet been received in exchange for goods or services already delivered. The right to receive cash in the future from this revenue is an asset.
3. A   In exchange for payment for six months of future insurance coverage, the company gets an asset, Prepaid insurance, because the company will receive future benefit from the insurance policy. Adjusting entries are needed to turn the asset into an expense as the coverage is used up.
4. B   The company has not done anything yet to earn the advance payment it has received. The company should record a liability because it owes its customer services now that it has accepted payment in advance.
5. C   Supplies are an expense when they are used to earn revenue. Purchasing supplies creates an asset called Supplies which the company has on hand to use in the future. Payment for supplies removes a liability to pay for items already received.

7.   D   Revenue is recorded when it is earned by performing services for clients. It doesn't matter when cash is collected.

8.   C   The last payday of the accounting period rarely is the same as the date of the financial statements. However, the income statement must show as an expense all that employees earned for the period. Any amounts that have not been paid in cash yet are shown as Salaries payable, a liability on the balance sheet. Almost every company will routinely show Salaries payable because of timing differences. So it doesn't mean a company is unable to pay its employees. (However, if Salaries payable are very large when compared with Salary expense for the year, it might mean the company has some financial problems.)

9.   B   Accounts receivable are created when a company earns revenue and has the right to receive cash from customers.

10. A   The missing entry would record Depreciation expense and Accumulated depreciation. Depreciation expense, like all expenses, decreases net income, retained earnings, and total stockholders' equity. Without the missing expense, net income, retained earnings, and total stockholders' equity are all too high, not too low. Accumulated depreciation is a contra-asset that decreases total assets. Neither Depreciation expense nor Accumulated depreciation has any effect on liabilities.

Matching

H 1. Subscription revenue/ Unearned revenue
F 2. Interest revenue/ Interest receivable
D 3. Interest expense/ Interest payable
A 4. Depreciation expense/ Accumulated depreciation
B 5. Supplies expense/ Supplies
G 6. Insurance expense/ Prepaid insurance
E 7. Salary expense/ Salaries payable
C 8. Rent expense/ Prepaid rent

Exercises

1		Assets =	Liabilities +	Owners' Equity
a	On December 31, made an adjusting entry to accrue $3,000 of sales revenue earned that has not yet been billed to a customer. *The income statement must show all revenue earned during the year.*	$3,000 Accounts receivable		$3,000 Sales
b	On January 2, billed the customer for $3,000. *No entry is required because revenue has already been recorded in the previous accounting period.*	No entry	No entry	No entry
c	On January 15, collected all $3,000 in cash. *Revenue is recorded in December, when it is earned, not when cash is collected.*	3,000 Cash (3,000) Accounts receivable		

49

2		Assets =	Liabilities +	Owners' Equity
a	On October 31, paid $2,400 for six months' rent in advance. *This prepayment is an asset because it will provide future benefit. No expense will be recorded until the rent is used up.*	(2,400) Cash 2,400 Prepaid rent		
b	Made the adjusting entry required on December 31. *Two months of rent have been used up. $2,400/6 x 2 months = $800*	(800) Prepaid rent		(800) Rent expense

3		Assets =	Liabilities +	Owners' Equity
a	On June 1, borrowed $10,000 for two years at 9% interest. Interest will be paid when the loan is repaid. *No interest expense is recorded until the company has used the $10,000 for a period of time.*	10,000 Cash	10,000 Notes payable	
b	Made the adjusting entry required on December 31. *The company has used the borrowed cash for seven months. $10,000 x .09 x 7/12 = $525*		525 Interest payable	(525) Interest expense

4		Assets =	Liabilities +	Owners' Equity
a	On August 1, loaned $20,000 for two years at 12% interest. Interest will be collected when the loan is repaid. *Interest is earned as time goes by. However, on the date of the loan, no time has elapsed so no interest is recorded yet.*	20,000 Notes receivable (20,000) Cash		
b	Made the adjusting entry required on December 31. *The loan has earned interest for 5 months. $20,000 x .12 x 5/12 = $1,000*	1,000 Interest receivable		1,000 Interest revenue

5		Assets =	Liabilities +	Owners' Equity
a	On December 30, the last working day of the year, employees have earned $1,800. They will not be paid for another week. Make the adjusting entry required on December 31. *Expenses are recorded when they are used to earn revenue.*		1,800 Salaries payable	(1,800) Salary expense

		Assets =	Liabilities +	Owners' Equity
b	Paid employees $4,000 for work done in December and January. *$1,800 of the cash has already been recorded as an expense in December. $4,000 – 1,800 = $2,200*	(4,000) Cash	(1,800) Salaries payable	(2,200) Salary expense

6		Assets =	Liabilities +	Owners' Equity
a	Noticed that only $100 of office supplies are left in the back room. Bought $700 more office supplies on account. *The supplies will be used in the future, so they are recorded as an asset.*	700 Supplies	700 Other payables	
b	Paid the vendor for the office supplies purchased in (6a) above. *No expense is recorded when cash is paid for a liability.*	(700) Cash	(700) Other payables	
c	On December 31, $200 of office supplies are left in the back room. Made the adjusting entry required on December 31. *Supplies used are an expense. $100 + 700 – 200 = $600*	(600) Supplies		(600) Supplies expense

7		Assets =	Liabilities +	Owners' Equity
a	On June 21, paid $9,000 for rent for the six months beginning August 1. *This rent will be used in the future, so it is recorded as an asset.*	9,000 Prepaid rent (9,000) Cash		
b	Made the adjusting entry required on December 31. *Five month's rent has been used up. $9,000/6 months x 5 months = $7,500*	(7,500) Prepaid rent		(7,500) Rent expense
c	On December 21, paid $10,000 for rent for the six months beginning February 1 of next year.	10,000 Prepaid rent (10,000) Cash		
d	Made the adjusting entry required on December 31. *No entry is required because none of the rent prepaid on December 21 has expired yet.*	no entry	no entry	no entry

8		Assets =	Liabilities +	Owners' Equity
a	On December 28, received a $75 bill for electric service used between Nov. 25 and December 25. Payment is not due until January 10. *The electricity was used to earn revenue in December, so it should be an expense in December even though it has not been paid in cash.*		75 Other payables	(75) Utilities expense
b	On January 10, paid December's $75 electric bill. *The $75 was already recorded as an expense in December. Expenses are not recorded when liabilities are paid.*	(75) Cash	(75) Other payables	
c	On December 31, the company still had not received the December bill from the gas company. This bill usually runs about $225 for winter months. *The company must estimate and record the expense so December's utility expense will be included on the income statement.*		225 Other payables	(225) Utilities expense
d	December's gas bill for $230 arrived on January 3. The bill was paid on January 15. *Most of the December bill was accrued as an expense in December, and should not be expensed in January, too. The December estimate was $5 too low, so January's income statement will include $5 extra expense. Estimates are never perfect, but this $5 is immaterial.*	(230) Cash	225 Other payables	(5) Utilities expense

9		Assets =	Liabilities +	Owners' Equity
a	On January 1, bought a $3,600 copy machine, which is expected to last for three years. *The equipment is an asset because it will benefit future accounting periods.*	3,600 Equipment (3,600) Cash		
b	Made the adjusting entry required on December 31. *The cost of the equipment must be spread out over all the years it will be used.* *$3,600 / 3 years = $1,200*	(1,200) Accumulated depreciation		(1,200) Depreciation expense

CHAPTER 4
KEEPING THE BOOKS: THE MECHANICS OF AN ACCOUNTING SYSTEM

Chapter Overview

This chapter covers the accounting cycle, the process by which financial events are recorded, summarized, and reported. Many companies still use a traditional general ledger system for this accounting cycle, which starts with recording business events in a journal using debits and credits. Entries are posted from the journal to the general ledger. After preparing an unadjusted trial balance, the accountant prepares and posts adjusting journal entries. An adjusted trial balance is used to prepare the four basic financial statements and the temporary accounts are closed so they can be used in the following fiscal period. A postclosing trial balance verifies the closing process.

Although this traditional system is still widely used, many large companies now use sophisticated database systems called enterprise resource planning systems that include accounting information along with information used by other functional areas of the company.

Chapter Highlights

1.   The accounting equation worksheet that we have been using to record business events is too awkward to use for a real-world company that has a large number of transactions. Traditionally, accountants have used a **general ledger system** to keep track of a company's financial transactions. Information from this system can be used to prepare the four basic financial statements. For many companies, accounting information is now only part of the data stored in a larger system, an **enterprise-wide resource planning system**, or **ERP**, which also stores data for other parts of the business like marketing, production, and human resources. However, this chapter will describe a manual general ledger system so that you can understand how information is recorded, classified, and summarized for the financial

statements. Many companies use a computerized system that is very much like this.

2.   As transactions occur, they are recorded by a bookkeeper in a **journal**. Some companies have separate journals for frequently recurring events like sales, cash receipts, and cash payments. Each journal entry shows the date of the transaction, the specific accounts and dollar amounts involved, and a brief explanation of the event. Since the journal lists events in chronological order, it is as difficult to use in preparing financial statements as the accounting equation worksheet when there are many transactions. To make statement preparation easier, all events that affect a particular account need to be grouped together. The transactions listed in the journal are copied, or **posted**, to another book, called the general ledger, which has a separate page for each account. The general ledger page for a particular account shows all the increases and decreases to that account and calculates a running balance.

- Every company must decide how many accounts it wants to use to keep track of financial events. Some companies that want to have detailed information will have many hundreds of accounts, while smaller companies may have only a few dozen. A **chart of accounts** is a complete list of all the accounts in a company's general ledger. Most companies combine similar accounts when they prepare financial statements, so the statements do not show all the underlying detail that is in the general ledger.

- Before a company prepares financial statements, it will prepare a **trial balance**, a list of all the accounts in the general ledger with their balances. The trial balance is reviewed to decide which accounts need adjustments so that the income statement will reflect all revenue that has been earned and all expenses incurred during the accounting period.

3. Accountants use a system of debits and credits to record financial events in the journal and ledger. **Debit (DR)** means the left side of an account and **credit (CR)** means the right side. Look at the accounting equation:

Assets = Liabilities + Owners' equity

- Assets are on the left-hand side of the accounting equation, and are increased with left-handed, debit entries. If debits make assets go up, then credits make them go down.

- Liabilities are on the right-hand side of the accounting equation, and are increased with right-handed, credit entries. If credits make liabilities go up, then debits make them go down.

- Owners' equity, on the right-hand side of the accounting equation, is increased with right-handed, credit entries. Owners' equity is decreased by a distribution to owners, called a **withdrawal** if it is a distribution to the owner of a sole proprietorship. Distributions to corporate shareholders are called **dividends**.

- Revenue, which increases owners' equity, is increased with a credit entry. Expenses decrease owners' equity. An increase in an expense is a decrease in owners' equity, a debit entry.

- Recording a debit entry is called **debiting** an account. Recording a credit entry is called **crediting** an account.

4. The general ledger, which has a separate page for each account, usually has separate columns for debits, credits, and each account's running balance. Accountants often use **T-accounts** to represent pages in the general ledger.

- The **normal balance** of an account is the type of entry (either debit or credit) that increases the account. For example, the normal balance of an asset account is a debit balance, because debits increase assets. If you know the kind of entry that increases each type of account, you don't need to memorize the kind of entry that decreases it, because you can figure it out.

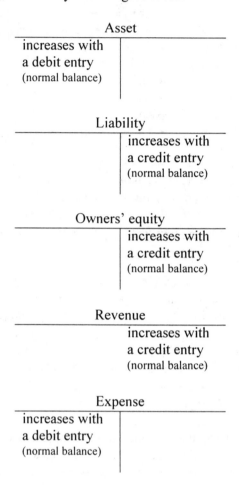

- For any journal entry, the dollars of debits must always equal the dollars of credits, just as the accounting equation must always balance.

5. The **accounting cycle** is a system for recording and summarizing financial information to produce financial statements.

- The first step in the accounting cycle is recording journal entries as business events take place. For example, if a business collects $500 in cash for services performed for a client, the business needs to record a $500 increase in the asset Cash and $500 of Revenue, which increases owners' equity.

54

Ref	Date	Transaction	Debit	Credit
1-1	1/1/01	Cash	500	
		Revenue		500
To record revenue earned				

The debit entry is always shown first. Some entries might have more than one debit. The credit entry follows all of the debit(s) and is always indented. Some entries might have more than one credit. Each journal entry also includes the date and a brief explanation of the business event that is being recorded. The number in the "Ref" column refers to the page number in the journal. It is posted to the ledger along with the debit and credit entries, so that they can be traced back from the ledger to the journal.

- The next step in the accounting cycle is posting from the journal to the general ledger. This is usually done on a daily or weekly basis. Using T-accounts to represent pages in the general ledger, the revenue transaction shown above would be posted like this:

Cash

1-1   500

Revenue

               500   1-1

- At the end of every accounting period, the accountant prepares an **unadjusted trial balance**, a three-column list of all accounts in the general ledger with their debit or credit ending balances.

Account	DR	CR

The debits and credits are shown in separate columns (with the debits on the left, of course) so that the accountant can see that total debits equal total credits. The accountant uses this unadjusted trial balance to review all of the account balances and identify those accounts that require adjusting entries. These are needed so that the income statement will properly reflect all revenue earned and all expenses incurred during the accounting period. Adjustments always affect balance sheet accounts, too.

- Step four is to prepare adjusting journal entries: 1) Accrued revenues must be recorded for revenue earned, even if cash has not yet been collected. 2) Adjustments are also needed to accrue expenses, so that the income statement will show all expenses incurred to earn revenue, even if payment has not yet been made. 3) Deferred revenues are recorded as Unearned revenue, a liability, when cash is received from customers before goods or services are delivered. The accountant examines all deferred revenue accounts to determine whether or not revenue has finally been earned. Dollar amounts for revenue earned are shifted out of the liability accounts and into Sales or Service revenue accounts. 4) Finally, deferred expenses, where the company paid in advance for items before they were used in the business, need adjustment too. The dollar amounts of prepaid goods and services that have been used up to generate revenue must be transferred from asset accounts to expense accounts.

- The next step in the accounting cycle is to prepare an **adjusted trial balance**. Like all trial balances, this is simply a three-column list of all the accounts in the general ledger with their debit or credit balances. If the total debits equal the total credits, and all accounts that need adjustment have been properly adjusted, this adjusted trial balance can be used to prepare the financial statements.

- Preparation of the four basic financial statements is the next step. The accountant prepares the income statement, statement of changes in owners' equity, balance sheet and statement of cash flows.

- After the financial statements have been prepared, the accountant must get the general ledger ready to record events for the next fiscal year. Revenue accounts, expense accounts, and Dividends are **temporary accounts**. All amounts in these accounts are transferred to Retained earnings through a process called **closing the accounts**. Their balances are reduced to zero so that they can be used to accumulate revenues, expenses, and dividends for the next year. The current year's revenue, expenses and dividends will not be combined with next year's revenue, expenses, and dividends. It will be easy to separate the current year's income and dividends from next year's income and dividends.

- Revenue accounts are closed by debiting the separate revenue accounts for the amount of their ending, credit balances, and making a single, offsetting credit to Retained earnings. For example, suppose the Sales account has a credit balance of $400,000, representing all of the sales revenue the company has earned for the fiscal year. This account would be closed by debiting Sales for $400,000 and crediting Retained earnings for $400,000. Now the balance in Sales is zero and Retained earnings has increased by $400,000. The Sales account can now be used to record sales for the next fiscal year.

- All expense accounts are closed in a similar way. However, expense accounts normally have debit balances. They usually are closed by making a single debit entry to Retained earnings for the total of all expenses, and making separate credit entries to each individual expense account. After this journal entry is posted, all of the expense accounts have zero balances and Retained earnings has decreased by the amount of all the fiscal year's expenses. The expense accounts are now ready to be used for the next year.

- Corporations often use an account called Dividends that is debited when dividends are declared by the board of directors.

Although dividends are not expenses, this account is also closed to Retained earnings by debiting Retained earnings and crediting Dividends.

- After **closing entries** have been made, the balance in Retained earnings, an owners' equity account, has been increased by revenues and decreased by expenses and dividends. Now the balance sheet should balance because total assets equal total liabilities plus total owners' equity.

- Asset accounts, liability accounts, and owners' equity accounts are **permanent accounts** or **real accounts**. Their balances are not reduced to zero at the end of the fiscal year. Instead, the ending balances in these accounts become the beginning balances for the following year.

- The final step in the accounting cycle is preparing a **postclosing trial balance**. Like any other trial balance, this is a three-column list of accounts with their debit or credit balances. However, only balance sheet accounts appear on the postclosing trial balance because the revenue, expense, and Dividends accounts have zero balances. The accountant uses this trial balance to check that debits equal credits and to make sure that all the temporary accounts have been properly closed.

6. The general ledger system is a double-entry accounting or bookkeeping system. Each individual journal entry must balance, which keeps the accounting equation in balance, too. The system has built-in checks and balances to make it easy to keep the accounting equation in balance. Furthermore, information is stored in a way that makes the financial statements easy to prepare. Many companies now use computerized general ledger systems that automatically post entries from the journal to the ledger and prepare financial statements. These computerized systems are faster and more accurate than the traditional manual system.

The problem with the general ledger system is that it records and stores information only for the financial statements. Companies need more information to support functions like marketing, which needs to have a list of customers with their credit and purchase histories. An enterprise resource planning system (ERP) is a software system that stores all of a company's information in a single database. Accounting information is only one part of this system. An ERP allows a company to 1) automate and integrate many of its business processes such as purchases and production, 2) share data across the organization, and 3) produce and access information at the same time. This has many benefits for a company such as reducing costs, improving communication among departments, and helping to identify and solve problems. Sharing data company-wide means that functional areas like marketing, production, and human resources no longer need to have their own separate systems. However, ERPs are very expensive to purchase and install. In spite of this, most large companies use ERPs.

7. Information processing risk is the risk that a company will not properly record financial information about its transactions. The accounting system must have controls to ensure that information in the journal is complete and accurate and that posting to the general ledger is done correctly. The double-entry system is a control for some errors and preparing the three trial balances helps to check that the controls are working. The relationship among the financial statements helps to ensure their accuracy. The balance sheet should balance after Retained Earnings is increased for the amount of net income minus any dividends declared. The accountant should thoroughly review the statements before they are released.

Featured Exercise

The following events took place in 2005:

January 1	John Doe began Hits for Hire, a consulting services corporation, by contributing $6,000 of his own money for stock in the company.
January 2	The company bought $5,000 of equipment and signed a one-year, 35% note payable. The equipment is expected to last for four years.
February 3	Paid $500 cash for supplies.
February 14	The company paid $1,000 cash for advertising in *Pen Pals*, a monthly magazine for Federal prison inmates.
March 5	The company accepted a $20,000 payment in advance for future services to be performed.
July 9	The company spent $10,000 to send John Doe out of town on "special assignment."
August 15	John Doe completed services for the client who made the advance payment in March. The client was billed for an additional $80,000.
October 31	Collected the full amount due from the client.
December 1	The company declared and paid a cash dividend of $50,000 to its owner John Doe.

A. Use the following chart of accounts to record these transactions for Hits for Hire in the journal:

Cash	Unearned revenue	Consulting fees
Accounts receivable	Notes payable	Travel expense
Supplies	Interest payable	Advertising expense
Equipment	Common stock	Supplies expense
Accumulated depreciation	Retained earnings	Depreciation expense
	Dividends	Interest expense

Ref.	Date	Transaction	Debit	Credit
1-1				
1-2				
1-3				
1-4				
1-5				
1-6				
1-7				
1-8				
1-9				

B. Post your journal entries to general ledger T-accounts.

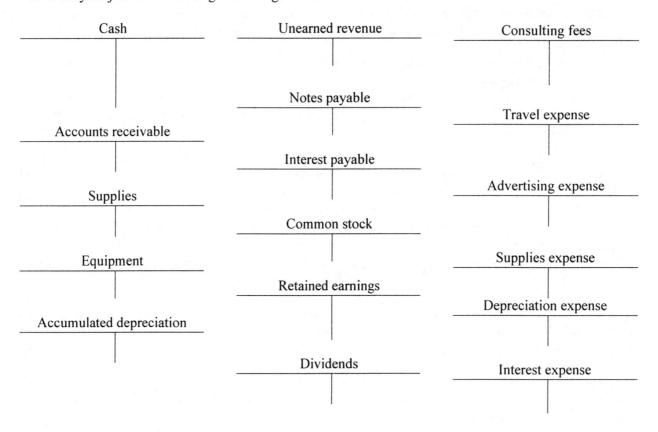

C. Prepare an unadjusted trial balance at December 31, 2005.

Hits for Hire, Inc. Unadjusted Trial Balance December 31, 2005		
Cash		
Accounts receivable		
Supplies		
Equipment		
Accumulated depreciation		
Unearned revenue		
Notes payable		
Interest payable		
Common stock		
Retained earnings		
Dividends		
Consulting fees		
Travel expense		
Advertising expense		
Supplies expense		
Depreciation expense		
Interest expense		
Totals		

D. Make the necessary adjusting journal entries and post them to the general ledger T-accounts you used before. For Hits for Hire, four adjustments must be made before the financial statements can be prepared. They are:
1. one year's interest accrued on the note payable;
2. one year's depreciation on the equipment;
3. the adjustment for unearned revenue that has now been earned; and
4. the adjustment for supplies used. John Doe counted the supplies on December 31 and found that $100 of supplies remain.

Ref.	Date	Transaction	Debit	Credit
adj-1				
adj-2				
adj-3				
adj-4				

E. Prepare an adjusted trial balance at December 31, 2005.

Hits for Hire, Inc. Adjusted Trial Balance December 31, 2005		
Cash		
Accounts receivable		
Supplies		
Equipment		
Accumulated depreciation		
Unearned revenue		
Notes payable		
Interest payable		
Common stock		
Retained earnings		
Dividends		
Consulting fees		
Travel expense		
Advertising expense		
Supplies expense		
Depreciation expense		
Interest expense		
Totals		

60

F. Use the adjusted trial balance to prepare the four basic financial statements.

Hits for Hire, Inc.
Income Statement
For the Year Ended December 31, 2005

Hits for Hire, Inc.
Statement of Changes in Shareholder's Equity
For the Year Ended December 31, 2005

Hits for Hire, Inc.
Balance Sheet
December 31, 2005

Hits for Hire, Inc.
Statement of Cash Flows
For the Year Ended December 31, 2005

G. Make the closing journal entries and post them to the same general ledger T-accounts you used before.

Ref.	Date	Transaction	Debit	Credit
c-1				
c-2				
c-3				

H. Prepare a postclosing trial balance at December 31, 2005.

Hits for Hire, Inc. Postclosing Trial Balance December 31, 2005		
Cash		
Accounts receivable		
Supplies		
Equipment		
Accumulated depreciation		
Unearned revenue		
Notes payable		
Interest payable		
Common stock		
Retained earnings		
Dividends		
Consulting fees		
Travel expense		
Advertising expense		
Supplies expense		
Depreciation expense		
Interest expense		
Totals		

Solution

A.

Ref.	Date	Transaction	Debit	Credit
1-1	1/01/05	Cash	6,000	
		Common stock		6,000
		To record owner contributions		
1-2	1/02/05	Equipment	5,000	
		Notes payable		5,000
		To record the purchase of equipment in exchange for a one-year, 35% note payable		
1-3	2/3/05	Supplies	500	
		Cash		500
		To record the purchase of supplies		
1-4	2/14/05	Advertising expense	1,000	
		Cash		1,000
		To record payment for advertising in Pen Pals		
1-5	3/05/05	Cash	20,000	
		Unearned revenue		20,000
		To record payment received from client for future services		

1-6	7/09/05	Travel expense	10,000	
		Cash		10,000
		To record cost of sending John Doe on special assignment		
1-7	8/15/05	Accounts receivable	80,000	
		Consulting Fees		80,000
		To record additional fees billed to client		
1-8	10/31/05	Cash	80,000	
		Accounts receivable		80,000
		To record collection of accounts receivable		
1-9	12/01/05	Dividends	50,000	
		Cash		50,000
		To record the payment of dividends to John Doe		

B., D., and G.

Cash
1-1	6,000	500	1-3
1-5	20,000	1,000	1-4
1-8	80,000	10,000	1-6
		50,000	1-9

Accounts receivable
| 1-7 | 80,000 | 80,000 | 1-8 |

Supplies
| 1-3 | 500 | 400 | adj-4 |

Equipment
| 1-2 | 5,000 | | |

Accumulated depreciation
| | | 1,250 | adj-2 |

Unearned revenue
| adj-3 | 20,000 | 20,000 | 1-5 |

Notes payable
| | | 5,000 | 1-2 |

Interest payable
| | | 1,750 | adj-1 |

Common stock
| | | 6,000 | 1-1 |

Retained earnings
| c-2 | 14,400 | 100,000 | c-1 |
| c-3 | 50,000 | | |

Dividends
| 1-9 | 50,000 | 50,000 | c-3 |

Consulting fees
| c-1 | 100,000 | 80,000 | 1-7 |
| | | 20,000 | adj-3 |

Travel expense
| 1-6 | 10,000 | 10,000 | c-2 |

Advertising expense
| 1-4 | 1,000 | 1,000 | c-2 |

Supplies expense
| adj-4 | 400 | 400 | c-2 |

Depreciation expense
| adj-2 | 1,250 | 1,250 | c-2 |

Interest expense
| adj-1 | 1,750 | 1,750 | c-2 |

C.

Hits for Hire, Inc. Unadjusted Trial Balance December 31, 2005		
Cash	$ 44,500	
Accounts receivable		
Supplies	500	
Equipment	5,000	
Accumulated depreciation		
Unearned revenue		$ 20,000
Notes payable		5,000
Interest payable		
Common stock		6,000
Retained earnings		
Dividends	50,000	
Consulting fees		80,000
Travel expense	10,000	
Advertising expense	1,000	
Supplies expense		
Depreciation expense		
Interest expense		
Totals	$111,000	$111,000

D.

Ref.	Date	Transaction	Debit	Credit
adj-1	12/31/05	Interest expense	1,750	
		Interest payable		1,750
		To accrue one year's interest on the note payable: $5,000 x 0.35 x 1 year		
adj-2	12/31/05	Depreciation expense	1,250	
		Accumulated depreciation		1,250
		To record depreciation expense: $5,000 / 4 years		
adj-3	12/31/05	Unearned revenue	20,000	
		Consulting fees		20,000
		To record fees earned		
adj-4	12/31/05	Supplies expense	400	
		Supplies		400
		To record the cost of supplies used: $500 – 100 = $400		

E.

Hits for Hire, Inc. Adjusted Trial Balance December 31, 2005		
Cash	$ 44,500	
Accounts receivable		
Supplies	100	
Equipment	5,000	
Accumulated depreciation		$ 1,250
Unearned revenue		
Notes payable		5,000
Interest payable		1,750
Common stock		6,000
Retained earnings		
Dividends	50,000	
Consulting fees		100,000
Travel expense	10,000	
Advertising expense	1,000	
Supplies expense	400	
Depreciation expense	1,250	
Interest expense	1,750	
Totals	$114,000	$114,000

F.

Hits for Hire, Inc.
Income Statement
For the Year Ended December 31, 2005

Revenue		
Consulting fees		$100,000
Expenses		
Travel	$10,000	
Advertising	1,000	
Supplies	400	
Depreciation	1,250	
Interest	1,750	
Total expenses		14,400
Net income		$ 85,600

Hits for Hire, Inc.
Statement of Changes in Shareholder's Equity
For the Year Ended December 31, 2005

Beginning contributed capital	$ 0	
Stock issued during the year	6,000	
Ending contributed capital		$ 6,000
Beginning retained earnings	$ 0	
Net income for the year	85,600	
Dividends	(50,000)	
Ending retained earnings		35,600
Total stockholder's equity		$41,600

Hits for Hire, Inc.
Balance Sheet
December 31, 2005

Assets		**Liabilities + Owner's equity**	
		Notes payable	$ 5,000
Cash	$ 44,500	Interest payable	1,750
Supplies	100	Total liabilities	6,750
Equipment (net of $1,250		Common stock	6,000
Accumulated depreciation)	3,750	Retained earnings	35,600
		Total liabilities +	
Total assets	$48,350	owner's equity	$48,350

Hits for Hire, Inc.
Statement of Cash Flows
For the Year Ended December 31, 2005

Cash from operating activities
Cash collected from customers	$100,000	
Cash paid for travel	(10,000)	
Cash paid for advertising	(1,000)	
Cash paid for supplies	(500)	
Total cash from operations		$88,500

Cash from investing activities   0

Cash from financing activities
Cash received from sale of stock	6,000	
Cash paid for dividends	(50,000)	
Total cash used for financing		(44,000)

Net increase in cash $44,500

A $5,000 note payable was issued to buy equipment.

G.

Ref.	Date	Transaction	Debit	Credit
c-1	12/31/05	Consulting fees	100,000	
		Retained earnings		100,000
		To close the revenue account		
c-2	12/31/05	Retained earnings	14,400	
		Travel expense		10,000
		Advertising expense		1,000
		Supplies expense		400
		Depreciation expense		1,250
		Interest expense		1,750
		To close the expense accounts		
c-3	12/31/05	Retained earnings	50,000	
		Dividends		50,000
		To close dividends		

H.

Hits for Hire, Inc. Postclosing Trial Balance December 31, 2005		
Cash	$44,500	
Accounts receivable		
Supplies	100	
Equipment	5,000	
Accumulated depreciation		$ 1,250
Unearned revenue		
Notes payable		5,000
Interest payable		1,750
Common stock		6,000
Retained earnings		35,600
Dividends		
Consulting fees		
Travel expense		
Advertising expense		
Supplies expense		
Depreciation expense		
Interest expense		
Totals	$49,600	$49,600

Review Questions and Exercises

Completion Statements

Fill in the blank(s) to complete each statement.

1. As transactions occur, they are recorded in by a bookkeeper in a _____.

2. The transactions listed in the journal are copied to another book called the _____.

3. The process of entering data in the general ledger is called _____.

4. A _____ is a complete list of all accounts in a company's general ledger. It does not show any dollar amounts for these accounts.

5. A(n) _____ is a list of all accounts and their debit or credit balances.

6. Distributions to corporate shareholders are called _____.

7. Expenses are increased with _____ entries.

8. Asset accounts, liability accounts, and owners' equity accounts are _____ accounts because their balances are not reduced to zero at the end of the fiscal year.

9. Revenue accounts, expense accounts, and Dividends are _____ accounts because their balances are reduced to zero at the end of a fiscal year by transferring amounts to Retained earnings.

10. ERP stands for _____ system.

True/False

Indicate whether each statement is true (T) or false (F).

_____1. The general ledger accounting system described in the chapter is no longer widely used.

_____2. The journal groups together transactions that affect a particular account.

_____3. Assets are decreased with debit entries.

_____4. Revenue accounts are closed by debiting them and crediting Retained Earnings.

_____5. Preparing a postclosing trial balance is an unnecessary extra step because it just repeats the information found on the balance sheet.

_____6. Revenue accounts, expense accounts and Dividends must be closed before financial statements can be prepared.

_____7. Accounting information is only one part of an enterprise-wide resource planning system.

_____8. For every journal entry, the dollar amount of debits must equal the dollar amount of credits.

_____9. All accounts begin each fiscal year with zero balances.

_____10. Adjusting entries must be prepared before financial statements are prepared.

Multiple Choice

Select the best answer for each question.

_____1. The adjusting entry to accrue interest on a note payable will include:
A. a debit to Interest revenue.
B. a debit to Interest receivable.
C. a debit to Interest expense.
D. a debit to Interest payable.

_____2. The adjusting entry to record depreciation on equipment will include:
A. a credit to Equipment.
B. a credit to Depreciation expense.
C. a credit to Accumulated depreciation.
D. a credit to Cash.

_____ 3. Which of the following events will cause the adjusted trial balance to be out of balance?
  A. An adjusting entry to record the cost of supplies used was recorded as a $200 debit to Supplies expense and a $200 debit to Supplies.
  B. An adjusting entry to record the amount of prepaid insurance that had expired was recorded as a $100 debit to Insurance expense and a $100 credit to Prepaid insurance. However, the $100 amount of the adjusting entry was wrong because $300 of insurance had actually expired.
  C. Both A and B will cause the adjusted trial balance to be out of balance.
  D. Neither A nor B will cause the adjusted trial balance to be out of balance.

_____ 4. On October 1, Tim's Ware accepted a $500 advance payment from a customer. This event was recorded as a debit to Cash and a credit to Unearned revenue. On October 10, Tim's Ware delivered the merchandise to the customer, but made no additional journal entry. Before Tim's Ware prepares financial statements, the company must:
  A. do nothing. The cash receipt was properly recorded when the advance payment was received from the customer.
  B. prepare a closing entry to reduce the balance in Unearned revenue to zero.
  C. record another journal entry that debits Cash and credits Sales.
  D. prepare an adjusting entry that debits Unearned revenue and credits Sales.

_____ 5. Which of the following events will cause the adjusted trial balance to be out of balance?
  A. An entire day's worth of transactions were not posted from the journal to the general ledger.
  B. An adjusting entry to record the $400 of prepaid rent that had expired was recorded as a debit to Prepaid rent and a credit to Rent expense.
  C. Both A and B will cause the adjusted trial balance to be out of balance.
  D. Neither A nor B will cause the adjusted trial balance to be out of balance.

_____ 6. Which of the following items are increased with debit entries?
  A. Assets and liabilities
  B. Assets and revenues
  C. Assets and expenses
  D. Assets and owners' equity

_____ 7. Debits are _____ better than credits.
  A. sometimes
  B. usually
  C. always
  D. never

_____ 8. Closing entries:
  A. are prepared to prove that debits equal credits.
  B. are prepared before financial statements.
  C. get the temporary accounts ready for the next accounting period.
  D. always increase a corporation's retained earnings.

_____ 9. An ERP includes:
  A. accounting information for financial statements.
  B. human resources information.
  C. information about production and distribution of products.
  D. all of these.

Exercises

1. First put an X in the appropriate box to identify each of these accounts as an asset, liability, owners' equity, revenue, or expense account. Then indicate the normal balance of the account with a DR or CR. Finally, identify each account as permanent (P) or temporary (T).

	Account	Asset	Liability	Owners' equity	Revenue	Expense	Normal balance	Permanent or temporary
a	Cash							
b	Accounts receivable							
c	Sales							
d	Unearned revenue							
e	Inventory							
f	Cost of goods sold							
g	Accounts payable							
h	Prepaid insurance							
i	Insurance expense							
j	Notes receivable							
k	Interest revenue							
l	Interest receivable							
m	Notes payable							
n	Interest expense							
o	Interest payable							
p	Equipment							
q	Depreciation expense							
r	Accumulated depreciation							
s	Salary expense							
t	Salaries payable							
u	Common stock							
v	Retained earnings							
w	Dividends							
x	Prepaid rent							
y	Rent expense							
z	Other payables							

2. Prepare the journal entries needed for each of the following situations.
   a. On April 1, 2005, Tim's Ware sold merchandise for $800. Twenty percent of the customers paid cash and the rest promised to pay next month. The merchandise originally cost Tim's Ware $500.

   Record the sale.

Ref.	Date	Transaction	Debit	Credit
2a				

Record the cost of goods sold.

Ref.	Date	Transaction	Debit	Credit
2a				

b. On December 31, 2005, the unadjusted trial balance shows Supplies of $300. However, only $50 of supplies remain. Prepare the adjusting journal entry at December 31, 2005.

Ref.	Date	Transaction	Debit	Credit
2b				

c. In March of 2004, Able Bakery bought a delivery van that cost $25,000, expecting to use the van for five years. Able Bakery does not prepare monthly financial statements, so it makes adjusting entries only once a year. Prepare the adjusting journal entry at December 31, 2005.

Ref.	Date	Transaction	Debit	Credit
2c				

d. On October 5, 2005, *Tanks a Lot*, the monthly magazine for tropical fish fanciers, received payment for one-year subscriptions from twenty new subscribers. A subscription to *Tanks a Lot* costs $24 for twelve monthly issues. All twenty new subscriptions will begin November 1, 2005.

Record the cash received October 5, 2005.

Ref.	Date	Transaction	Debit	Credit
2d				

Tanks a Lot does not prepare monthly financial statements, so it makes adjusting entries only once a year. Prepare the adjusting journal entry at December 31, 2005.

Ref.	Date	Transaction	Debit	Credit
2d				

e. On December 31, 2005, the unadjusted trial balance for Tim's Ware shows Prepaid insurance of $2,400. This represents the amount the company paid in August for a two-year policy effective September 1, 2005. Tim's Ware does not prepare monthly financial statements, so it makes adjusting entries only once a year. Prepare the adjusting journal entry at December 31, 2005.

Ref.	Date	Transaction	Debit	Credit
2e				

f. On December 31, 2005, the adjusted trial balance for Tim's Ware shows Sales of $50,000 and Dividends of $10,000.

Record the closing entry for Sales at December 31, 2005.

Ref.	Date	Transaction	Debit	Credit
2f				

Record the closing entry for Dividends at December 31, 2005.

Ref.	Date	Transaction	Debit	Credit
2f				

Completion Statements

1.   journal
2.   ledger or general ledger
3.   posting
4.   chart of accounts
5.   trial balance (can be unadjusted, adjusted or postclosing)
6.   dividends
7.   debit
8.   permanent (or real)
9.   temporary
10.   enterprise-wide resource planning

True/False

1.   False   Although many large companies now use ERPs, many other companies still use the traditional general ledger system described in the chapter. It might be a computerized system, but it is still the same basic general ledger system.
2.   False   The journal shows financial events in chronological order, the same order in which they take place. The general ledger groups together transactions that affect a particular account.
3.   False   Assets are on the left-hand side of the accounting equation. They are increased with left-handed, debit entries. Assets are decreased with credit entries.
4.   True
5.   False   The postclosing trial balance is used to verify that debits still equal credits after closing entries have been made in the journal and posted to the general ledger. The accountant also reviews the postclosing trial balance to make sure that all of the temporary accounts have

zero balances. Furthermore, since many companies group accounts together and show them as a single financial statement line item, the postclosing trial balance might show more detail than the balance sheet.

6.　　False　Financial statements are prepared after adjusting entries but before closing entries. Since closing reduces the balances in temporary accounts to zero, it would be impossible to prepare an income statement after closing, because it would show $0 revenue and $0 expenses.

7.　　True

8.　　True

9.　　False　Only in the first year of a company's operations is it true that all accounts begin with zero balances. In subsequent years, only the temporary accounts (revenues, expenses, and Dividends) begin the fiscal year with zero balances. Permanent accounts (asset, liability, and owners' equity accounts) have balances carried forward from the end of the previous fiscal year.

10.　　True

Multiple Choice

1. C　The adjustment for accrued interest on a note payable includes a debit to Interest expense and a credit (not a debit) to Interest payable. The adjusting entry to accrue interest on a note receivable (not payable) would include a debit to Interest receivable and a credit (not a debit) to Interest revenue.

2. C　The adjusting entry for depreciation on equipment includes a debit (not a credit) to Depreciation expense and a credit to Accumulated depreciation. Although the entry decreases the carrying value of the equipment, it is not made directly to the Equipment account. Depreciation does not require a payment of cash, so the entry will not decrease (credit) the Cash account.

3. A　For every journal entry, the dollars of debits must equal the dollars of credits. A journal entry that involves two debit entries with no offsetting credit(s) will cause the general ledger and the adjusted trial balance to be out of balance. Since debits equal credits, the error described in B. will not cause the adjusted trial balance to be out of balance. Even though the dollar amounts are wrong for two of the accounts, total debits will still equal total credits.

4. D　It is true that the cash receipt was recorded properly on October 1. No additional debit to Cash should be recorded. However, the company also recorded Unearned revenue, a liability to deliver goods in the future. Now that the merchandise has been delivered, an adjusting entry is needed to remove the liability and record the sale that has finally taken place. A closing entry would reduce the balances in revenue, expense, and Dividends accounts to zero, but it would not affect the Unearned revenue account, which is a liability.

5. D　Although the dollar amounts for many of the accounts may be incorrect, the debits will still equal the credits. Even a backwards entry like B. will not make the trial balance out of balance, since the entry has both a debit and a credit for the same amount.

6. C　Assets are on the left-hand side of the accounting equation and are increased with left-handed, debit entries. Liabilities and owners' equity are on the right-hand side of the accounting equation and are increased with right-handed, credit entries. It follows that liabilities and owners' equity are decreased with debit entries. Since expenses decrease owners' equity, an increase in an expense account is recorded with a debit.

7. A　Debits and credits are neither good nor bad by themselves. The terms simply mean "left " and "right." An increase in cash is recorded as a debit to Cash. Most companies would consider this debit to be good. On the other hand, most companies are pleased when sales increase. Sales are recorded with credits to revenue accounts.

8. C　Closing entries reduce the balance in the temporary accounts (revenues, expenses and

Dividends) to zero. Closing entries also increase Retained earnings for revenues. However, closing entries also decrease Retained earnings for expenses and dividends. If expenses and dividends are greater than revenues for an accounting period, closing entries will decrease (not increase) Retained earnings.

9. D   An enterprise resource planning system stores data that is shared by many departments company-wide.

Exercises

1.

	Account	Asset	Liability	Owners' equity	Revenue	Expense	Normal balance	Permanent or temporary
a	Cash	X					DR	P
b	Accounts receivable	X					DR	P
c	Sales				X		CR	T
d	Unearned revenue		X				CR	P
e	Inventory	X					DR	P
f	Cost of goods sold					X	DR	T
g	Accounts payable		X				CR	P
h	Prepaid insurance	X					DR	P
i	Insurance expense					X	DR	T
j	Notes receivable	X					DR	P
k	Interest revenue				X		CR	T
l	Interest receivable	X					DR	P
m	Notes payable		X				CR	P
n	Interest expense					X	DR	T
o	Interest payable		X				CR	P
p	Equipment	X					DR	P
q	Depreciation expense					X	DR	T
r	Accumulated depreciation	X					CR	P
s	Salary expense					X	DR	T
t	Salaries payable		X				CR	P
u	Common stock			X			CR	P
v	Retained earnings			X			CR	P
w	Dividends			X			DR	T
x	Prepaid rent	X					DR	P
y	Rent expense					X	DR	T
z	Other payables		X				CR	P

2.

Ref.	Date	Transaction	Debit	Credit
2a	4/01/05	Cash	160	
		Accounts receivable	640	
		Sales		800
		To record sales		

Ref.	Date	Transaction	Debit	Credit
2a	4/01/05	Cost of goods sold	500	
		Inventory		500
		To record cost of goods sold		

Ref.	Date	Transaction	Debit	Credit
2b	12/31/05	Supplies expense	250	
		Supplies		250
		To record supplies used: $300 - 50 = $250		

Ref.	Date	Transaction	Debit	Credit
2c	12/31/05	Depreciation expense	5,000	
		Accumulated depreciation		5,000
		To record depreciation expense $25,000 / 5 years = $5,000		

Ref.	Date	Transaction	Debit	Credit
2d	10/05/05	Cash	480	
		Unearned revenue		480
		To record cash received for subscriptions		

Ref.	Date	Transaction	Debit	Credit
2d	12/31/05	Unearned revenue	80	
		Subscription revenue		80
		To record revenue earned $24 / 12 months times 2 months times 20 subscribers = $80		

Ref.	Date	Transaction	Debit	Credit
2e	12/31/05	Insurance expense	400	
		Prepaid insurance		400
		To record insurance expense $2,400 / 24 months times 4 months = $400		

Ref.	Date	Transaction	Debit	Credit
2f	12/31/05	Sales	50,000	
		Retained earnings		50,000
		To close the Sales account		

Ref.	Date	Transaction	Debit	Credit
2f	12/31/05	Retained earnings	10,000	
		Dividends		10,000
		To close the Dividends account		

CHAPTER 5
ACQUISITIONS: PURCHASE AND USE OF BUSINESS ASSETS

Chapter Overview

When a business begins it must first obtain financing. Then it must set up the infrastructure for the company by acquiring **long-term** (or **fixed**) **assets** such as property, plant, and equipment. From Chapter 5, you should understand how the financial statements show the purchase, use, and sale of these long-term assets that last for longer than 1 year.

Chapter Highlights

1. There are two types of long-term assets. **Tangible assets** are assets used in the business to help generate revenue. They can be seen and touched and include property, plant, equipment, and natural resources. **Intangible assets**, whose true value resides in the rights and privileges given to the owners, include copyrights, patents, franchises, trademarks, and goodwill.

2. When a long-term asset is purchased its cost is **capitalized**, meaning the cost is recorded as an asset rather than an expense. Since the asset is used to generate revenue, the matching principle requires the cost of the asset to be allocated to an expense on the income statement over the periods it is used. This process of **expensing (writing off)** the cost of a long-term asset to expense is called **depreciation** for plant and equipment, **depletion** for natural resources, and **amortization** for intangible assets. Land is the only long-term asset that remains on the books at cost.

3. The **historical cost principle** requires the long-term assets be recorded at the purchase price plus any costs necessary to get the asset in place and ready to use. Such additional costs include freight-in, transportation insurance, installation costs, commissions, architect and attorney fees, construction costs, and the costs of renovating, repairing, or preparing the asset for use.

4. Two or more long-term assets are sometimes bought for a single price. These assets may depreciate at different rates or not at all (land). Thus the assets must be recorded separately. The process of splitting the cost is called a **basket purchase allocation**. The **relative fair market value method** is a common method used to assign the joint costs to the individual assets using the individual assets' market values at the time of purchase. The fair market value of a single asset is divided by the sum of the assets' fair market values to arrive at a percent. This percent is then multiplied by the total cost to get the asset's individual cost.

5. **Depreciation** is a systematic, rational allocation of the cost of a fixed asset to expense over the periods benefited and does not measure the actual physical deterioration or decrease in market value of the asset. The **book value** (or **carrying value**) of an asset is the cost of the asset minus **accumulated depreciation** (all the depreciation taken to date).

6. GAAP allows three common methods of depreciation for financial statements. (Methods used for income tax returns are in accordance with the tax codes, not GAAP). The effect of the adjusting entry to record depreciation (or use of an asset) during an accounting period is the same regardless of the method used:

Assets	Liabilities	Owners' equity
- Accumulated depreciation		- Depreciation expense

The income statement will show depreciation expense for the accounting period. The balance sheet will show:

Cost
Less accumulated depreciation
Net book value

Accumulated depreciation, unlike depreciation expense, increases so the balance equals all the depreciation taken to date, not just the current period's depreciation. The net book value is the amount of usefulness left in the asset. Depreciation expense is a non-cash expense, so the statement of cash flows will never show cash paid for depreciation.

- **Straight-line depreciation** calculates depreciation expense as the depreciable base divided by the estimated useful life of the asset. The **depreciable base** equals the cost of the asset minus the residual value. The **residual value** (or salvage value) is what the company estimates it can sell the asset for when it is done using it. The **estimated useful life** is the number of periods the company estimates it will benefit from the use of the asset. The amount of depreciation will be the same each accounting period, which makes this a simple method to use.

- **Activity (units of production) depreciation** calculates the depreciation rate as the depreciable base divided by the estimated total units of activity the asset will provide. This depreciation rate is then multiplied by the actual number of units used or produced during the accounting period. The activity and straight-line methods differ in that the activity method 1) uses units (not time) in the denominator, 2) requires multiplying the number of actual units used or produced during the accounting period by the depreciation rate, and 3) may result in different depreciation expense each period depending on the amount of use.

- **Declining-balance method** is an **accelerated method** that allows for more depreciation expense in the early years and less in the later years of an asset's life. A common rate used is 200% and is called **double-declining balance** because the rate at which an asset is depreciated is 200% or twice that of the straight-line rate. For example, if the life of an asset is 5 years, the straight-line rate is 1/5 or 20% and the double-declining balance rate is twice that, or 2/5 or 40%. Depreciation expense for the period is calculated by multiplying the net book value by the double-declining balance rate. Since the net book value is cost minus accumulated depreciation, the net book value will become smaller every period the asset is depreciated. Thus, each later period's

depreciation expense is smaller than the prior period's expense. Since the residual value is not built into the double declining balance calculation, the depreciation will need to be adjusted to ensure the net book value equals the residual value by the end of its useful life.

7. Any expenditure that will benefit more than one accounting period is called a **capital expenditure**. **Capitalizing** a cost means to record the cost as an asset on the balance sheet. As the asset is used to help generate revenue, it will become an expense on the income statement. A **revenue expenditure** has no future benefit beyond the current accounting period, and is an expense on the income statement. The matching principle requires **expensing** the cost in the same period as the related revenue, hence the term revenue expenditure. Companies usually have policies that dictate whether a cost is a capital expenditure (an asset) or revenue expenditure (an expense).

- For the sake of efficiency, the materiality principle allows companies to expense certain small dollar capital expenditures rather than capitalizing the cost and later having to depreciate the asset over time. An example would be the purchase of a $10 wastebasket.

- Betterments are capital expenditures that either increase the useful life, efficiency, or productivity of the asset. Remodeling and adding an addition to a building are examples of capital expenditures.

- Ordinary repairs are revenue expenditures because they are routine and do not significantly increase the life or efficiency of an asset. Painting, re-shingling a roof, and tune-ups for vehicles and machines are examples of revenue expenditures.

8. The asset's useful life and residual (or salvage) value are estimates made by managers that may later need to be revised because of additional information. Revising an estimate is not treated as an error; it does not require restating previous records and financial statements. The revision is used only for future

periods by adjusting the depreciation formula using the net book value (cost minus accumulated depreciation) and the new residual value or useful life.

- For example, an asset cost $1,000, had a residual value of $100, and useful life of 3 years. Its net book value at the end of the second year using straight-line was $600 (before making an adjusting entry for depreciation expense), at which time management decides to revise the residual value to $200 and the useful life to 4 more years. The depreciation will now be changed to equal the net book value ($600) minus the new residual value ($200) depreciated over the new estimated useful life of 4 years.

9. **Depletion** of natural resources (farms, forests, oil wells, and mines) is similar to the activity depreciation method in determining the amount of the cost of the natural resources to be shown as depletion expense in the current accounting period. The units of output are the units the natural resource produces such as tons of ore, units of lumber cut, etc.

10. **Amortization** of intangible assets (copyrights, patents, franchises, etc.) is similar to the straight-line method in determining the amount of the cost of the intangible asset to be shown as amortization expense in the current accounting period. GAAP limits the useful life to 40 years or less. GAAP requires research and development (R&D) costs to be expensed immediately (*i.e.*, not capitalized) since it is too uncertain as to whether the costs will result in future benefit.

11. When the company finally sells an asset at the end of its useful life, the price often differs from the net book value. The result is a gain if the amount received is greater than the net book value or a loss if the amount received is less than the net book value.

- A machine that originally cost $1,000 with accumulated depreciation of $800 at the end of its useful life has a net book value equal to its estimated residual value of $200. If the **proceeds** (or price the asset sells for) are $300, then a gain is recorded:

Assets	Liab.	Owners' equity
$ 300 Cash		
(1,000) Machine		
800 Accumulated depreciation		$200 Gain on sale of machine

If the machine sold for only $150, then a loss would be recorded:

Assets	Liab.	Owners' equity
$150 Cash		
(1,000) Machine		
800 Accumulated depreciation		$(50) Loss on sale of machine

- Gains or losses from sales of assets not sold in the ordinary course of business are reported on the income statement, usually below the subtotal "operating income."

12. GAAP are the rules followed in preparing financial statements. The Internal Revenue Code dictates the legal rules used for preparing tax returns. A significant difference in the rules is the method of depreciating assets. A common method used in calculating the deduction for depreciation on tax returns (not financial statements) is the **Modified Accelerated Cost Recovery System** (or **MACRS**). This method results in assets being written off very quickly. The high deduction for depreciation results in lower taxes. The tax authorities intended to provide an incentive for companies to invest the excess cash, due to lower taxes, in more fixed assets, which in turn should spur the economy.

13. The financial statements provide useful information for decision-makers regarding long-term assets. The balance sheet reports the cost, the accumulated depreciation (depletion or amortization), and the net book value of long-term assets that reflects the future usefulness of the assets. The income statement includes depreciation (depletion and amortization) expense (not necessarily as separate line items). The expense reflects the use of the asset during the current accounting period matched with the related revenue the asset helped to generate. Finally, the notes to the financial statements provide additional useful information such as the depreciation methods used and the useful lives of the long-term assets.

14. A ratio that measures how well a company is using its assets to generate revenue is **return on assets** (or ROA) and equals net income divided by average total assets. Since ROA is a measure of how well owners' (not creditors') money is used, some argue it is better to add interest expense (which is the creditors' return on their money) back into net income in the numerator. ROA is meaningful only when compared to ROA from other years or other companies. Before an asset is purchased, companies often calculate the ROA for that particular asset as net income from the asset divided by the investment in that asset.

15. Safeguarding assets is one of the main purposes of an internal control system in minimizing the risk of theft or damage. Limiting access to the assets is a key control. Separating duties is also important. Those responsible for record keeping should be separate from those who have physical custody of the assets. The assets and related records and controls should be monitored on an on-going basis.

Featured Exercise

On January 1, 2004, the San Diego Sea World purchased Arco the whale from the Washington Coast Aquarium. Arco cost $500,000 plus 5% sales tax. The transportation costs included $4,000 for an 11-ton truck and crane, $100,000 for airfare, and $1,000 transportation insurance premiums. The San Diego Sea World paid $50,000 in fish food, $6,000 annual insurance premiums, and $20,000 in training and maintenance costs for Arco during 2004. Arco's estimated useful life is 10 years and 8,000 performances. The residual value for Arco is 5,000 pounds at $2 per pound. Arco performed in 750 performances during 2004 and 820 during 2005.

Required:

Part A: Identify which costs the San Diego Sea World should capitalize (*i.e.*, capital expenditures) and which costs should be expensed (*i.e.*, revenue expenditures) for the year ended December 31, 2004.

Part B: What is the effect of depreciation on San Diego Sea World's accounting equation.

Part C: Calculate the depreciation expense, accumulated depreciation and the net book value of Arco the whale using the three depreciation methods (straight-line, activity, and double-declining balance methods) for the years ended December 31, 2004 and 2005.

Part D: Show the effect of the sale of Arco for $14,000 at the end of its useful life assuming a net book value of $10,000 at the time of sale.

Solution

Part A: The costs to get Arco in place and ready to perform that should be capitalized:

Whale	$500,000
Sales tax (0.05 x $500,000)	25,000
Truck and crane rental	4,000
Airfare	100,000
Transportation insurance	1,000
Total cost of whale	$630,000

The costs that are revenue expenditures are as follows:

Fish food	$ 50,000
Insurance premiums	6,000
Training and maintenance	20,000
Depreciation	
(amount depends on method used)	

Part B:

Assets	Liabilities	Owners' equity
-Accumulated depreciation		-Depreciation expense

Part C: **Straight-line method**:

Depreciation expense on the income statement for the year ended December 31, 2004 is $62,000.

$$\frac{\text{Cost - residual value}}{\text{Estimated useful life}} = \frac{\$630,000 - (\$2 \times 5,000 \text{ pounds})}{10 \text{ years}} = \$62,000$$

Accumulated depreciation on the balance sheet at December 31, 2004 is $(62,000)

The net book value of Arco on the balance sheet at December 31, 2004 is $568,000 or the cost minus accumulated depreciation ($630,000 - 62,000).

Depreciation expense on the income statement for the year ended December 31, 2005 is $62,000.

$$\frac{\text{Cost - residual value}}{\text{Estimated useful life}} = \$62,000 \text{ (same for each year)}$$

Accumulated depreciation (a contra asset) on the balance sheet at December 31, 2005 is $(124,000) or $(62,000) for each of the two years combined.

The net book value of Arco on the balance sheet at December 31, 2005 is $506,000 or the cost minus accumulated depreciation ($630,000 - 124,000).

Activity method:

Depreciation expense on the income statement for the year ended December 31, 2004 is $58,125.

$$\text{Depreciation rate} = \frac{\text{Cost - residual value}}{\text{Estimated total performances}} = \frac{\$630,000 - 10,000}{8,000} = \$77.50 \text{ per performance}$$

Depreciation expense = Depreciation rate x performances in 2004 = $77.50 x 750 = $58,125.

Accumulated depreciation on the balance sheet at December 31, 2004 is $(58,125).

The net book value of Arco on the balance sheet at December 31, 2004 is $571,875 or the cost minus accumulated depreciation ($630,000 - 58,125).

Depreciation expense on the income statement for the year ended December 31, 2005 is $63,550.

Depreciation rate x performances in 2005 = $77.50 x 820 = $63,550.

Accumulated depreciation on the balance sheet at December 31, 2005 is $(121,675) or $(58,125) beginning accumulated depreciation plus (63,550) accumulated depreciation for 2005.

The net book value of Arco on the balance sheet at December 31, 2005 is $508,325 or the cost minus accumulated depreciation or ($630,000 - 121,675).

Double-declining balance method:

Depreciation expense on the income statement for the year ended December 31, 2004 is $126,000.

$$\text{Net book value} \times \frac{2}{\text{Estimated useful life}} = (\$630,000 - 0) \times \frac{2}{10} = \$126,000.$$

Accumulated depreciation on the balance sheet at December 31, 2004 is $(126,000).

The net book value of Arco on the balance sheet at December 31, 2004 is $504,000 or the cost minus accumulated depreciation ($630,000 - 126,000).

Depreciation expense on the income statement for the year ended December 31, 2005 is $100,800.

$$\text{Net book value} \times \frac{2}{\text{Estimated useful life}} = (\$630,000 - 126,000) \times \frac{2}{10} = \$100,800.$$

Accumulated depreciation on the balance sheet at December 31, 2005 is $(226,800) or $(126,000) beginning accumulated depreciation plus (100,800) accumulated depreciation for 2005.

The net book value of Arco on the balance sheet at December 31, 2005 is $403,200 or the cost minus accumulated depreciation or ($630,000 - 226,800).

Part D: Proceeds minus net book value = $14,000 - 10,000 = $4,000 gain on sale of Arco.

Assets	Liabilities	Owners' equity
$14,000 Cash (630,000) Whale 620,000 Accumulated depreciation		$4,000 Gain on sale of whale

Review Questions and Exercises

Completion Statements

Fill in the blank(s) to complete each sentence.

1. _____ can be seen and touched and include property, plant, equipment, and natural resources.

2. _____ whose true value resides in the rights and privileges given to the owners, include copyrights, patents, franchises, trademarks, and goodwill.

3. When a long-term asset is purchased its cost is _____ or is recorded as an asset rather than an expense.

4. The process of splitting the cost among assets purchased together is called a _____. The _____ is a common method used to assign the joint costs to the individual assets using the individual assets' market values at the time of purchase.

5. The cost of an asset minus its accumulated depreciation is called _____.

6. The depreciation expense using the straight-line method equals _____.

7. The depreciation expense using the activity method equals _____.

8. _____ is an _____ that allows for more depreciation expense in the early years and less in the later years of an asset's life.

9. A _____ is the opposite of a capital expenditure which benefits only the current accounting period and it is an expense on the income statement.

10. _____ are capital expenditures that either increase the useful life, efficiency, or productivity of the asset.

True/False

Indicate whether each statement is true (T) or false (F).

1. Capital expenditures are costs that are found on the balance sheet as assets; revenue expenditures are costs that are found on the income statement as expenses.

2. Depreciation expense will always be higher in the first year of an asset's life when the double-declining balance method is used instead of the straight-line method.

3. MACRS is a depreciation method used only for financial reporting and not tax reporting.

4. A gain on the sale of a long-term asset will result when the salvage value is greater than the proceeds.

5. A basket purchase allocation is required when the items purchased are all revenue expenditures and the costs are less than their relative fair market values.

6. Despite the method of depreciation chosen by a company, the amount of accumulated depreciation will be the same at the end of the asset's useful life.

7. Despite the method of depreciation chosen by a company, the amount of depreciation expense will be the same each accounting period.

8. Despite the method of depreciation chosen by a company, the effect on the accounting equation is to decrease assets and decrease owners' equity.

9. The return on assets will increase if a company purchases inventory on account instead of paying cash.

10. Internal controls surrounding the safeguarding of assets include monitoring the assets by comparing the physical assets to what is recorded in the information system.

Multiple Choice

Select the best answer for each question.

_____1. Which of the following should be recorded as an intangible asset?
A. Research and development costs on a new project
B. Cost of advertising a new product
C. Cost of employee education
D. Cost to obtain exclusive rights to manufacture a unique product.

_____2. Which financial statement shows how much cash was paid for newly acquired property plant and equipment?
A. Statement of financial position
B. Statement of operations
C. Statement of cash flows
D. Statement of changes in stockholders' equity.

_____3. Which of the following accounting treatments violates the matching principle?
A. A capital expenditure is recorded as an asset when acquired and expensed as it generates revenue.
B. A revenue expenditure is recorded as an expense.
C. A long-term asset is expensed over its useful life using one of the depreciation methods in accordance with GAAP.
D. None of the above violates the matching principle.

_____4. The bookkeeper did not record depreciation expense for the period. As a result:
A. assets will be understated.
B. liabilities will be understated.
C. owners' equity will be overstated
D. There is no effect on the accounting equation because accumulated depreciation is a contra asset account that offsets depreciation expense.

_____5. The bookkeeper recorded a capital expenditure as an asset. As a result:
A. assets will be understated.
B. liabilities will be understated.
C. owners' equity will be overstated
D. There is no effect on the accounting equation because capital expenditures should be recorded as assets, not expenses.

_____6. The net book value (or carrying value) of an asset is
A. increased when the market value of the asset increases.
B. the original cost of the asset minus its salvage value minus its accumulated depreciation.
C. the amount for which the asset could be sold.
D. the original cost of the asset minus its accumulated depreciation.

_____7. E-buy, Inc. purchased a mainframe computer for $500,000 with state sales tax of $20,000. It cost $1,000 to transport and $5,000 to install and $10,000 to test the computer. Six months later the computer was cleaned for $500 and a programmer was paid $300 to make adjustments to the programs that back up the accounting information system. The proper treatment in recording these events is to:
A. capitalize $500,000 as an asset on the balance sheet and show $36,800 as expenses on the income statement.
B. capitalize $520,000 as an expense on the balance sheet and $16,800 as revenue expenditures on the balance sheet.
C. capitalize $536,000 as an asset on the balance sheet and show $800 as expenses on the income statement.
D. capitalize $536,800 as an asset on the balance sheet.

_____8. The process of expensing the cost of an intangible asset over its useful life is called:
A. amortization.
B. depreciation.
C. depletion.
D. accumulated depreciation.
E. None of the above. An intangible asset is not expensed over its useful life.

_____9. The process of expensing the cost of a natural resource over its useful life is called:
A. amortization.
B. depreciation.
C. depletion.
D. accumulated depreciation.
E. None of the above. Natural resources are not expensed over their useful lives.

_____10. Fair Market, Inc. purchased land, a warehouse and a delivery truck for $450,000. The appraised values for the items are $300,000, $150,000, and $50,000, respectively. Fair Market should record this purchase:
A. as an expense of $450,000 on the income statement.
B. as assets on the balance sheet: $270,000 for the land, $135,000 for the building, and $45,000 for the delivery truck.
C. as assets on the balance sheet: $300,000 for the land, $150,000 for the building, and $50,000 for the delivery truck.
D. as assets on the balance sheet: $500,000 for basket purchase minus $50,000 accumulated depreciation.

Exercises

For Exercises 1 - 4: Fill in the correct dollar amount and put an "X" in the column of the financial statement where the item will most likely be found.

1. On April 1, AAA, Inc. paid $36,000 cash for a truck. AAA plans to use the truck for 5 years and then sell it for $6,000. The straight-line depreciation method was used. Any necessary adjusting entries were correctly made at the end of April and at the end of May.

Financial statement line item:	Amount as of or for the month ended April 30	Select one for each line item:		
		Income Statement	Balance Sheet	Statement of Cash Flows
a. Cash paid for truck				
b. Depreciation expense				
c. Accumulated depreciation				
d. Truck (net of accumulated depreciation)				

Financial statement line item:	Amount as of or for the month ended May 31	Select one for each line item: (if applicable)		
		Income Statement	Balance Sheet	Statement of Cash Flows
e. Cash paid for truck				
f. Depreciation expense				
g. Accumulated depreciation				
h. Truck (net of accumulated depreciation)				
i. Cash paid for depreciation expense				

2. On January 1, 2003, E-commerce began operations and purchased a truck for $25,000 cash. This truck has an estimated useful life of 4 years and a salvage value of $5,000. The straight-line depreciation method was used.

Financial statement line item:	Amount as of or for the year ended December 31, 2003	Select one for each line item:		
		Income Statement	Balance Sheet	Statement of Cash Flows
a. Depreciation expense				
b. Accumulated depreciation				
c. Truck (net of accumulated depreciation)				

Financial statement line item:	Amount as of or for the year ended December 31, 2004	Select one for each line item:		
		Income Statement	Balance Sheet	Statement of Cash Flows
d. Depreciation expense				
e. Accumulated depreciation				
f. Truck (net of accumulated depreciation)				

On January 1, 2005, E-commerce sold the truck (in 2. above) for $12,000.

Financial statement line item:	Amount as of or for the year ended December 31, 2005	Select one for each line item:		
		Income Statement	Balance Sheet	Statement of Cash Flows
g. Gain (loss) on sale of truck				
h. Proceeds from sale of truck				

3. On January 1, 2005, Slippery Slope, Inc. purchased equipment for $400,000 cash. This equipment has an estimated useful life of 10 years and a salvage value of $20,000. The **double-declining depreciation method** was used.

Financial statement line item:	Amount as of or for the year ended December 31, 2005	Select one for each line item:		
		Income Statement	**Balance Sheet**	**Statement of Cash Flows**
a. Depreciation expense				
b. Accumulated depreciation				
c. Equipment (net of accumulated depreciation)				

Financial statement line item:	Amount as of or for the year ended December 31, 2006	Select one for each line item:		
		Income Statement	**Balance Sheet**	**Statement of Cash Flows**
d. Depreciation expense				
e. Accumulated depreciation				
f. Equipment (net of accumulated depreciation)				

4. On January 1, 2000, Tons-of-Coal, Inc. purchased mining equipment for $70,000, which had an estimated useful life of five years or 200,000 tons of coal and an estimated residual value of $10,000. Tons-of-Coal used the activity method of depletion and the machine produced 35,000 tons in 2000 and 40,000 in 2001.

Financial statement line item:	Amount as of or for the year ended December 31, 2000	Select one for each line item:		
		Income Statement	Balance Sheet	Statement of Cash Flows
a. Depreciation expense				
b. Accumulated depreciation				
c. Machinery (net of accumulated depreciation)				

Financial statement line item:	Amount as of or for the year ended December 31, 2001	Select one for each line item:		
		Income Statement	Balance Sheet	Statement of Cash Flows
d. Depreciation expense				
e. Accumulated depreciation				
f. Machinery (net of accumulated depreciation)				

5. Show the effect on the accounting equation for each of the following:

	Assets	Liabilities	Owners' equity
a. On January 1, 2001, Ridof, Inc. sold its van for $1,000 cash. The van had cost $20,000 and had $18,000 in accumulated depreciation. Record the sale of the van.			
b. Changes, Inc. revised its truck's estimated useful life from 5 years to 4 years at the beginning of its 3rd year. Record depreciation for year 3 given the truck cost $60,000, had accumulated depreciation of $20,000, a residual value of $10,000 and uses the straight-line method.			
c. Safety, Inc. paid $200 for a special insurance policy to cover the delivery of a new machine.			
d. Fixit, Inc. paid $100 to pay for routine repairs of its copy machine.			
e. Expand, Inc. built a $50,000 addition to its building by borrowing from the bank.			
f. Expand, Inc. paid $500 in architect fees related to the addition to its building in e., above.			
g. Tops, Inc. paid $3,000 for a newly shingled roof.			
h. Accume, Inc. recorded $1,000 amortization on its copyright.			
i. Accume, Inc. recorded $3,000 depreciation on its fixed assets.			
j. Rand, Inc. spent $800,000 on research and development during the year.			

6. Calculate the 2002 return on assets for Rachio, Inc. given the selected information from its financial statements:

As of or for the year ended	December 31, 2003	December 31, 2002
Current assets	$18,000	$20,000
Long-term assets	$27,000	$35,000
Current liabilities	$10,000	$10,000
Long-term liabilities	$15,000	$15,000
Sales	$100,000	$100,000
Net income	$4,000	$5,000

Completion Statements

1. Tangible assets
2. Intangible assets
3. capitalized
4. basket purchase allocation; relative fair market value method
5. net book value (or carrying value)
6. (Cost – residual value) / estimated useful life
7. ((Cost – residual value) / estimated total units) times the units produced or used during the period.
8. Declining-balance method, accelerated method
9. Revenue expenditure
10. Betterments

True/False

1. True
2. True
3. False MACRS is a depreciation method used only for tax reporting. The accelerated method used for financial reporting is the declining balance method.
4. False A gain on the sale of a long-term asset will result when the net book value is less than the proceeds.
5. False A basket purchase allocation is needed when the items are purchased together for a single price. The costs must be separated and can be allocated based on their relative fair market values.
6. True
7. False Depreciation expense may differ depending on the method of depreciation used. Straight-line will result in the same expense each accounting period; depreciation expense using the activity method will vary depending on the level of activity; and depreciation expense using the declining-balance method will be higher in the early periods compared to the later years of the life of the asset.
8. True
9. False The return on assets will decrease if a company purchases inventory on account because the denominator will increase while the numerator would be the same as if cash had been paid instead.
10. True

Multiple Choice

1. D Research and development costs, employee education and training costs, and advertising are all revenue expenditures that are expensed, not capitalized.
2. C The cash flow from investing activities section of the statement of cash flows shows how much cash was spent on purchases of long-term assets. The balance sheet shows the balances of long-term assets, their related accumulated depreciation (depletion or amortization), and their net book value. The income statement shows the depreciation (depletion or amortization) expense for the period.
3. D The matching principle requires costs to be expensed in the period the items help generate revenue. Capital expenditures and long-term assets are not expensed because they will help to generate revenues in the future. Revenue expenditures are expensed in the current period since they benefit the current period.

4. C The adjusting entry to record depreciation (depletion and amortization) is to reduce assets and reduce owners' equity. Owners' equity and the assets were not properly reduced, so they will be overstated.

5. D A capital expenditure should be recorded as an asset since it will provide future benefit.

6. D The net book value of an asset is found on the balance sheet and represents the undepreciated balance (or cost minus accumulated depreciation).

7. C All costs incurred to get an asset in place and ready to use are capitalized. Once the asset is in place and being used, the costs for ordinary repairs and upkeep are expensed (revenue expenditures).

8. A The process of expensing the cost of an intangible asset is amortization, the cost of expensing a fixed asset (except land) is depreciation, and the cost of expensing natural resources is depletion.

9. C The process of expensing the cost of an intangible asset is amortization, the cost of expensing a fixed asset (except land) is depreciation, and the cost of expensing natural resources is depletion.

10. B The relative fair market value method allocates the cost as follows:
Land: ($300,000/($300,000 + $150,000 + $50,000)) X $450,000 = $270,000
Warehouse: ($150,000/($300,000 + $150,000 + $50,000)) X $450,000 = $135,000
Truck: ($50,000/($300,000 + $150,000 + $50,000)) X $450,000 = $45,000.

Exercises

1. Financial statement line item:	Amount as of or for the month ended April 30	Income Statement	Balance Sheet	Statement of Cash Flows
a. Cash paid for truck	$36,000			X
b. Depreciation expense	$\frac{\$36,000 - 6,000}{60 \text{ months}} = \$500$	X		
c. Accumulated depreciation	$500		X	
d. Truck (net of accumulated depreciation)	$36,000 - 500 = $35,500		X	

1. (continued) Financial statement line item:	Amount as of or for the month ended May 31	Income Statement	Balance Sheet	Statement of Cash Flows
e. Cash paid for truck	$0			Not shown
f. Depreciation expense	$\frac{\$36,000 - 6,000}{60 \text{ months}} = \$500$	X		
g. Accumulated depreciation	$1,000		X	
h. Truck (net of accumulated depreciation)	$36,000 - 1,000 = $35,000		X	
i. Cash paid for depreciation expense	$0			Not shown

2. Financial statement line item:	Amount as of or for the year ended December 31, 2003	Select one for each line item: Income Statement	Balance Sheet	Statement of Cash Flows
a. Depreciation expense	$25,0000-5,000 =$5,000 / 4 years	X		
b. Accumulated depreciation	$5,000		X	
c. Truck (net of accumulated depreciation)	$25,000 - 5,000 = $20,000		X	

2. (continued) Financial statement line item:	Amount as of or for the year ended December 31, 2004	Select one for each line item: Income Statement	Balance Sheet	Statement of Cash Flows
d. Depreciation expense	$25,0000-5,000 =$5,000 / 4 years	X		
e. Accumulated depreciation	$5,000 + 5,0000 = $10,000		X	
f. Truck (net of accumulated depreciation)	$25,000 - 10,000 = $15,000		X	

2. (continued) Financial statement line item:	Amount as of or for the year ended December 31, 2005	Select one for each line item: Income Statement	Balance Sheet	Statement of Cash Flows
g. Gain (loss) on sale of truck	$12,000 - 15,000 = ($3,000)	X		
h. Proceeds from sale of truck	$12,000			X

3. Financial statement line item:	Amount as of or for the year ended December 31, 2006	Select one for each line item: Income Statement	Balance Sheet	Statement of Cash Flows
a. Depreciation expense	$400,000 x 2/10 = $80,000	X		
b. Accumulated depreciation	$80,000		X	
c. Equipment (net of accumulated depreciation)	$400,000 - 80,000 = $320,000		X	

3. (continued) Financial statement line item:	Amount as of or for the year ended December 31, 2006	Select one for each line item: Income Statement	Balance Sheet	Statement of Cash Flows
d. Depreciation expense	$320,000 x 2/10 = $64,000	X		
e. Accumulated depreciation	$80,000 + 64,000 = $144,000		X	
f. Equipment (net of accumulated depreciation)	$400,000 - 144,000 =$256,000		X	

4. Financial statement line item:	Amount as of or for the year ended December 31, 2000	Income Statement	Balance Sheet	Statement of Cash Flows
a. Depreciation expense	(($70,000 - 10,000)/200,000 tons) x 35,000 tons = $10,500	X		
b. Accumulated depreciation	$10,500		X	
c. Machinery (net of accumulated depreciation)	$70,000 - 10,500 = $59,500		X	

4. (continued) Financial statement line item:	Amount as of or for the year ended December 31, 2001	Income Statement	Balance Sheet	Statement of Cash Flows
d. Depreciation expense	(($70,000 - 10,000)/200,000 tons) x 40,000 tons = $12,000	X		
e. Accumulated depreciation	$10,500 + 12,000 = $22,500		X	
f. Machinery (net of accumulated depreciation)	$70,000 - 22,500 = $47,500		X	

5.	Assets	Liabilities	Owners' equity
a.	$1,000 (20,000) 18,000		$(1,000)
b.	(15,000) or $60,000 - 20,000 - 10,000 = $15,000 2 years		(15,000)
c.	200 (200)		
d.	(100)		(100)
e.	50,000	50,000	
f.	500 (500)		
g.	(3,000)		(3,000)
h.	(1,000)		(1,000)
i.	(3,000)		(3,000)
j.	(800,000)		(800,000)

6.

As of or for the year ended	December 31, 2003	December 31, 2002
Current assets	$18,000	$20,000
Long-term assets	$27,000	$35,000
Total assets	$45,000	$55,000
Net income	$4,000	$5,000

ROA = Net income/Total average assets = $5,000/(($55,000 + 45,000)/2) = 0.1 or 10%

CHAPTER 6
INVENTORY COST FLOW ASSUMPTIONS AND TAXES

Chapter Overview

A significant business process for merchandising companies is the acquisition of, and payment for, inventory - the acquisition/payment cycle. Chapter 6 will help you to understand how a company acquires and accounts for inventory and liabilities and how this information is reported in the financial statements.

Chapter Highlights

1. The acquisition process is well controlled when a company requires the use of the following documents and procedures:

- A **purchase requisition**, a document requesting goods or services needed by someone in the company, should be sent to the company's purchasing agent who obtains the required authorizations and determines the best place to obtain the goods or services.

- The purchasing agent sends copies of a **purchase order** to the selected vendor, the receiving department, and the accounts payable department.

- The receiving department prepares a **receiving report** after it inspects and counts the goods received and compares the information to the purchase order. The quantity, however, is intentionally left blank on the receiving department's *blind* purchase order to encourage an independent count of the goods received. Copies of the receiving report are sent to the purchasing agent and inventory manager so they know the goods have arrived and can update the formal accounting records. A copy is sent to the accounts payable department, so an employee can compare what was received to the purchase order and invoice from the vendor before making payment.

2. The acquisition of inventory affects the accounting records by increasing **Merchandise inventory**, a current asset, and increasing Accounts payable, a current liability (or decreasing Cash if purchased for cash). Later, the Accounts payable is reduced when cash is paid. The matching principle requires that inventory be expensed as cost of goods sold in the same accounting period as the related sale.

3. **Purchase returns and allowances** reflect the amount of defective goods the company returned and price reductions the vendor allowed for defective goods kept by the company. *Gross purchases* less purchase returns and allowances equal *net purchases*. Purchase discounts also reduce the cost of the purchase of inventory. Discounts are expressed in terms such as 2/10, n/30, which means that the buyer gets a 2% discount if the bill is paid within 10 days. Otherwise, no discount will be given and the full amount of the bill is due within 30 days.

4. If the terms of purchase are **FOB shipping point**, then the buyer pays the shipping cost. **Freight-in** is the cost paid by the purchasing company and is included in the buyer's cost of the goods. If the terms are **FOB destination**, then the seller pays the shipping cost. **Freight-out** is the delivery expense for the seller and is an operating expense on the seller's income statement.

5. In calculating cost of goods sold on the income statement, companies do not have to track the actual cost of each specific inventory item sold. It is time-consuming and costly for companies that make many purchases at continually changing costs. GAAP allows companies to select one of several inventory cost flow assumptions when determining the amount of cost of goods sold. The method used does not have to be consistent with the actual physical flow of the goods. Since the various methods can result in significantly differing amounts, GAAP requires the company to disclose the amounts and methods used in its notes to the financial statements. The four basic methods used to calculate cost of goods sold and the cost of ending inventory are:

- **Specific identification method**. The cost of goods sold equals the actual cost of the specific goods that have been sold. This method is the only method where the cost flow is consistent with the physical flow of the goods. This method is time-consuming and costly and is typically used by companies that purchase a small quantity of large, luxury items.

- **Weighted-average method**. An average unit cost is calculated by dividing the total cost of goods available for sale by the total number of units available for sale. The average unit cost is then multiplied 1) by the number of units sold to arrive at cost of goods sold on the income statement and 2) by the number of units remaining to arrive at ending inventory on the balance sheet.

- **First-in, first-out method (FIFO)**. Regardless of which specific items are sold, FIFO assumes the first goods purchased are sold first. Thus, the cost of goods sold is the cost of the older items and ending inventory is the cost of the most recent purchases.

- **Last-in, first-out method (LIFO)**. Regardless of which specific items are sold, LIFO assumes the most recently purchased goods are sold first. Thus, the cost of goods sold is the cost of the newer items and ending inventory is the cost of the older items.

6. A company has to decide not only which inventory cost flow method to use, but also when to record its cost of goods sold. A company will use one of two options:

- A **perpetual inventory** system records cost of goods sold and updates the inventory balance after every sale.

- A **periodic inventory** system records cost of goods sold and updates the inventory balance only periodically - at the end of each accounting period. The amount of cost of goods sold is determined as follows:

Beginning inventory	XX
+Purchases	XX
Goods available for sale	XX
-Ending inventory	(XX)
Cost of goods sold	XX

7. Cost of goods sold is the largest expense in most merchandising companies and on a multi-step income statement it would be presented as follows:

Revenue from sales (or net sales)
-Cost of goods sold (or cost of sales)
Gross margin from sales (or gross profit)
-Operating expenses
Income before income taxes
-Income taxes
Net income

8. The effect of an error in ending inventory on cost of goods sold and net income is as follows:

Beginning inventory	correctly stated
+Purchases	correctly stated
Goods available for sale	correctly stated
-Ending inventory	if overstated
Cost of goods sold	then understated

On the income statement, the understated cost of goods sold causes net income to be overstated. The overstated net income is closed into Retained earnings and Retained earnings will be overstated along with Inventory on the balance sheet.

If the error is not discovered before the next year's financial statements are prepared, then the overstated ending inventory becomes next year's overstated beginning inventory. The effect will be:

Beginning inventory	overstated
+Purchases	correctly stated
Goods available for sale	overstated
-Ending inventory	correctly stated
Cost of goods sold	overstated

On the income statement, the overstated cost of goods sold causes net income to be understated. The understated net income is closed into an already overstated Retained earnings, offsetting the previous year's mistake. Retained earnings and ending inventory on the balance sheet at the end of the second year will be correctly stated.

9. The **gross profit method** provides a means of estimating inventory instead of actually counting the inventory. A company may use this method for estimating inventory for monthly or quarterly financial statements or for estimating lost inventory for insurance claims. Estimated inventory is calculated by first estimating the company's typical gross profit percentage (gross profit divided by sales) from prior periods. Second, the company multiplies the sales for the period by the estimated gross profit percentage to arrive at an estimated gross profit margin. Third, the sales minus the estimated gross profit margin equals the estimated cost of goods sold. Fourth, the ending inventory can then be determined by subtracting the estimated cost of goods sold from the goods available for sale (beginning inventory plus purchases).

10. GAAP requires inventory to be valued on the balance sheet at the lower of its cost (per the accounting records using one of the cost flow assumptions such as LIFO or FIFO) or the market value at the balance sheet date, whichever is lower. This rule is to help prevent inventory from being overstated. Market value is the replacement cost, that is, the cost to buy similar inventory. If the market value is lower than the cost of inventory, then the inventory must be reduced as follows:

Assets	Liab.	Owners' Equity
- Inventory		- Loss on inventory write-down

The inventory is never written back up if the market value increases.

11. Financial statements and related footnotes provide information concerning inventory such as the cost of goods sold (an expense on the income statement), inventory balance (a current asset on the balance sheet), and cost flow assumptions used (in the notes to the financial statements). This information is helpful in determining how quickly a company is selling and replacing its inventory and how much its gross margin on sales ratio contributes to profits. These measures are calculated as follows:

$$\text{Inventory Turnover Ratio} = \frac{\text{Cost of goods sold}}{\text{Average inventory}}$$

$$\text{Gross Margin on Sales Ratio} = \frac{\text{Gross margin}}{\text{Sales}}$$

12. In the acquisition process described in section 1, acquiring goods involved a number of steps. The accounts payable department records a liability after an employee reviews and compares the purchase order for items requested, the receiving report for items received, and the invoice from the vendor to confirm its accuracy. The invoice is marked for payment and filed by its date due in a tickler file. A request for payment (a check requisition) is prepared prior to the invoice due date. After payment is made, the invoice is marked as paid.

13. A liability is recognized on the balance sheet when an obligation is incurred as a result of a past transaction. The liabilities are classified on the balance sheet as either current, where the amounts are due within a year, or noncurrent, where the amounts are due beyond a year. The amount of the liability is the amount due or fair market value of the goods or services required to be delivered to satisfy the obligation. Certain liabilities, such as interest payable and unearned revenue, require end-of-period adjustments.

14. Liabilities can be classified into three types. **Definitely determinable liabilities**, such as accounts payable, can be measured exactly. **Estimated liabilities**, such as warranty payable, have some uncertainty in the amount. **Contingent liabilities,** such as lawsuits and tax disputes, are potential obligations from past events that are not recorded as liabilities unless they are both probable and reasonably estimable.

15. Hiring and paying employees is a large component of the acquisition/payment process. An effective payroll system includes a great deal of information about an employee such as marital status, number of dependents, the hours worked based on time cards, pay rates, and payroll taxes. The disbursement of an

employee's pay check affects a company's accounting equation as follows:

Assets	Liabilities	Owners' Equity
- Cash (net pay)	+ Income taxes payable + Social Security and Medicare payable	- Salary expense (gross pay)

The employee's take-home (net pay) is much less than the amount earned (gross pay). The difference is the taxes withheld (payables) from the employee's pay. The company is required by law to act as an agent for the government by sending the money to the proper authorities. These taxes include income taxes, Social Security taxes (currently 6.2% of gross pay) and Medicare taxes (currently 1.45% of gross pay). The employer is also required to match the amount of Social Security taxes and Medicare taxes. When the company pays these taxes the effect on the accounting equation is as follows:

Assets	Liabilities	Owners' Equity
- Cash	- Income taxes payable - Social Security and Medicare payable	- Employers' payroll tax expense

The cash paid includes the employee's taxes and the employer's portion of Social Security and Medicare taxes.

16. There are risks associated with the acquisition and payment of inventory and payroll that must be minimized by implementing internal control policies and procedures. In addition to the controls mentioned previously in section 1., limiting access to inventory by using locked storage rooms and separating the duties of those who keep the inventory records from those who have physical access to the inventory are important controls surrounding inventory. For payroll controls, it is important to ensure that only legitimate employees are paid and that duties are separated so the people who prepare the payroll checks do not distribute the checks.

Featured Exercise

The Ultimate Snowboard Shop's records showed the following information about its beginning inventory, purchases, and sales of snowboards for January 2005:

	Units	Unit Price
Beginning inventory, January 1	10	$200
Purchase, January 15	10	$210
Purchase, January 18	20	$220
Sale, January 20	36	$450
Purchase, January 23	10	$230

For each question below, fill in the correct dollar amount and circle the correct financial statement on which it appears, using the following code:

IS for the income statement for the month ended January 31, 2005
BS for the balance sheet at January 31, 2005
SOCF for the statement of cash flows for the month ended January 31, 2005

1. Assume Ultimate uses a **LIFO perpetual** inventory system.

   a. Cost of goods sold of $_____ appears on the: **IS   BS   SOCF**

   b. Inventory of $_____ appears on the: **IS   BS   SOCF**

   c. Sales of $_____ appears on the: **IS   BS   SOCF**

   d. Gross margin of $_____ appears on the   **IS   BS   SOCF**

2. Assume Ultimate uses a **LIFO periodic** inventory system.

   a. Cost of goods sold of $_____ appears on the: **IS   BS   SOCF**

   b. Inventory of $_____ appears on the: **IS   BS   SOCF**

   c. Sales of $_____ appears on the: **IS   BS   SOCF**

   d. Gross margin of $_____ appears on the   **IS   BS   SOCF**

3. Assume Ultimate uses a **FIFO perpetual** inventory system.

   a. Cost of goods sold of $_____ appears on the: **IS   BS   SOCF**

   b. Inventory of $_____ appears on the: **IS   BS   SOCF**

   c. Gross margin of $_____ appears on the   **IS   BS   SOCF**

4. Assume Ultimate uses a **FIFO periodic** inventory system.

    a. Cost of goods sold of $_____ appears on the: **IS   BS   SOCF**

    b. Inventory of $_____ appears on the: **IS   BS   SOCF**

    c. Gross margin of $_____ appears on the   **IS   BS   SOCF**

5. Assume Ultimate uses a **weighted average periodic** inventory system.

    a. Cost of goods sold of $_____ appears on the: **IS   BS   SOCF**

    b. Inventory of $_____ appears on the: **IS   BS   SOCF**

    c. Gross margin of $_____ appears on the: **IS   BS   SOCF**

6. Which method, LIFO, FIFO, or Weighted-average method, is the right answer for the following questions?

    a. Which method results in the highest net income?

    b. Which method results in the lowest taxes?

    c. Which method results in the highest inventory turnover rate?

    d. Which method results in the highest current ratio?

    e. Which method results in the highest gross margin on sales percentage?

Solution

1. LIFO perpetual:
    a. (20 x $220) + (10 x $210) + (6 x $200) = $7,700; IS
    b. (4 x $200) + (10 x $230) = $3,100; BS
    c. 36 x $450 = $16,200; IS
    d. $16,200 - 7,700 = $8,500; IS

2. LIFO periodic:
    a. (10 x $230) + (20 x $220) + (6 x $210) = $7,960; IS
    b. (10 x $200) + (4 x $210) = $2,840; BS
    c. 36 x $450 = $16,200; IS
    d. $16,200 - 7,960 = $8,240; IS

3. FIFO perpetual:
    a. (10 x $200) + (10 x $210) + (16 x $220) = $7,620; IS
    b. (10 x $230) + (4 x $220) = $3,180; BS
    c. $16,200 - 7,620 = $8,580; IS

4. FIFO periodic: same answers as in FIFO perpetual (3. above).

5. Weighted average periodic: Weighted average cost = $\dfrac{\text{cost of goods available for sale}}{\text{total snowboards available for sale}}$

$$= \frac{(10 \times \$200) + (10 \times \$210) + (20 \times \$220) + (10 \times \$230)}{10 + 10 + 20 + 10} = \frac{\$10,800}{50} = \$216 \text{ per snowboard}$$

   a. 36 snowboards x $216 = $7,776; IS
   b. (50 – 36) x $216 = $3,024; BS
   c. $16,200 - 7,776 = $8,424; IS

6. a. FIFO The cost of snowboards has been rising. The FIFO method assumes the older, less expensive items are part of cost of goods sold. A lower cost of goods sold results in higher net income.

    b. LIFO The cost of snowboards has been rising. The LIFO method assumes the newer, more expensive items are part of cost of goods sold. A higher cost of goods sold results in lower net income and lower income taxes.

    c. LIFO Inventory turnover equals cost of goods sold divided by inventory. The cost of goods sold in the numerator is higher using LIFO, which assumes the newer, more expensive items are sold first, and the inventory in the denominator is smaller since the older, less expensive items are left in inventory.

    d. FIFO The current ratio equals current assets divided by current liabilities. Inventory is a current asset. FIFO results in a higher inventory balance in times of rising prices than the other methods, because with FIFO the newer, more expensive items are left in inventory. Accounts payable is a current liability and would be the same balance, for the amount owed to the vendors, regardless of which method is used.

    e. FIFO The gross margin on sales percentage equals the gross margin (or sales less cost of goods sold) divided by the sales. In times of rising prices, the FIFO method assumes the older, less expensive items are part of cost of goods sold. A lower cost of goods sold results in a higher gross margin. Since sales in the denominator is the same regardless of which inventory method is used, FIFO will result in the higher percentage.

Review Questions and Exercises

Completion Statements

Fill in the blank(s) to complete each statement.

1. The acquisition process is well controlled when a company requires the use of three documents: _____, _____, and _____.

2. Purchase _____ and _____ reflect the amount of defective goods the company returned and price reductions the vendor allowed for defective goods kept by the company.

3. If the terms of purchase are _____, then the buyer pays the shipping cost. _____ is the cost paid by the purchasing company and is included in the buyer's cost of the goods.

4. If the terms of purchase are _____, then the seller pays the shipping cost. _____ is the delivery expense to the seller and is an operating expense on the seller's income statement.

5. When using the _____ method, the cost of goods sold equals the exact cost of the actual goods that have been sold. This method is the only method where the cost flow is the same as the physical flow of the goods.

6. When using the _____ method, a unit cost is calculated by dividing the total cost of goods available for sale by the total number of units available for sale.

7. The _____ method assumes the first goods purchased are sold first. Thus, the cost of goods sold is the cost of the older items and ending inventory is the cost of the most recent purchases.

8. The _____ method assumes the most recently purchased goods are sold first. Thus, the cost of goods sold is the cost of the newer items and ending inventory is the cost of the older items.

9. A _____ system records cost of goods sold and updates the inventory balance after every sale.

10. A _____ system records cost of goods sold and updates the inventory balance only at the end of each accounting period.

11. The _____ provides a means of estimating inventory instead of actually counting the inventory. A company may use this method for estimating inventory for monthly or quarterly financial statements or for estimating lost inventory for insurance claims.

12. Liabilities can be classified into three types:
_____, such as accounts payable, can be measured exactly.
_____, such as warranty payable, have some uncertainty in the amount.
_____, such as lawsuits and tax disputes, are potential obligations from past events that are not recorded as liabilities unless they are both probable and reasonably estimable.

True/False

Indicate whether each statement is true (T) or false (F).

_____1. The purchase of inventory is recorded as an expense called cost of goods sold.

_____2. A company that uses the last-in, first-out method of valuing cost of goods sold must sell its newer inventory before selling any of its older inventory, even though some of the older items may be perishable.

_____3. A blind purchase order, which does not show the quantity of inventory ordered, is given to the receiving department to encourage an independent count of the inventory.

_____4. The employer must pay the same amount as the employee for Social Security and Medicare.

_____5. An example of a definitely determinable liability is warranty payable.

_____6. The gross profit method is used to estimate cost of goods sold and ending inventory when the actual amounts are not available.

_____7. Goods available for sale equals beginning inventory less cost of goods sold.

_____8. Cost of goods sold can be expressed as goods available for sale less ending inventory.

_____9. A company has a gross margin on sales of 40%. This means that for every $1 of sales the company's cost of goods sold is $0.40.

_____10. For payroll controls, it is important to ensure duties are separated so that the people who prepare the payroll checks do not distribute them.

Multiple Choice

Select the best answer for each question.

_____1. Inventory would be found in:
   A. the current liabilities section of the balance sheet.
   B. the current assets section of the statement of financial position.
   C. the operating section of the statement of operations.
   D. the noncurrent assets section of the balance sheet.

_____2. Which of the following accounting treatments violates the matching principle?
   A. The use of the LIFO cost flow method when the company is a grocery store.
   B. Inventory is expensed in the period it is sold.
   C. Inventory is expensed when purchased.
   D. More than one of the above violate the matching principle.

_____3. The lower-of-cost-or-market rule requires a company to:
   A. use the LIFO method in times of rising prices.
   B. adjust the inventory balance downward if its replacement cost is lower than cost.
   C. adjust the cost of goods sold downward if the inventory's replacement cost is lower than cost.
   D. use this method if its inventory has been destroyed or lost.

_____4. The gross margin on sales of Proffits, Inc., increased from 45% in 2005 to 50% in 2006. Which of the following is true?
   A. Proffits made more sales in 2006 than in 2005.
   B. Proffits' net income was greater in 2006 than in 2005.
   C. Proffits' cost of sales was lower relative to sales in 2006 than in 2005.
   D. Proffits' markup on its goods was less in 2006 than in 2005.

_____5. The company's lawyer believes $10 million of unsettled lawsuits filed by customers are probably going to result in a loss and will not be settled within one year.
   A. The company should report a $10 million noncurrent liability on its balance sheet.
   B. The company does not need to report the amount since it is a contingent liability and it is not certain that the company will lose.
   C. The company should report a current liability of $10 million on its income statement.
   D. The company should report a $10 million current liability on its balance sheet.

_____6. Labor services of employees have been used but not yet paid for. Payment will be made in the next accounting period, January 15th. This type of liability is called:

A. a contingent liability.
B. a definitely determinable liability.
C. an estimated liability.
D. a fixed liability.

_____7. The excess of sales over cost of goods sold is:

A. net income.
B. income before taxes.
C. operating income.
D. gross margin.

_____8. Redux, Inc., purchased $2,500 of inventory on account with terms of 2/10, n/30 and paid the bill within the discount period. How much was the amount paid by Redux?

A. $2,500
B. $2,450
C. $2,300
D. $2,250

_____9. FOB shipping point means:

A. the purchaser pays the shipping costs and records an expense called freight-in.
B. the purchaser pays the shipping costs and records the cost as a part of inventory.
C. the seller pays the shipping costs and records an expense called freight-out.
D. the seller pays the shipping costs and records a contra-revenue account called freight-out.

_____10. Which of the following may be a problem with an unusually high inventory turnover ratio?

A. The inventory may be too low, causing goods to be out of stock and sales to be lost.
B. The inventory may not be selling as quickly as it was in the past.
C. The inventory may have been bought in quantities that are too large, causing goods to be on hand for too long.
D. More than one of the above may be the cause of a high inventory turnover ratio.

_____11. With a periodic inventory system, an undiscovered error that overstates the 2005 year-end inventory will cause:

A. an overstatement of 2005 net income and an understatement of 2006 net income.
B. an understatement of assets on the 2005 balance sheet.
C. an overstatement of 2005 cost of goods sold.
D. An overstatement of 2005 net income and no effect on 2006 net income.

_____12. If a business' inventory on hand was destroyed by fire but the accounting records were saved, the method that would probably be used to estimate the amount of inventory lost would be:

A. the LIFO method.
B. the weighted average cost method.
C. the gross profit method.
D. the specific identification method.

Exercises

For exercises 1. – 8., show the effect on the accounting equation. Include the proper account titles.

1. The effect of the purchase of inventory on account is:

Assets	Liabilities	Owners' Equity

2. The effect of paying the invoice for merchandise previously purchased on account is:

Assets	Liabilities	Owners' Equity

3. The effect of the sale of merchandise to a customer on account is (ignore the cost of the sale):

Assets	Liabilities	Owners' Equity

4. The effect of recording the cost of the merchandise sold is:

Assets	Liabilities	Owners' Equity

5. The effect of the entry to record the collection of an account receivable is:

Assets	Liabilities	Owners' Equity

6. The effect of the adjusting entry to reduce inventory to market required by the lower-of-cost-or-market rule is:

Assets	Liabilities	Owners' Equity

7. The effect of the entry to record the disbursement of net pay to employees is:

Assets	Liabilities	Owners' Equity

8. The effect of the entry to record the payment of the employees' and employers' portions of payroll taxes:

Assets	Liabilities	Owners' Equity

9. Put an "X" in the column that indicates the best place to find each of the following items:

		Balance Sheet	Statement of Cash Flows	Income Statement	Notes to the Financial Statements
a.	The cost of inventory sold				
b.	The amount of merchandise on hand				
c.	The amount paid for inventory				
d.	The amount owed for inventory				
e.	The gross margin				
f.	The inventory method used				

10. Put an "X" in the column that indicates whether the item is overstated, understated, or correctly stated as a result of a company overstating its December 31, 2005 inventory balance.

		Overstated	Understated	Correctly stated
a.	Inventory, January 1, 2005			
b.	Purchases during 2005			
c.	Goods available for sale in 2005			
d.	Inventory, December 31, 2005	X		
e.	Cost of goods sold in 2005			
f.	Net income in 2005			
g.	Retained earnings, December 31, 2005			
h.	Purchases during 2006			
i.	Goods available for sale in 2006			
j.	Inventory, December 31, 2006			
k.	Cost of goods sold in 2006			
l.	Net income in 2006			
m.	Retained earnings, December 31, 2006			

11. Stockit, Inc., has the following inventory information available from a recent month:

Date	Description	Units	Unit Cost / Price	Total
12/1	Beginning inventory	10	$10	$100
12/6	Purchase	20	$12	$240
12/18	Purchase	30	$16	$480
12/20	Sale	55	$30	$1,650
12/24	Purchase	10	$18	$180

Using the information above, fill in the following table:

	Cost flow method:	Cost of goods sold	Ending inventory
a.	Perpetual LIFO		
b.	Periodic LIFO		
c.	Perpetual FIFO		
d.	Periodic FIFO		
e.	Periodic weighted average (round the unit cost to the nearest cent)		

12. S. Mates, Inc., filed an insurance claim for inventory destroyed by a storm. The inventory at the beginning of the year was $20,000. Purchases were $140,000 and sales were $240,000 for the year up to the storm. The gross margin percentage has historically been 45%. How much inventory should this company claim was lost?

13. Paywell, Inc., has gross payroll of $200,000, federal income tax withheld of $50,000, and Social Security and Medicare taxes withheld of $15,300. Show the effect of paying its employees on the accounting equation:

Assets	Liabilities	Owners' Equity

14. Calculate the gross margin on sales and the inventory turnover ratio for the year ended December 31, 2005:

For the year ended	December 31, 2005	December 31, 2004
Inventory	$20,000	$30,000
Sales	$400,000	$380,000
Cost of goods sold	$180,000	$170,000

Completion Statements

1. purchase requisition, purchase order, receiving report
2. returns, allowances
3. FOB shipping point, Freight-in
4. FOB destination, Freight-out
5. specific identification
6. weighted-average
7. First-in, first-out (FIFO)
8. Last-in, first-out (LIFO)
9. perpetual
10. periodic
11. gross profit method
12. Definitely determinable liabilities, Estimated liabilities, Contingent liabilities

True/False

1. False   Inventory is a current asset until it is sold. When the inventory is sold, the cost of the sale is matched with the related sale in the same accounting period (the matching principle).
2. False   GAAP allows companies to select one of several inventory cost flow assumptions when determining the amount of cost of goods sold. The method used does not have to be consistent with the actual physical flow of the goods. Thus, a company that uses the LIFO method can physically sell its older inventory before its newly purchased items.
3. True
4. True
5. False   Warranty payable is an estimated liability, not a definitely determinable liability. The matching principle requires companies to record an estimated amount of warranty expense in the same period as the related sale. The exact amount will not be known until a later period, when the customer returns the item for repair or replacement.
6. True
7. False   Goods available for sale equals beginning inventory plus purchases.
8. True
9. False   The gross margin on sales of 40% means that for every $1 of sales, the cost of goods sold is $0.60 and the gross margin is $0.40.
10. True

Multiple Choice

1. B   Inventory is a current asset since it should be sold within the year. Another name for the balance sheet is the statement of financial position.
2. C   Inventory is an asset until it is sold. The matching principle requires the cost of the goods sold be reported in the same period as the related sale. The cost flow assumptions, such as LIFO and FIFO, are used to estimate the amount of cost of goods sold. GAAP allows companies to use estimates instead of tracking the actual physical flow and actual cost of each item sold.
3. B   Companies are required by GAAP to reduce the inventory balance downward if the cost of the inventory is higher than the market value or cost to replace the inventory. This rules helps to prevent companies from overstating their inventory. The effect of the write-down of inventory on the accounting equation is to reduce assets (inventory) and reduce owners' equity (loss on inventory write-down).
4. C   The gross margin on sales is calculated by dividing gross margin (or sales less cost of sales) by sales. When the cost of sales is lower relative to sales, than the percentage increases since the

numerator, gross margin, is larger. Choice A is incorrect because sales can increase at the same rate as cost of sales, causing the gross margin to remain the same. Choice B is incorrect because other operating expenses may have increased, offsetting any increase in the gross margin on sales. Choice D is incorrect because a higher gross margin results when a company increases its markup on goods.

5. A   A liability must be recorded if a contingent liability is both probable and able to be estimated. Since the contingent liability is not expected to be settled within the year, then the liability should be classified as noncurrent.

6. B   The exact amount of payroll is known at the end of the accounting period and thus is a definitely determinable liability. Payroll liability is not an estimated liability since the exact amount is known. It is not a contingent liability since the outcome is certain.

7. D   Sales less cost of goods sold (or cost of sales) is the gross margin (or gross profit). It represents the markup on a company's goods.

8. B   The discount term, 2/10, n/30, means the buyer will receive a 2% discount if the invoice is paid within 10 days, otherwise the entire amount is due within 30 days. A 2% discount on $2,500 is $50. The buyer will pay $2,450 ($2,500 – 50).

9. B   FOB (free on board) shipping point means the purchaser pays the shipping costs. The shipping cost is considered part of the cost of buying the inventory and is thus included as inventory along with the purchase price. If the terms were FOB destination, then the shipper pays and records the cost as an expense, freight-out.

10. A   The inventory turnover equals cost of goods sold divided by average inventory. If the inventory is low, the result would be a high turnover, which is typically good. However, if inventory is too low, the result would be loss of sales if the goods are temporarily out of stock. A low inventory turnover is usually not good and may be a result of not being able to sell the goods quickly enough and/or having too much inventory on hand.

11. A   Cost of goods sold is calculated by subtracting ending inventory from goods available for sale. If too much is subtracted as ending inventory, cost of goods sold will be too low. Low cost of goods sold results in high net income for 2005. In 2006, the high amount of beginning inventory increases the cost of goods available for sale. If the correct ending inventory for 2006 is subtracted from a number that is too large, cost of goods sold is too high for 2006 and net income is too low. Choice B is incorrect because assets on the balance sheet will be too large at the end of 2005. Choice C is incorrect because cost of goods sold in 2005 is too low, not too high. Choice D is incorrect because the error in 2005 ending inventory also has an effect on the income reported in 2006.

12. C   The gross profit method is the only method that can be used to calculate inventory without knowing the actual number of units in ending inventory. For both choices A and B, the number of units in inventory must be multiplied by the appropriate prices to calculate inventory cost. For Choice D, both the number of units and the actual cost of those units must be known.

Exercises

	Assets	Liabilities	Owners' Equity
1.	+Inventory	+Accounts payable	
2.	-Cash	-Accounts payable	
3.	+Accounts receivable		+Sales
4.	-Inventory		-Cost of goods sold
5.	+Cash -Accounts receivable		
6.	-Inventory		-Loss on inventory write-down
7.	-Cash	+Payroll taxes payable	-Salary expense
8.	-Cash	-Payroll taxes payable	-Employer's payroll tax expense

9.		Balance Sheet	Statement of Cash Flows	Income Statement	Notes to the Financial Statements
a.	The cost of inventory sold			X	
b.	The amount of merchandise on hand	X			
c.	The amount paid for inventory		X		
d.	The amount owed for inventory	X			
e.	The gross margin			X	
f.	The inventory method used				X

10.		Overstated	Understated	Correctly stated
a.	Inventory, January 1, 2005			X
b.	Purchases during 2005			X
c.	Goods available for sale in 2005			X
d.	Inventory, December 31, 2005	X		
e.	Cost of goods sold in 2005		X	
f.	Net income in 2005	X		
g.	Retained earnings, December 31, 2005	X		
h.	Purchases during 2006			X
i.	Goods available for sale in 2006	X		
j.	Inventory, December 31, 2006			X
k.	Cost of goods sold in 2006	X		
l.	Net income in 2006		X	
m.	Retained earnings, December 31, 2006			X

11.	Cost flow method:	Cost of goods sold	Ending inventory
a.	Perpetual LIFO	$(30 \times \$16) + (20 \times \$12) + (5 \times \$10)$ = $770	$(5 \times \$10) + (10 \times \$18)$ = $230
b.	Periodic LIFO	$(10 \times \$18) + (30 \times \$16) + (15 \times \$12)$ = $840	$(10 \times \$10) + (5 \times \$12)$ = $160
c.	Perpetual FIFO	$(10 \times \$10) + (20 \times \$12) + (25 \times \$16)$ = $740	$(10 \times \$18) + (5 \times \$16)$ = $260
d.	Periodic FIFO	$(10 \times \$10) + (20 \times \$12) + (25 \times \$16)$ = $740	$(10 \times \$18) + (5 \times \$16)$ = $260

e.	Periodic weighted average $\dfrac{(\$100 + 240 + 480 + 180)}{(10 + 20 + 30 + 10)} =$ $\dfrac{\$1{,}000 \text{ cost of goods available}}{70 \text{ units available for sale}}$ $= \$14.29$ per unit (rounded)	55 x $14.29 = $785.95	$1,000 Cost of goods available for sale - $785.95 Cost of goods sold = $214.05

12. First estimate cost of goods sold:

Sales	100%	$240,000
-Cost of goods sold	- 55%	132,000	((100%-45%) x $240,000)
Gross margin	45%	$108,000

Then estimate inventory:

Beginning inventory	$ 20,000
+Purchases	140,000
Goods available for sale	$160,000
-Estimated cost of goods sold	(132,000) (see cost of goods sold above)
Estimated ending inventory	$ 28,000

13.

Assets	Liabilities	Owners' Equity
$(134,700) Cash	$50,000 Income Taxes Withheld 15,300 Social Security & Medicare Withheld	$(200,000) Salary Expense

14. Gross margin on sales:

$$\frac{\text{gross margin}}{\text{sales}} = \frac{\$400{,}000 - 180{,}000}{\$400{,}000} = .55 \text{ or } 55\%$$

$$\text{Inventory turnover ratio} = \frac{\text{Cost of goods sold}}{\text{Average inventory}} = \frac{\$180{,}000}{((\$20{,}000 + \$30{,}000)/2)} = 7.2 \text{ times}$$

CHAPTER 7
THE SALES/COLLECTION CYCLE

Chapter Overview

Once the necessary assets, such as inventory, have been acquired in the acquisition/payment cycle, the company will want to sell its services or products and collect cash from its customers. Chapter 7 will help you to understand the sales/collection cycle. You will see how a company accounts for sales, cash, and accounts receivable and how this information is reported in the financial statements.

Chapter Highlights

1. In making a sale, a company must be sure 1) a customer's credit is approved to help assure collection; 2) picking and packing slips and shipping notices are properly prepared so the customer will receive what he or she ordered; 3) an accurate sales invoice (bill) is sent to the customer; and 4) the money collected is properly deposited in the company's bank account. The financial statements and footnotes must provide information about these sales and collections.

2. The revenue recognition principle states that revenue is recognized when "the earnings process is virtually complete," and collection is reasonably assured. There are times when revenue is earned before or after the cash is collected. Sometimes cash is received before revenue is earned, and a liability called unearned revenue is recorded instead of revenue. Sometimes revenue is earned before cash is received, and an asset called account receivable is recorded.

3. Most companies' income statements show revenues as net sales. Discounts and returns are subtracted from sales to arrive at net sales. Sales discounts are similar to purchase discounts. They are expressed in terms such as 2/10, n/30, which means that the customer gets a 2% discount if the bill is paid within 10 days. Otherwise, no discount will be given and the full amount of the bill is due within 30 days. The Sales discount is a contra-revenue account and is subtracted from sales to reflect revenue actually

earned. Sales returns is also a contra-revenue account and reflects the goods customers returned.

4. Internal controls surrounding cash are important to help safeguard the cash and ensure that sales and cash collections are properly recorded. Controls include limiting access to the cash, segregating the duties of record keeping from custody of cash, and monitoring cash by preparing a cash reconciliation.

5. A cash reconciliation, also known as a bank reconciliation, is a crucial control that compares the bank statement balance with the balance per the company's books and helps determine the company's true cash balance for the financial statements.

*   A cash reconciliation is prepared as follows:

Balance per bank statement	XX
+ Deposits in transit	XX
+ Bank errors in bank's favor	XX
- Bank errors in company's favor	(XX)
- Outstanding checks	(XX)
= Correct (true) cash balance	XX

Balance per books	XX
+ Notes collected by bank	XX
+ Interest earned	XX
+ Company errors in bank's favor	XX
- Company errors in company's favor	(XX)
- NSF checks	(XX)
- Bank charges	(XX)
= Correct (true) cash balance	XX

A cash reconciliation is prepared properly only if the correct (true) cash balances are the same coming from the bank to books and from the books to the bank. Any discrepancies must be investigated.

*   Since the cash reconciliation is a worksheet it does not directly affect the company's accounting records. Adjusting entries are required to adjust the cash balance per books to the correct (true) cash balance. All items

112

needed to get the balance per books equal to the true cash balance require adjusting entries.

6. **Accounts receivable**, also called **receivables**, are current assets arising from credit sales to customers. Unfortunately a company cannot expect to collect 100% of its receivables. There are always some customers who do not pay. GAAP requires a company to estimate its uncollectible accounts. This estimated bad debt expense is matched with the same period as the related sales. This is called the **allowance method**. The adjusting entry required is:

Assets	Liab.	Owners' equity
- Allowance for un-collectible accounts		- Bad debts expense

7. The **Allowance for uncollectible accounts** is a **contra-asset** account. Accounts receivable is not reduced directly because at the time of the adjusting entry the company does not know exactly which accounts are not going to be collected. The allowance account represents only an estimate of uncollectible accounts. On the balance sheet, accounts receivable is shown as a current asset below cash:

Accounts receivable	XX
Allowance for uncollectible accounts	(XX)
Net realizable value	XX

The **net realizable value** or simply **net receivables** represents the amount the company believes it will collect from its customers. This is also called the carrying value or book value of accounts receivable.

7. The **Bad debts expense**, or **Uncollectible accounts expense**, reduces net income on the income statement. The matching principle requires the estimated expense be recorded in the same accounting period as the related sales.

8. When the company finds out that a specific customer is unable to pay, a company will write off the customer's account as follows:

Assets	Liab.	Owners' equity
+ Allowance for un-collectible accounts - Accounts receivable		

Notice the write-off of the specific account does not affect the net realizable value of accounts receivable.

9. There are two ways under the allowance method to estimate the amount of uncollectible accounts, the sales method and the accounts receivable method. The adjusting entry is the same (see 6.) regardless of which method is used. It's the amount of the estimate that may differ. The entry and amount to write off a specific customer's account (see 8.) will be the same regardless of which method is used.

- The **sales method** focuses on the income statement. Management estimates the bad debt expense as a percentage of credit sales (or sales if cash and credit sales are not easily separated). Notice the sales method ignores the unadjusted balance in the Allowance for uncollectible accounts in estimating bad debts expense.

- The **accounts receivable method** focuses on the balance sheet. Management analyzes accounts receivable by preparing an aging schedule of receivables. Based on this schedule, management estimates the percentage of accounts receivable that will not be collected. This method is more involved than the sales method because the amount of the adjustment depends on the unadjusted balance already in the Allowance for uncollectible accounts.

10. The allowance method (using either the sales or accounts receivable methods) results in a better, more realistic measure of net income and accounts receivable than if the company were to wait until specific customers' accounts were determined to be uncollectible. Companies may ignore the allowance method only if their uncollectible accounts are very small. If they are immaterial, GAAP allows companies to use the **direct write-off method**. The company waits to write off a specific customer's account instead of making an adjusting entry for estimated bad

debts in the same period as the related sales. This method violates the matching principle because the sale and the write-off of the uncollectible account may occur in different accounting periods. The write-off is recorded as:

Assets	Liab.	Owners' equity
- Accounts receivable		- Bad debts expense

11. Credit card sales are not as risky as credit sales and are recorded as:

Assets	Liab.	Owners' equity
+ Accounts receivable (credit card company)		+ Sales - Credit card expense

The credit card company, for a fee, will pay the company daily (or weekly):

Assets	Liab.	Owners' equity
+ Cash - Accounts receivable (credit card company)		

The company must compare the fee with the benefits of credit card sales such as having the credit card company pursue non-paying customers.

12. When a company sells its product or service with a warranty, the matching principle requires the company to estimate and record warranty expense in the same period as the related sale:

Assets	Liabilities	Owners' equity
	+ Estimated warranty liability (or payable)	- Warranty expense

Later, the company will reduce this liability as it meets its warranty obligations to customers:

Assets	Liabilities	Owners' equity
- Cash *or* - Inventory	- Warranty payable	

13. Financial statements and related footnotes provide sales and accounts receivable information to help users assess a company's ability to collect its receivables and pay its obligations. Two ratios help to assess the company's ability to meet its short-term obligations: 1) the current ratio, which equals current assets divided by current liabilities, and 2) the quick (or acid-test) ratio, which equals cash plus short-term investments plus net accounts receivable in the numerator and current liabilities in the denominator. Another important ratio is the **accounts receivable turnover ratio**, that measures the company's ability to collect cash from its credit customers. It is calculated by dividing net sales by average net accounts receivable. This ratio can also be expressed as the average number of days it takes to collect for a sale by dividing the ratio into 365 days. The footnotes to the financial statements provide further detail about sales and collection policies.

14. There are three types of controls surrounding sales, cash, and accounts receivable. **Preventive controls** such as keeping cash locked up are designed to prevent an error or irregularity (an intentional error). **Detective controls** such as preparing cash reconciliations are designed to find an error or irregularity. **Corrective controls** such as denying future credit to slow paying or non-paying customers are designed to fix errors.

Featured Exercise

Part A. Fill in the accounting equation below for Tina'sWare, Inc.'s events that occurred during 2006.

Tina's Ware, Inc.		Assets =	Liabilities +	Owners' equity
	Beginning balances, January 1, 2006	Cash $ 500 Accounts receivable 7,500 Allowance for uncol- lectible accounts (450) Inventory 5,000 Prepaid insurance 600 Truck (net) 16,000	Accounts payable $6,000 Interest payable 700 Notes payable 7,000	Common stock $6,000 Retained earnings 9,450
a	Purchased $32,000 of inventory on account.			
b	Made sales of $55,000 on account, 2/10, n/30. The cost of the sales was $35,000.			
c	$50,000 of receivables with sales discount terms of 2/10,n/30 were collected within the discount period.			
d	Wrote off $400 of specific customer accounts considered uncollectible.			
e	Paid $34,000 for the amounts owed to its supplier.			
f	Paid $2,400 in advance for an insurance policy that covers two years beginning July 1.			
g	One year of insurance coverage has expired.			
h	Adjusting entries are $4,000 for depreciation and $700 for interest owed.			
i.	In December, Tina's Ware began offering warranties and expects warranty costs on this year's sales to be $100.			
j.	Tina's Ware uses the accounts receivable allowance method and estimates that 5% of its accounts receivable will be uncollectible.			

Part B: Tina's Ware's financial statement line items:	Fill in the correct dollar amount: Amount as of or for the year ended December 31	Put an "X" in the column of the statement where the item will most likely appear:		
		Income Statement	Balance Sheet	Statement of Cash Flows
a. Cash paid to suppliers				
b. Accounts payable				
c. Inventory				
d. Cost of goods sold				
e. Sales (net of sales discounts)				
f. Cash received from customers				
g. Accounts receivable				
h. Allowance for uncollectible accounts				
i. Bad debts expense				
j. Warranty payable				
k. Warranty expense				

Part C:

1. When should Tina's Ware record revenue from the sales of its wares?

2. What should Tina's Ware record in January 2007 when a customer brings a product under warranty back to be fixed. The repair costs Tina's Ware $60?

Assets	Liabilities	Owners' equity

3. Identify a preventive control Tina's Ware should have in place to safeguard its cash.

4. Identify a detective control Tina's Ware should have in place to find errors in its cash.

5. Assume Tina's Ware uses the sales method instead of the accounts receivable method to estimate bad debts expense. It believes 1% of its sales (not net sales) are uncollectible. What would be the adjusting entry?

Assets	Liabilities	Owners' equity

6. Calculate Tina's Ware's 2005 (not 2006) current ratio and quick ratio. The note payable and related interest are due in 2009.

7. Calculate Tina's Ware's 2006 (not 2005) accounts receivable turnover ratio.

Solution

Part A. Tina's Ware, Inc.	Assets =	Liabilities +	Owners' equity
	Beginning balances, January 1, 2006	Cash $ 500 Accounts receivable 7,500 Allowance for uncol- lectible accounts (450) Inventory 5,000 Prepaid insurance 600 Truck (net) 16,000	Accounts payable $6,000 Interest payable 700 Notes payable 7,000	Common stock $6,000 Retained earnings 9,450
a	Purchased $32,000 of inventory on account.	32,000 Inventory	32,000 Accounts payable	
b	Made sales of $55,000 on account, 2/10, n/30. The cost of the sales was $35,000.	55,000 Accounts receivable (35,000) Inventory		55,000 Sales (35,000) Cost of goods sold
c	$50,000 of receivables with sales discount terms of 2/10,n/30 were collected within the discount period.	49,000 Cash (50,000) Accounts receivable *$50,000 – (2% x 50,000)*		(1,000) Sales discounts
d	Wrote off $400 of specific customer accounts considered uncollectible.	400 Allowance for uncol- lectible accounts (400) Accounts receivable		
e	Paid $34,000 for the amounts owed to its supplier.	(34,000) Cash	(34,000) Accounts payable	
f	Paid $2,400 in advance for an insurance policy that covers two years beginning July 1.	(2,400) Cash 2,400 Prepaid insurance		
g	One year of insurance coverage has expired.	(1,200) Prepaid insurance		(1,200) Insurance expense
h	Adjusting entries are $4,000 for depreciation and $700 for interest owed.	(4,000) Accumulated depreciation	700 Interest payable	(4,000) Depreciation expense (700) Interest expense
i.	In December, Tina's Ware began offering warranties and expects warranty costs on this year's sales to be $100.		100 Warranty payable	(100) Warranty expense
j.	Tina's Ware uses the accounts receivable allowance method and estimates that 5% of its accounts receivable will be uncollectible.	(555) Allowance for un- collectible accounts (see * below)		(555) Bad debts expense

* $7,500 + 55,000 - 50,000 - 400 = $12,100 Accounts receivable;

$12,100 x (5%) = $(605) adjusted Allowance for uncollectible accounts; $(450)+ 400 + X = $(605); X = (555)

117

Part B. Tina's Ware's financial statement line items:		Fill in the correct dollar amount: **Amount** as of or for the year ended December 31	Put an "X" in the column of the statement where the item will most likely appear:		
			Income Statement	**Balance Sheet**	**Statement of Cash Flows**
a.	Cash paid to suppliers	$34,000			X
b.	Accounts payable	$4,000		X	
c.	Inventory	$2,000		X	
d.	Cost of goods sold	$35,000	X		
e.	Sales (net of sales discounts)	$54,000	X		
f.	Cash received from customers	$49,000			X
g.	Accounts receivable	$12,100		X	
h.	Allowance for uncollectible accounts	$(605) =$12,100 x(5%)		X	
i.	Bad debts expense	$555	X		
j.	Warranty payable	$100		X	
k.	Warranty expense	$100	X		

Part C:

1. When the earnings process is virtually complete and collection is reasonably assured.

2.	**Assets**	**Liabilities**	**Owners' equity**
	(60) Cash	(60) Warranty payable	

3. Limiting access to cash by placing cash in locked cash drawers or safes and depositing cash in the bank as soon as possible are good preventive controls.

4. Preparing a cash reconciliation is an important detective control designed to find errors in cash.

5.	**Assets**	**Liabilities**	**Owners' equity**
(550)	Allowance for uncollectible accounts *(1%) x $55,000 = $(550)*		(550) Bad debts expense

6. Current ratio = $\dfrac{\text{current assets}}{\text{current liabilities}}$ = $\dfrac{\text{cash + accounts receivable (net) + inventory + prepaid insurance}}{\text{accounts payable}}$
(2005)

$$= \frac{\$500 + (7{,}500 - 450) + 5{,}000 + 600}{\$6{,}000} = 2.2$$

Quick ratio = $\dfrac{\text{cash + accounts receivable (net)}}{\text{current liabilities}}$ = $\dfrac{\$500 + (7{,}500 - 450)}{\$6{,}000}$ = 1.3
(2005)

7. A/R turnover = $\dfrac{\text{Net sales}}{\text{Average net AR}}$ = $\dfrac{\$54{,}000}{((\$7{,}500-450)+(12{,}100-605))/2}$ = 5.8 times
(2006)

118

Review Questions and Exercises

Completion Statements

Fill in the blank(s) to complete each statement.

1. In making a sale, a company must be sure a customer's _____ is approved to help assure collection.

2. _____ and _____ slips and shipping notices are properly prepared so the customer will receive what he/she ordered.

3. The revenue recognition principle states that revenue is recognized when "the earnings process is _____," and _____ is reasonably assured.

4. GAAP allows companies to use the _____ to write off customers' accounts instead of the allowance method only if the amount of uncollectible accounts is immaterial.

5. The _____, or simply net receivables, represents the amount the company believes it will collect from its customers. This is also called the _____ value or _____ value of accounts receivable.

6. A ratio that measures the company's ability to collect cash is calculated by dividing net sales by average net accounts receivable is called the _____ ratio.

7. _____ controls such as keeping cash locked up are designed to prevent an error or irregularity.

8. _____ controls such as preparing a cash reconciliation are designed to find an error or irregularity.

9. _____ controls such as denying future credit to slow paying or non-paying customers are designed to fix errors.

10. The _____ principle requires bad debts expense and warranty expense be recorded in the same period as the related sales.

True/False

Indicate whether each statement is true (T) or false (F).

_____1. The adjusting entry for bad debts is the same whether a company uses the direct write-off method or the sales method.

_____2. The quick ratio is a measure of a company's ability to pay its short-term obligations.

_____3. The lower the accounts receivable turnover ratio the longer it takes the company to collect its credit sales on average.

_____4. Sales discounts and sales returns are contra-asset accounts and are subtracted from accounts receivable to arrive at net realizable value.

_____5. The direct write-off method is better than the allowance method because it results in a better matching of bad debt expense with the related sales.

_____6. When using the sales method, bad debts expense equals the net sales times the percentage management considers uncollectible plus any balance already in the unadjusted Allowance for uncollectible accounts.

_____7. The sales discount term 2/7, n/30 means a customer gets a 2% discount if he or she pays within 7 to 30 days from delivery of the product.

_____8. Corrective controls include adjusting entries that are recorded in order to ensure the financial statements have correct balances.

_____9. The revenue recognition principle requires the allowance for uncollectible accounts to be shown as a contra-revenue account in the period of the write-off.

_____10. The matching principle requires bad debts expense be estimated and recorded in the period in which the sale is made, not in the period in which a specific receivable is later written off.

Multiple Choice

Select the best answer for each question.

_____1. The Allowance for uncollectible accounts on the balance sheet shows:
   A. how much a company wrote off as uncollectible during the period.
   B. how much a company recorded as bad debts expense during the period.
   C. the amount of receivables that a company believes it will not collect.
   D. the accumulation of all the uncollectible accounts since the beginning of the business.

_____2. Using the accounts receivable method, a company determines the Allowance for uncollectible accounts should have an adjusted balance of $(1,000). Using the sales method, the company determines bad debt expense should equal $1,000. If the unadjusted balance of the Allowance for uncollectible accounts is $(100), which allowance method would result in a larger decrease in owners' equity?
   A. Accounts receivable method
   B. Sales method
   C. Both will result in the same decrease in owners' equity.
   D. Neither will result in a decrease in owners' equity.

_____3. Rite On, Inc. uses the allowance method and decided to write off an account receivable from I.M. Broke that is considered uncollectible. When Rite On writes off the account:
   A. total assets will increase.
   B. total assets will decrease.
   C. total assets will remain unchanged.
   D. retained earnings will decrease.
   E. Both B. and D. are correct.

_____4. Which method will result in an Allowance for uncollectible accounts account?
   A. Accounts receivable method
   B. Direct write-off method
   C. Sales method
   D. Both A. and C. are correct.

_____5. Which method ignores the unadjusted balance in Allowance for uncollectible accounts when recording the adjusting entry for bad debts expense?
   A. Accounts receivable method
   B. Direct write-off method
   C. Sales method
   D. Both B. and C. are correct.

_____6. Which of the following is an effective segregation of duties in controlling cash? The employee who has access to cash should not:
   A. take the deposits to the bank.
   B. prepare the cash reconciliation.
   C. open the mail since it often includes checks.
   D. take sales orders from customers.
   E. All of the above are proper segregation of duties.

_____7. Collectibles, Inc. estimated that $20,000 of its receivables will be uncollectible based on an aging of its accounts receivable. Why then did Collectibles, Inc. record bad debts expense of only $18,000?
   A. Collectibles, Inc. purposely understated its expenses.
   B. Collectibles, Inc. had already written off $2,000 of its accounts receivable during the year.
   C. Collectibles, Inc. already had a $(2,000) balance in its Allowance for uncollectible accounts.
   D. Collectibles, Inc. had underestimated its bad debts expense in the prior year.

_____8. The matching principle requires a company to:
   A. expense the bad debts expense in the same period as the related sale.
   B. write off an uncollectible account in the period the account is found to be uncollectible.
   C. match the balance in the Allowance for uncollectible accounts with the Bad debts expense.
   D. match the Allowance for uncollectible accounts with the net realizable value of accounts receivable.

_____9. Which one of the following items from a cash reconciliation does the company need to record in its accounting records?
   A. Deposits in transit
   B. NSF checks
   C. Outstanding checks
   D. None of the above since the company already has recorded these items prior to preparing its cash reconciliation.

_____10. Which of the following is true for a company that accepts credit cards?
   A. The company is more assured of collecting credit card sales.
   B. The company must compare the cost of the credit company's fees with the benefit of receiving cash sooner and the benefit of not needing to pursue non-paying customers.
   C. The company records a credit card expense when it records the related sale.
   D. All of the above are true.

Exercises

1. Complete the May 31, 2004 bank reconciliation for Well Balanced, Inc. given the following:

   a. Outstanding checks: No. 975...$1,260; No. 991...$300; No. 1073...$1,300
   b. Check no. 1018 (for repair expense) was written for $483 but erroneously recorded in Well Balanced's records as $843.
   c. Deposits in transit of $3,370
   d. NSF check from I.M. Broke of $440
   e. Bank service charge of $20

Well Balanced, Inc. Bank Reconciliation, May 31, 2004				
Balance per bank statement	$15,700		Balance per books	$16,310
Add:			Add:	
Deduct:			Deduct:	
True cash balance			True cash balance	

2. Which of the above reconciling items (a. - e.) require adjusting entries in Well Balanced's records?

3. Liquidators, Inc. uses the sales method in estimating bad debts expense and has found that such expense has consistently approximated 1% of net sales. At December 31 of the current year, Accounts receivable total $100,000 and the Allowance for uncollectible accounts has a $(300) balance prior to adjustment. Net sales for the current year were $800,000. The appropriate adjusting entry is:

Assets	Liabilities	Owners' equity

4. Macrohard, Inc., after aging its accounts receivable, estimated that 2% of its $125,000 receivables on hand would probably prove uncollectible. The Allowance for uncollectible accounts contained a balance of $(300) prior to adjustments. The appropriate adjusting entry is:

Assets	Liabilities	Owners' equity

5. A customer used a credit card to purchase a $100 battery from Chargemup, Inc. What entry should Chargemup, Inc. record if the credit card company charges a 4% fee for its service.

Assets	Liabilities	Owners' equity

For Exercises 6. – 9., show the effect on the accounting equation by circling either increase, decrease, or no effect in each column.

6. The adjusting entry to record the estimate for warranty obligations is:

Assets	Liabilities	Owners' Equity
Increase	Increase	Increase
Decrease	Decrease	Decrease
No effect	No effect	No effect

7. The adjusting entry to record the estimate for bad debts expense is:

Assets	Liabilities	Owners' Equity
Increase	Increase	Increase
Decrease	Decrease	Decrease
No effect	No effect	No effect

8. The entry to record the collection of an account receivable is:

Assets	Liabilities	Owners' Equity
Increase	Increase	Increase
Decrease	Decrease	Decrease
No effect	No effect	No effect

9. The writing-off of a specific account receivable for a company that uses the allowance method is:

Assets	Liabilities	Owners' Equity
Increase	Increase	Increase
Decrease	Decrease	Decrease
No effect	No effect	No effect

10. Cycles, Inc.'s net credit sales for the current year are $6,000,000, and net accounts receivable at the beginning of the year was $700,000 and at the end was $800,000. Calculate the accounts receivable turnover. Also calculate the average number of days its takes Cycles to collect its receivables (assume 365 days to a year).

Completion Statements

1. credit
2. picking, packing
3. virtually complete, collection
4. direct write-off method
5. net realizable value, carrying, book
6. accounts receivable turnover
7. Preventive
8. Detective
9. Corrective
10. matching

True/False

1. False   The direct write-off method does not require an adjusting entry for bad debts expense, thus it violates GAAP (the matching principle).
2. True
3. True
4. False   Sales discounts and sales returns are contra-revenue accounts and are subtracted from sales to get net sales.
5. False   The allowance method (GAAP) is better than the direct write-off method (not GAAP).
6. False   The sales method estimates bad debts expense as net sales times the percentage management considers uncollectible. The balance left in the unadjusted Allowance for uncollectible accounts is not part of the calculation. (However, it is part of the calculation of bad debts expense when a company uses the accounts receivable method).
7. False   The sales discount term 2/7, n/30 means a customer gets a 2% discount if he or she pays within 7 days, otherwise the full amount is due within 30 days.
8. False   Corrective controls are internal controls designed to fix errors, not adjusting entries.
9. False   The allowance for uncollectible accounts is a contra-asset account. The matching principle, not the revenue recognition principle, requires bad debts expense to be recorded as an expense, not a contra-revenue account, in the period of the related sale, not in the period of the write-off.
10. True

Multiple Choice

1. C   The Allowance for uncollectible accounts, a contra-asset on the balance sheet, is subtracted from accounts receivable to show the net realizable value (the amount the company believes it will collect from its customers).
2. B   The accounts receivable method requires bad debt expense (which reduces owners' equity) to be only $900 since there is already a $(100) balance in the allowance account. The sales method does not consider what is left in the allowance account and thus the bad debts expense is the entire $1,000 estimate.
3. C   The write-off of a specific account receivable has no effect on the net realizable value of receivables (accounts receivable minus allowance for uncollectible accounts) or on total assets:

Assets	Liabilities	Owners' equity
- Accounts receivable + Allowance for uncollectible accounts		

4. D   The direct write-off method, which violates the matching principle, does not require an allowance account since no attempt is made to record the estimated amount of bad debts expense in the same period as the related sales. Accounts receivable are written off (expensed) in the period the receivables are considered uncollectible.

5. D   The sales method's bad debt expense equals the percentage of sales management believes to be uncollectible times the credit sales; the adjusting amount is not dependent on the balance in the allowance account. The direct write-off method's bad debt expense is the actual amount of the specific accounts receivable written off; there is no allowance account needed with this method.

6. B   Employees who have access to cash should not have any record-keeping responsibilities. Otherwise an employee could steal cash and manipulate the cash reconciliation to conceal the theft.

7. C   Management based its estimate on an aging of its accounts receivable and thus uses the accounts receivable method. The estimated $20,000 is the balance needed in the Allowance for uncollectible accounts, not Bad debts expense. The Bad debts expense amount is dependent on the unadjusted balance in the Allowance for uncollectible accounts which must have had a $(2,000) unadjusted balance since the expense was only $18,000.

8. A   The matching principle is extremely important for companies to follow since it results in net income being a more realistic, consistent, and comparable measure of profitability.

9. B   The items in a cash reconciliation that require adjustment to the company's books are the items added or subtracted from the cash per the company's books to arrive at the true cash balance. These reconciling items include NSF checks and errors made by the company, collections made by the bank on the company's behalf, bank charges and interest earned.

10. D   Credit card companies typically pay for credit card sales daily or weekly. The credit card company takes on the risk of non-paying customers, relieving the company of bad debts expense. The cost of the credit card sales is a fee that is recorded as an expense at the same time as the related credit card sale.

Exercises

1.	Well Balanced, Inc. Bank Reconciliation, May 31, 2004			
Balance per bank statement	$15,700		Balance per books	$16,310
Add:			Add:	
Deposits in transit	3,370		Correction of an error ($843-483)	360
Deduct:			Deduct:	
Check: no. 975	(1,260)		NSF check	(440)
Check no. 991	(300)		Bank service charge	(20)
Check no. 1073	(1,300)			
True cash balance	$16,210		True cash balance	$16,210

2. Which of the above reconciling items (a. - e.) require adjusting entries in Well Balanced's records?

The error the company made (b), the NSF check (d), and the bank service charge (e) are all reconciling items that need to be recorded in Well Balanced's records.

3.	Assets	Liabilities	Owners' equity
	$(8,000) Allowance for uncollectible accounts		$(8,000) Bad debts expense *(1%) x $800,000*

4.	Assets	Liabilities	Owners' equity
	$(2,200) Allowance for uncollectible accounts *((2%) x $125,000) + $300*		$(2,200) Bad debts expense

5.	Assets	Liabilities	Owners' equity
	$96 Accounts receivable		$100 Sales (4) Credit card expense

	Assets	Liabilities	Owners' equity
6.	No effect	Increase	Decrease
7.	Decrease	No effect	Decrease
8.	No effect	No effect	No effect
9.	No effect	No effect	No effect

10. $$\text{AR turnover} = \frac{\text{Net sales}}{\text{Average net AR}} = \frac{\$6,000,000}{(\$700,000 + 800,000)/2} = 8 \text{ times per year}$$

$$\frac{365 \text{ days}}{\text{AR turnover}} = \frac{365}{8} = 45.6 \text{ days}$$

CHAPTER 8
SPECIAL ACQUISITIONS: FINANCING A BUSINESS WITH DEBT

Chapter Overview

This chapter discusses how companies get long-term financing from creditors. You will learn about the time value of money and how to calculate the payments on long-term installment notes. You will also learn about bonds, which are a special type of long-term borrowing available to large companies.

Chapter Highlights

1. Financing is the first concern of someone who is starting a new business, both to cover start-up costs and to pay for future operations, improvements, or expansion. **Debt financing** means obtaining money from creditors, who lend money for a specific period of time at a specific rate. **Interest**, which is the cost of borrowing, is usually stated as an annual rate. Creditors' claims to business assets come before owners' claims. However, no matter how successful the business may be, creditors receive only repayment of the loan principal and the specified amount of interest. Only owners, who take on more risk, have the opportunity to share in a firm's profits and earn a higher return.

2. A company can borrow money for short-term operations by establishing a **line of credit**, an arrangement with a bank that lets it borrow an amount ranging from zero up to a specified limit whenever it wants. The term for this type of loan is short, usually 60 to 90 days, and the interest rate, while lower than the usual credit card interest rate, is higher than the rate on most short-term loans for specific dollar amounts and longer repayment periods.

Lines of credit are available only to profitable, established businesses with predictable cash flows, where they are helpful for temporary cash shortages and serve as a backup for future potential cash flow problems. Lines of credit should not be used to finance long-term assets, which should be financed with long-term loans at lower interest rates. Companies with permanent cash flow problems or difficulties paying employees should find other, more permanent sources of financing.

3. **Short-term notes** are debts that are due in less than one year. **Long-term notes** like car loans are usually repaid with a series of equal installments over the life of the note. Some of each payment is interest and some is repayment of principal.

- Part of each installment payment decreases the outstanding principal of the loan. As the balance of the loan gets smaller, the interest for the next period gets smaller, too. Since the total amount of the installment payment stays the same, more of the next payment is used to repay loan principal because less of it is needed to cover interest.

- A **mortgage** is a special type of long-term note used to purchase property. It gives the lender a claim against the property until the loan is repaid.

- Payments on installment notes are calculated using the time value of money. A dollar received today is worth exactly $1. A dollar received a year ago is worth more than $1 today. It is worth the original dollar plus the interest that has been earned for the year gone by. A dollar received one year in the future is worth less than a dollar today. The $1 future receipt includes interest to compensate you for waiting. When you remove the interest, called **discounting** the future payment to calculate its value to you today (its **present value**), you have less than $1 today. The interest rate used in present value problems of this type is called the **discount rate**.

- Future installment payments on a loan include interest on any outstanding principal as well as part of the principal itself. The bank calculates the amount of interest it would receive over the life of the loan, adds it to the principal, and then figures the installment payments to be made. The discounted future installment payments, with interest removed, are equal to the amount being borrowed today, which is the present value of the loan.

4. Suppose you buy property by signing a $100,000, three-year, 8% mortgage note, with annual payments to be made at the end of each year. When the first installment payment of $38,803.35 is made, the interest component of this payment is $8,000 (Interest = principal x rate x time, or $100,000 x .08 x 1 year). The payment's effect on the accounting equation is:

- a $38,803.35 reduction in assets (Cash),
- a $30,803.35 reduction in liabilities (Mortgage payable), and
- an $8,000 reduction in Retained earnings (Interest expense).

For the second year of the loan, the balance now owed on the mortgage is $69,196.65 ($100,000 – 30,803.35). When the second installment payment of $38,803.35 is made, the interest component of the payment is $5,535.73 ($69,196.65 x .08 x 1 year). The remaining $33,267.62 of the payment is applied to the loan principal, reducing the principal to $35,929.03 ($69,196.65 – 33,267.62).

When the final installment payment of $38,803.35 is made, the interest component of the payment is $2,874.32 ($35,929.03 x .08 x 1 year). The remaining $35,929.03 of the payment is applied to the loan principal, reducing the principal to zero.

Look at the amortization schedule in Exhibit 8-2 of your text. Each year the interest component of the loan payment is smaller because the loan principal is smaller, and more of each payment is used to repay principal.

5. Simple interest is calculated on only the principal of a loan. Compound interest is calculated on the principal plus any interest that has been earned but not yet collected or paid. Money invested at compound interest grows much faster than money invested at simple interest, because with compound interest the amount on which interest is calculated gets bigger each year.

6. Using compound interest, you can calculate the future value of an amount using the formula:

$$FV_n = PV(1 + i)^n$$

where

FV_n = future value of the investment at the end of n periods
PV = present value or original amount invested
i = interest rate for each period
n = number of periods when compounding occurs

- Rather than using this formula, you can find the future value of an investment by using a future value table, like *The Future Value of a Single Amount ($1)* table found in Appendix B of your textbook. To use a future value table, find the column that corresponds to the interest rate in the problem (*i*). Go down the column to find the factor for the proper number of periods (*n*). Multiply this factor times the amount of the investment (*PV*).

- Interest rates quoted by lenders are usually annual interest rates. If interest is compounded more than once a year, both the interest rate (*i*) and the number of periods (*n*) must be adjusted. If 10% interest is compounded semiannually (twice a year) for three years, then use a 5% interest rate (10% divided by two compoundings per year) for six periods (three years times two compoundings per year).

- You can also use a financial calculator to find the future value of an investment. Instructions are in your textbook.

7. An **annuity** is a series of payments where the dollar amount of each payment is the same, and the time period between payments is also the same. With an **ordinary annuity**, also called an annuity in arrears, the investor makes payments at the end of each time period. With an **annuity due**, the investor makes payments at the beginning of each period. The future value of an ordinary annuity is smaller than the future

value of an annuity due for the same interest rate and time period.

- An investment made in the form of a five-year ordinary annuity will earn interest for only four years. The first payment is made at the end of the first year and earns no interest for that year. The fifth payment is made at the end of the fifth year and earns no interest at all.

- An investment made in the form of a five-year annuity due earns interest for all five years because the first payment is made at the beginning of the first year.

8.   You can find the future value of an annuity by using the formula for finding the future value of a single amount. Apply the formula to each separate annuity payment for the appropriate number of periods, then add together the future values of all the separate payments.

- Rather than using the formula, you can find the future value of an ordinary annuity by using *The Future Value of an Annuity of $1 in Arrears* table found in Appendix B of your textbook. Multiply the factor from the table by the amount of one annuity payment.

- Instructions for using a financial calculator to find the future value of an ordinary annuity are in your textbook.

9.   A payment of $100 received a year from today has a present value of less than $100. The present value today, plus the interest it earns for one year, equals $100.You can find the present value of a single sum using the formula:

$$PV = FV_n \ \ \times \ \ \frac{1}{(1+i)n}$$

The factor for finding the present value is the inverse of the factor for finding the future value.

- You can also find the present value of a future amount using *The Present Value of a Single Amount ($1)* table in Appendix B of your textbook. The interest rate used in present value problems is called the discount rate.

- There are instructions in your textbook for finding the present value of a single amount using a financial calculator.

10. Most present value problems involving annuities use ordinary annuities, where equal payments are received at the end of each period. Installment payments received in the future include interest, the difference between the present value of the payments and the actual dollar amount of the payments.

- You can calculate the present value of an annuity by finding the present value of each payment separately, then adding them together.

- You can use *The Present Value of an Annuity of $1 in Arrears* table found in Appendix B of your textbook. This table assumes that it is an ordinary annuity, not an annuity due.

- You can use a financial calculator, following the instructions in your textbook.

11. The present value of a series of installment loan payments is the same as the principal amount. To calculate the dollar amount of installment payments, first make sure that the annual interest rate and number of time periods are adjusted to fit the payment schedule. If payments are made monthly, the annual interest rate must be divided by 12 and the number of years must be multiplied by 12. The amount being borrowed, the loan's present value, is equal to the unknown future installment payments times the appropriate factor from the Present Value of an Annuity Table. Divide the loan principal by the factor from the table and your answer is the amount of each installment payment. You can also use a financial calculator, following the instructions given in your textbook.

12. Firms that need to borrow a lot of money may issue (*i.e.*, sell) bonds, which are written agreements to pay interest and to repay the buyers of the bonds (the lenders) at the end of the bonds' term. Companies issue bonds rather than borrowing from a bank because: 1) the time

period for bonds may be 20, 30, or 50 years, longer than the term usually available from banks, and 2) the interest rate on bonds is also usually lower than the interest rate on bank loans. Investors like insurance companies and individuals buy bonds because there is a ready market, similar to the stock market, where they can sell their bonds at any time. Bond owners are creditors who have priority over stockholders, the who are owners of the business. Bondholders may also get extra protection from **covenants** that are included in the bond agreement, such as limits on the issuing company's future borrowing or requirements that the company maintain a particular current ratio.

13. The principal amount of a bond is also called the **face value, maturity value,** or **par value**. Most bonds are issued in multiples of $1,000. The length of the loan period is the bonds' **maturity**. Most bonds pay the face value to bondholders at the **maturity date**. In the United States, bonds usually make semiannual interest payments based on the **coupon rate** (also known as the **stated rate**), which is the interest rate quoted on the face of the bonds.

14. There are different types of bonds. **Secured bonds** give the bondholder a claim to a specific company asset if there is a default (failure to meet the bond's obligations). Unsecured bonds, called **debentures**, are backed by the general credit of the company. **Term bonds** all mature on the same date. **Serial bonds** mature over a period of years.

15. The selling price of a bond depends on the interest rate prevailing in the secondary bond market. When interest rates increase, a bond's price falls (and *vice versa*). This is because the bond's coupon rate is fixed. If overall interest rates have gone up and investors can earn a higher return elsewhere, the bond will be an unattractive investment unless the price of the bond goes down. Similarly, if the bond's coupon rate is higher than the prevailing market interest rate, investors will find the bond attractive and will bid up the price.

Bond prices are quoted as a percentage of face value:

- A bond selling at 100 sells for 100% of its face value, which is also known as selling at par.
- A bond selling below 100 sells at a discount.
- A bond selling above 100 sells at a premium.

16. When a company issues bonds, it records the cash received and the liability to repay the face value of the bonds, Bonds Payable. The periodic interest payments are calculated using the face value of the bonds times the coupon rate times the fraction of a year that has elapsed, even if the bonds sold for some amount other than the face value. The effect on the accounting equation is:

Assets	Liabilities	Owners' equity
- Cash		- Interest Expense

Bonds may be issued at par, at a premium, or at a discount. Often there is a delay between selecting the coupon rate for a bond issue and actually selling the bonds. If the market interest rate has changed in the meantime, the bonds will not sell at par.

- Bonds sell at par only if the coupon rate of interest is the same as the market rate of interest, which is the rate an investor can earn on another investment with the same risk and maturity.

- When the coupon rate is higher than the market rate of interest, the bonds will sell at a premium.

- When the coupon rate is lower than the market rate of interest, the bonds will sell at a discount.

17. The price at which a bond is issued is equal to the present value of the future cash flows to be received by the bondholder, discounted at the market rate of interest.

1) Calculate the amount of the periodic interest payments: face value of the bond times the coupon rate of the bond times the appropriate fraction of a year.

2) Calculate the present value of these future cash interest payments (the present value of an annuity).

3) Calculate the present value of the future payment of maturity value (the present value of a single amount).

4) Add the two present values together to determine the amount of cash the company will receive when the bond is issued.

If a $1,000, 10-year bond with annual interest payments of 11.5% was issued for $1,092.17 because the market rate of interest was 10%, the issuing company would record the premium as a separate liability, called an adjunct liability, which will be added to Bonds payable on the balance sheet:

Assets	Liabilities	Owners' equity
$1,092.17 Cash	$1,000 Bonds payable 92.17 Premium on bonds payable	

If a $1,000, 10-year bond with annual interest payments of 11.5% was issued for $971.74 because the market rate of interest was 12%, the issuing company would record the discount as a separate, negative liability, called a contra-liability, which will be subtracted from Bonds payable on the balance sheet:

Assets	Liabilities	Owners' equity
$971.74 Cash	$1,000 Bonds payable (28.26) Discount on bonds payable	

18. Bond premiums and discounts are written off (reduced to zero) over the life of the bond issue. Interest expense shown on the company's annual income statements will not be the same amount as the cash interest payments made to bondholders.

Using the **effective interest method**, calculate interest expense by multiplying the net value of the bond, times the market rate of interest in effect when the bond was issued, times the

appropriate fraction of a year. If a bond was issued at a discount, its net value, also called its carrying value or book value, is the amount of Bonds payable minus the related Discount on bonds payable. The difference between this interest expense and the actual interest payment made to bondholders (which is based on the par value, not the net value, and the coupon rate, not the market rate) is the amount of the premium or discount to be amortized for the period.

Continue to use the example above of a $1,000, 10-year bond with annual interest payments of 11.5% was that was issued for $971.74 because the market rate of interest was 12%. Interest expense for the first year would be:

$971.74 x 12% x 1 year = $116.61

while the annual cash interest payment is:

$1,000 x 11.5% x 1 year = $115.00

The $1.61 difference between interest expense and the cash payment is the amount of the bond discount to be amortized.

The effect of the interest payment and discount amortization on the accounting equation is:

Assets	Liabilities	Owners' equity
$(115) Cash	$1.61 Discount on bonds payable	$(116.61) Interest expense

As the bond discount is amortized it becomes smaller. For the first year, $(28.26) + 1.62 = $(26.65). This means that less will be subtracted from the $1,000 balance in Bonds payable and the carrying value of the bond increases ($1,000 – 26.65 = $973.35). At maturity, the discount will be zero and the carrying value of the bond will be equal to its $1,000 face value.

With the effective interest method, the interest expense shown on the income statement is based on the actual cash loaned to the company, $971.74, not the $1,000 face value of the bond. Interest expense also reflects the market rate of interest that investors demand, 12%, not the 11.5% coupon rate. The cash interest payment made to bondholders, however, is less than the interest expense. The difference increases the carrying value of the bond, so that interest expense will be calculated for the second year on a greater principal amount, compounding interest on interest.

At maturity, bondholders receive the $1,000 face value of the bond, not the $971.74 they loaned the company. The difference between the two, the original unamortized discount of $28.26, can be thought of as extra interest that bondholders earn over the life of the bond issue, so that in effect they earn 12% on $971.74 rather than 11.5% on $1,000.

19. Bond premiums can also be amortized using the effective interest method. Go back to the earlier example of a $1,000, 10-year bond with annual interest payments of 11.5% issued for $1,092.17 when the market rate of interest was 10%. Interest expense for the first year would be:

$1,092.17 x 10% x 1 year = $109.22

while the annual cash interest payment is:

$1,000 x 11.5% x 1 year = $115.00

The $5.78 difference between interest expense and the cash payment is the amount of the bond premium to be amortized. The effect of the interest payment and premium amortization on the accounting equation is:

Assets	Liabilities	Owners' equity
$(115) Cash	$(5.78) Premium on bonds payable	$(109.22) Interest expense

As the bond premium is amortized it becomes smaller. For the first year, $92.17 - 5.78 = $86.39. This means that less will be added to the $1,000 balance in Bonds payable and the carrying value of the bond decreases ($1,000 + 86.39 = $1,086.39). At maturity, the premium will be zero and the carrying value of the bond will be equal to its $1,000 face value.

20. A second way to calculate the dollar amount of premium or discount to be amortized is to use the straight-line method. Simply divide the premium or discount by the number of interest payment periods. An equal amount of premium or discount will be amortized each period. Straight-line amortization is easy, but it is not GAAP. However, it is allowed if the resulting interest expense and carrying value of bonds payable are not significantly different from those calculated using the effective interest method.

21. Some bonds, called **zero-coupon bonds**, do not make regular interest payments to bondholders because the coupon rate of interest on these bonds is 0%. Instead, they make only a single payment of the bond's face value at maturity. Calculating the issue price of these bonds is simply finding the present value of a single cash receipt. These bonds sell at a big discount, which is amortized over the life of the bond.

22. **Callable** bonds allow the issuing company to buy back a bond at any time before maturity. The call price, specified in the bond agreement, is usually greater than the face value of the bond. This allows a company to retire old debt if interest rates drop.

23. **Convertible** bonds can be exchanged for common stock whenever bondholders want. This makes them more attractive to investors, who then have the possibility of benefiting from increases in the stock price.

24. A company's capital structure is the mix of debt and equity that it uses to finance its assets. Borrowing money is a good idea for a company if the benefit to the company exceeds the cost of borrowing. This means the company has positive **financial leverage**, which is using borrowed money to increase earnings.

The **debt-to-equity ratio** compares the value of creditors' claims to the value of owners' claims. It is calculated as:

$$\frac{\text{Total Liabilities}}{\text{Shareholders' Equity}}$$

A company with a high ratio is referred to as highly-leveraged.

The **times-interest-earned ratio** measures a company's ability to make its interest payments:

$$\frac{\text{Income from Operations}}{\text{Interest Expense}}$$

A company with a low times-interest-earned ratio may have too much debt.

Details about a company's long-term debt are usually found in the notes to its financial statements.

25. Debt carries risk for both the issuing company and its creditors, which is the risk that the company will not meet its obligations. A company can reduce its risk by 1) a thorough cost-benefit analysis of any intended long-term borrowing to determine if it will earn more than it costs, and 2) studying the characteristics such as interest rates, borrowing terms, and ease of obtaining money for different types of borrowing available.

Featured Exercise

A company needs to borrow $1,000,000 to finance a major expansion. One financing alternative is a ten-year bank loan with an annual interest rate of 12%.

Part A: If the loan is repaid in ten annual installments made at the end of each year, calculate the amount of each payment and prepare an amortization schedule for the loan.

Mortgage balance	Annual payment	Interest portion of payment (12% x mortgage balance)	Amount of mortgage reduction (annual payment – interest portion)
Beginning balance $1,000,000			

133

Part B: Now assume that the company decides instead to issue $1,000,000 of ten-year, 8.5% mortgage bonds to finance the expansion. The bonds will pay interest annually.

1. If the market rate of interest is 9%, these bonds will sell at (circle one) a premium

   a discount

   par

2. How much cash will the company pay on each interest payment date? _____

3. How much cash will the company pay when the bonds mature? Assume the last interest payment has already been made separately. _____

4. Calculate the amount of cash the company will receive when it issues the bonds.

5. Check your answers to questions 1 through 4, then complete the amortization schedule for the first four years of the bond issue using the effective interest method.

Period	Carrying value at beginning of period	Annual interest expense	Interest payment (Cash)	Amortization of discount	Unamortized discount	Carrying value
0	At issue					
1						
2						
3						
4						

6. At maturity, the unamortized discount on the bonds will be _____ and the carrying value of the bonds will be _____.

7. If the market rate of interest is 8%, these bonds will sell at (circle one) a premium

                                                                            a discount

                                                                            par

8. How much cash will the company pay on each interest payment date? _____

9. How much cash will the company pay when the bonds mature? Assume the last interest payment has already been made separately. _____

10. Calculate the amount of cash the company will receive when it issues the bonds.

11. Check your answers to questions 7 through 10, then complete the amortization schedule for the first four years of the bond issue using the effective interest method.

Period	Carrying value at beginning of period	Annual interest expense	Interest payment (Cash)	Amortization of premium	Unamortized premium	Carrying value
0	At issue					
1						
2						
3						
4						

12. At maturity, the unamortized premium on the bonds will be _____ and the carrying value of the bonds will be _____.

Solution

Part A: Annual payments: $\dfrac{\$1,000,000}{5.65022} = \$176,984.26$

Mortgage balance	Annual payment	Interest portion of payment (12% x mortgage balance)	Amount of mortgage reduction (annual payment – interest portion)
Beginning balance $1,000,000	$176,984.26	$120,000.00 *1,000,000 x .12*	$56,984.26 *176,984.26 – 120,000*
943,015.74 *1,000,000 – 56,984.26*	176,984.26	113,161.89 *943,015.74 x .12*	63,822.37 *176,984.26 – 113,161.89*
879,193.37 *943,015.74 - 63,822.37*	176,984.26	105,503.20 *879,193.37 x .12*	71,481.06 *176,984.26 – 105,503.20*
807,712.31 *879,193.37 - 71,481.06*	176,984.26	96,925.48 *807,712.31 x .12*	80,058.78 *176,984.26 – 96,925.48*
727,653.53 *807,712.31 - 80,058.78*	176,984.26	87,318.42 *727,653.53 x .12*	89,665.84 *176,984.26 – 87,318.42*
637,987.69 *727,653.53 - 89,665.84*	176,984.26	76,558.52 *637,987.69 x .12*	100,425.74 *176,984.26 – 76,558.52*
537,561.95 *637,987.69 - 100,425.74*	176,984.26	64,507.43 *537,561.95 x .12*	112,476.83 *176,984.26 – 64,507.43*
425,085.12 *537,561.95 - 112,476.83*	176,984.26	51,010.21 *425,085.12 x .12*	125,974.05 *176,984.26 – 51,010.21*
299,111.07 *425,085.12 - 125,974.05*	176,984.26	35,893.33 *299,111.07 x .12*	141,090.93 *176,984.26 – 35,893.33*
158,020.14 *299,111.07 - 141,090.93*	176,982.56*	18,962.42 *158,020.14 x .12*	158,020.14

* The final payment is adjusted to equal the balance due on the mortgage plus the last year's interest ($158,020.14 + 18,926.42)

Part B: 1. a discount
2. $85,000 ($1,000,000 x .085 x 1 year)
3. $1,000,000
4. First, find the present value of the series of ten future interest payments of $85,000 each, discounted at the 9% market rate of interest: $85,000 x 6.41766 = $545,501.10
   Then find the present value of the single payment of $1,000,000 face value ten years from now at maturity, discounted at the 9% market rate of interest: $1,000,000 x 0.42241 = $422,410.00.
   Finally, add the two together:
   $545,501.10 + 422,410.00 = $967,911.10
5.

Period	Carrying value at beginning of period	Annual interest expense	Interest payment (Cash)	Amortization of discount	Unamortized discount	Carrying value
0	At issue				$32,088.90 *1,000,000 - 967,911.10*	$967,911.10
1	$967,911.10	$87,112.00 *967,911.10 x .09*	$85,000.00 *1,000,000 x .085*	$2,112.00 *87,112 - 85,000*	29,976.90 *32,088.90 - 2,112.00*	970,023.10 *1,000,000 - 29,976.90*

Period	Carrying value at beginning of period	Annual interest expense	Interest payment (Cash)	Amortization of discount	Unamortized discount	Carrying value
2	970,023.10	87,302.08 *970,023.10* *x .09*	85,000.00	2,302.08 *87,302.08 -* *85,000*	27,674.82 *29,976.90 -* *2,302.08*	972,325.18 *1,000,000 -* *27,674.82*
3	972,325.18	87,509.27 *972,325.18* *x .09*	85,000.00	2,509.27 *87,509.27 -* *85,000*	25,165.55 *27,674.82 -* *2,509.27*	974,834.45 *1,000,000 -* *25,165.55*
4	974,834.45	87,735.10 *974,834.45* *x .09*	85,000.00	2,735.10 *87,735.10 -* *85,000*	22,430.45 *25,165.55 -* *2,735.10*	977,569.55 *1,000,000 -* *22,430.45*

6. At maturity, the unamortized discount on the bonds will be $0 and the carrying value of the bonds will be $1,000,000.
7. a premium
8. $85,000 ($1,000,000 x .085 x 1 year)
9. $1,000,000
10. First, find the present value of the series of ten future interest payments of $85,000 each, discounted at the 8% market rate of interest: $85,000 x 6.71008 = $570,356.80.
   Then find the present value of the single payment of $1,000,000 face value ten years from now at maturity, discounted at the 8% market rate of interest: $1,000,000 x 0.46319 = $463,190.00.
   Finally, add the two together: $570,356.80 + 463,190.00 = $1,033,546.80.
11.

Period	Carrying value at beginning of period	Annual interest expense	Interest payment (Cash)	Amortization of premium	Unamortized premium	Carrying value
0	At issue				$33,546.80 *$1,033,546.80* *- 1,000,000*	$1,033,546.80
1	$1,033,546.80	$82,683.74 *$1,033,546.80* *x .08*	$85,000.00 *$1,000,000* *x .085*	$2,316.26 *$85,000 -* *82,683.74*	31,230.54 *$33,546.80 -* *2,316.26*	1,031,230.54 *$1,000,000 +* *31,230.54*
2	1,031,230.54	82,498.44 *$1,031,230.54* *x .08*	85,000.00	2,501.56 *$85,000 -* *82,498.44*	28,728.98 *$31,230.54 -* *2,501.56*	1,028,728.98 *$1,000,000 +* *28,728.98*
3	1,028,728.98	82,298.32 *$1,028,728.98* *x .08*	85,000.00	2,701.68 *$85,000 -* *82,298.32*	26,027.30 *$28,728.98 -* *2,701.68*	1,026,027.30 *$1,000,000 +* *26,027.30*
4	1,026,027.30	82,082.18 *$1,026,027.30* *x .08*	85,000.00	2,917.82 *$85,000 -* *82,082.18*	23,109.48 *$26,027.30 -* *2,917.82*	1,023,109.48 *$1,000,000 +* *23,109.48*

12. At maturity, the unamortized premium on the bonds will be $0 and the carrying value of the bonds will be $1,000,000.

Review Questions and Exercises

Completion Statements

Fill in the blank(s) to complete each statement.

1. _____ means obtaining money from creditors.

2. The cost of borrowing is called _____.

3. A _____ is an arrangement with a bank that lets a company borrow an amount ranging from zero up to a specified limit whenever it wants.

4. A _____ is a special type of long-term note used to purchase property. It gives the lender a claim against the property until the loan is repaid.

5. Removing the interest from a future payment to calculate its present value is called _____. The interest rate used in present value problems of this type is called the _____.

6. A series of payments where the dollar amount of each payment is the same and the time period between payments is also the same is called an _____.

7. Bondholders may get extra protection from _____ included in the bond agreement. These might place limits on the issuing company's future borrowing or require the company to maintain a particular current ratio.

8. Most bonds pay the face value to bondholders at the _____.

9. Unsecured bonds, called _____, are backed by the general credit of the company.

10. _____ bonds all mature on the same date, while _____ bonds mature over a period of years.

11. The formula for calculating the debt-to-equity ratio is _____.

12. The formula for calculating the times-interest-earned ratio is _____.

True/False

Indicate whether each statement is true (T) or false (F).

_____ 1. With an ordinary annuity, the investor makes payments at the end of each time period.

_____ 2. With an annuity due, the investor makes payments at the beginning of each period.

_____ 3. The future value of an ordinary annuity is larger than the future value of an annuity due for the same interest rate and time period.

_____ 4. If the market rate of interest is higher than a bond's coupon rate, the bond will sell at a premium.

_____ 5. A low times-interest-earned ratio may mean a company is having difficulty making its interest payments.

_____ 6. A company that is highly leveraged has very little debt.

_____ 7. If a company issues bonds at a discount, interest paid to bondholders during the period will be more than the interest expense shown on the company's income statement.

_____ 8. The carrying value of a bond sold at a premium is the face value of the bond plus the related premium.

_____ 9. Assume that a long-term note payable will be repaid with five equal annual installment payments. Interest expense reported from this loan will be the same for each of the five years.

_____ 10. At maturity, the discount on a bond sold below par is zero.

Multiple Choice

_____ 1. Bonds sell at par when the coupon rate is _____ the market rate of interest.
   A. higher than
   B. lower than
   C. the same as
   D. The answer cannot be determined from the information given.

_____ 2. _____ bonds can be exchanged for common stock whenever bondholders want.
   A. Convertible
   B. Callable
   C. Serial
   D. Term

USE THE FOLLOWING INFORMATION TO ANSWER THE NEXT SEVEN QUESTIONS:
On January 1, 2006, Debtor Corporation issued $2,000,000 of 20-year, 8% bonds at 96, when the market rate of interest was 8.5%. The bonds pay interest annually on December 31. The company uses the effective interest method of amortization.

_____ 3. These bonds sold at:
   A. a premium.
   B. a discount.
   C. par.

_____ 4. How much cash did Debtor Corporation receive when the bonds were issued?
   A. $960,000
   B. $1,920,000
   C. $2,000,000
   D. $1,840,000
   E. $1,830,000

_____ 5. How much cash will bondholders receive when the bonds mature? (Assume that the final payment of interest has already been made separately.)
   A. $60,000
   B. $1,920,000
   C. $2,000,000
   D. $1,840,000
   E. $1,830,000

_____ 6. How much cash will bondholders receive on December 31, 2006, the first interest payment date?
   A. $160,000
   B. $170,000
   C. $153,600
   D. $163,200

_____ 7. How much interest expense will Debtor Corporation report on its income statement for the year ended December 31, 2006?
   A. $160,000
   B. $170,000
   C. $153,600
   D. $163,200

_____ 8. With each annual payment of bond interest, the net value (or carrying value) of the bonds will:
   A. increase.
   B. decrease.
   C. remain the same.
   D. change in a way that cannot be predicted because it depends on the market rate of interest in effect at the end of each year.

_____ 9. With each annual payment of bond interest, the interest expense reported for the year will:
   A. increase.
   B. decrease.
   C. remain the same.
   D. change in a way that cannot be predicted because it depends on the market rate of interest in effect at the end of each year.

_____ 10. Bonds that make no annual interest payments to investors, but instead pay only the face value of the bonds at maturity, are:
   A. convertible bonds.
   B. serial bonds.
   C. premium bonds.
   D. zero-coupon bonds.

Exercises

1. On January 1, a company borrowed $40,000 at 11% interest. The loan will be repaid with four equal annual installment payments made on the last day of each year.

   Calculate the amount of each annual payment. Round your answer to the nearest dollar.

Complete the amortization schedule for the loan. Round your answers to the nearest dollar.

	Annual payment	Interest expense	Reduction in principal	Principal balance
0				$40,000
1				
2				
3				
4				0

2. Check your answers for the amortization table above, then answer the questions below. Fill in the correct dollar amount and circle the statement on which it appears, using the following code:
   IS is the income statement for the year described
   BS is the balance sheet at the end of the year described
   SOCF is the statement of cash flows for the year described

a. For Year 1, interest expense of $_____ appears on the   **IS**   **BS**   **SOCF**

b. For Year 1, cash paid for interest of $_____ appears on the   **IS**   **BS**   **SOCF**

c. For Year 1, notes payable of $_____ appears on the   **IS**   **BS**   **SOCF**

d. For Year 1, cash paid for loan principal of $_____ appears on the   **IS**   **BS**   **SOCF**

e. For Year 2, cash paid for loan principal of $_____ appears on the   **IS**   **BS**   **SOCF**

f. For Year 2, notes payable of $_____ appears on the   **IS**   **BS**   **SOCF**

g. For Year 2, interest expense of $_____ appears on the   **IS**   **BS**   **SOCF**

h. For Year 2, cash paid for interest of $_____ appears on the   **IS**   **BS**   **SOCF**

Completion Statements

1. Debt financing
2. interest
3. line of credit
4. mortgage
5. discounting, discount rate
6. annuity

7. covenants
8. maturity date
9. debentures
10. Term, serial
11. total liabilities divided by shareholders' equity
12. income from operations divided by interest expense

True/False

1. True
2. True
3. False   Payments for an ordinary annuity are made at the end of the period. Assume a three-year ordinary annuity of $1,000 per year. The first payment, made at the end of the first year, will earn only two years' interest because it earns nothing for the first year. Similarly, the second payment, made at the end of the second year, earns only one year's interest and the last payment, made at the end of the third year, earns no interest at all. This makes the future value of an ordinary annuity **smaller** than the future value of an annuity due, where payments are made at the beginning of each period. The first payment of a three-year annuity due, made at the beginning of the first year, earns a full three years of interest. Payment two, made at the beginning of the second year, earns two years of interest, and the third payment earns one year of interest.
4. False   If the market rate of interest is higher for other investments, investors will refuse to buy the bond unless the price is less than face value. The bond will sell at a discount.
5. True
6. False   Financial leverage is using borrowed money to increase earnings. A highly-leveraged company has a lot of debt.
7. False   If the bond was sold at a discount, the coupon rate on the bond must be lower than the market rate of interest in effect when the bond was issued. Using the effective interest method, interest expense on the income statement will reflect the higher, market interest rate, and be more (not less) than the cash paid for interest. Part of the current period's interest expense is paid to bondholders in cash, and the remainder is added to the carrying value of the discounted bond, to be paid to bondholders at maturity.
8. True
9. False   Part of each of the five installment payments is interest and part is principal. Since each of the payments makes the principal smaller, interest expense will be calculated on a smaller principal amount each period. Interest expense decreases with each successive payment, even though the total amount of the payment stays the same.
10. True

Multiple Choice

1. C   The law of supply and demand determines prices in the bond market. If the coupon interest rate is higher than the market interest rate, the rate investors can earn elsewhere, they will see the bond as a good investment and drive the price up above par. If the coupon interest rate is lower than the market interest rate, investors will not buy the bond unless the price is less than face value.
2. A   If the bonds are convertible, bondholders can exchange their bonds for stock at any time. The issuing company is allowed to buy back callable bonds whenever it wants. Term bonds all mature on the same date, while serial bonds mature over a period of years.
3. B   The price at which the bonds were issued is 96, which means 96% of face value. Since investors could earn the 8.5% market rate of interest elsewhere, they will not buy the bonds unless the price drops below par.

4. B 96% x $2,000,000 = $1,920,000

5. C Bondholders receive the full $2,000,000 face value of the bonds at maturity, regardless of the price that they paid for the bonds

6. A Interest payments are determined by the terms of the bond contract ($2,000,000 x .08 x 1 year).

7. D Using the effective interest method, interest expense is based on the carrying value (or net value) of the bond, x the effective interest rate when the bonds were issued, x the appropriate fraction of a year ($1,920,000 x .085 x 1 year).

8. A Each year the Discount on Bonds Payable will decrease by the difference between interest expense and the cash paid for interest. As the Discount on Bonds Payable becomes smaller, less is subtracted from the face value of the bonds, and the net value becomes larger.

9. A Using the effective interest method, interest expense is based on the carrying value (or net value) of the bond, times the effective interest rate when the bonds were issued (not the rate in effect at the end of each year). As the carrying value of the bonds increases from year to year, the interest expense will increase, too.

10. D Since the annual interest payment is based on the coupon rate times the face value of the bond, a zero-coupon bond, which has a coupon interest rate of 0%, does not make annual interest payments to bondholders.

Exercises

1	Annual payment	Interest expense *(principal balance x 11%)*	Reduction in principal *(payment – interest)*	Principal balance *(previous principal balance – reduction in principal)*
0				$40,000
1	$12,893 *40,000/ 3.10245, rounded to the nearest dollar*	$4,400 *40,000 x .11 x 1 year*	$8,493 *12,893 - 4,400*	31,507 *40,000 - 8,493*
2	12,893	3,466 *31,507 x .11 x 1 year*	9,427 *12,893 –3,466*	22,080 *31,507 - 9,427*
3	12,893	2,429 *22,080 x .11 x 1 year*	10,464 *12,893 – 2,429*	11,616 *22,080 - 10,464*
4	12,894* *11,616+1,278*	1,278 *11,616 x .11 x 1 year*	11,616*	0 *11,616 - 11,616*

* The final loan payment has been adjusted to pay off the principal balance completely, plus interest for the fourth year.

2. a. $4,400   IS
   b. $4,400   SOCF
   c. $31,507   BS
   d. $8,493   SOCF
   e. $9,427   SOCF
   f. $22,080   BS
   g. $3,466   IS
   h. $3,466   SOCF

CHAPTER 9
SPECIAL ACQUISITIONS: FINANCING A BUSINESS WITH EQUITY

Chapter Overview

When a business begins or wants to expand, it needs to obtain financing. The two sources of financing are debt financing (money from creditors), and equity financing (money from owners). Chapter 8 helps you to understand debt financing. Chapter 9 will help you to understand equity financing. You will see how the money a corporation receives from its owners, called stockholders, is obtained and shown on the financial statements. You will also see how the corporation reports its earnings and its distributions of these earnings to stockholders on the financial statements.

Chapter Highlights

1. All companies, whether they are sole proprietorships, partnerships, or corporations, receive contributions from owners. Corporation owners are called stockholders or shareholders. Stockholders' equity represents these owners' claims to the assets after the liabilities have been paid. Shareholders' equity is made up of **contributed capital** (owners' contributions) and **retained earnings** (earnings kept by the business).

2. To begin, a corporation must receive a corporate charter from the state where the firm is located. The charter authorizes the maximum number of shares a corporation is allowed to issue (sell). The number of shares a company issues cannot exceed the number authorized.

3. A corporation will sometimes buy back its own stock in the stock market for several reasons. It might want to give employees stocks for bonuses or stock option plans, try to increase the market price or the earnings per share, or try to reduce chances of a hostile takeover. The shares held by the corporation are called **treasury stock** because they are physically held in the corporation's "treasury" where it keeps its cash and other certificates of value. Treasury Stock is a **contra-equity** account that reduces total shareholders' equity.

- The number of shares issued always equals the number of shares outstanding plus the number of shares in treasury. The number of shares outstanding is the number of shares issued minus the number of shares in treasury.

- The **cost method** of recording a repurchase of treasury stock requires both assets (Cash) and shareholders' equity (Treasury Stock) to be decreased by the cost to repurchase the stock.

- If the stock is later reissued at a price that is more than this cost, the entry would be:

Assets	Liab.	Shareholders' equity	
		Contributed capital	**Retained earnings**
+ Cash		+ Treasury stock *(cost)* + Additional paid-in capital *(price – cost)*	

If the price is less than cost, then additional paid-in capital would be reduced (instead of increased) by the difference between the cost and the price. If insufficient Additional paid-in capital is available, then Retained earnings would be reduced for the remaining amount.

4. Contributed capital (or paid-in capital) is divided into two parts, **capital stock** and **additional paid-in capital**, that together represent the amount received from owners in cash (or sometimes other assets, like property).

- The amount of common stock equals the number of shares issued times the par value of the common stock. The **par value** is a fixed per-share amount stated on the stock certificate. It defines the maximum responsibility of a stockholder if a company goes out of business (i.e., it limits the stockholders' liability) and restricts a corporation from paying dividends if it would cause stockholders' equity to fall below this amount.

- The par value is not to be confused with the market price the stock sells for when issued. The par value is typically much lower than the market price. The difference between the market price (the value received from the shareholder) and the par value, when the stock is issued, is called **additional paid-in capital** or **paid-in capital in excess of par**.

5. All corporations have **common stock** which has specific rights: 1) to vote for members of the board of directors; 2) to share in the corporation's profits; 3) to share in any assets left if the corporation is to dissolve; and 4) to acquire more shares when the corporation issues new stock. Shareholders take risks in hope of receiving cash **dividends** and an increase in the stock's market value. The board of directors determines how much and when a dividend will be paid and are not legally obligated to do so until the dividend is declared.

- The declaration date is the date the board of directors decides a dividend will be paid. A legal liability is created and recorded as:

Assets	Liabilities	Shareholders' equity	
		Contribu-ted capital	Retained earnings
	+ Dividends payable		- Dividends

- The record date determines who will receive the dividends. Stocks are frequently traded on the stock market, so whoever owns the stock on the record date will receive the full dividend (even if the new stockholder held the stock for only one day). After this date the stock is said to trade ex-dividend.

- The payment date is when the cash is actually paid to the shareholders. The effect on the accounting equation is to reduce assets (Cash) and reduce liabilities (Dividends Payable).

6. Some corporations issue **preferred stock** that has preference over common stock for dividends and claims on assets if the corporation were to dissolve. Common stockholders, however, typically have other rights that preferred stockholders do not, such as voting rights and the right to receive new shares of stock.

- The amount of dividends a preferred stockholder receives equals the dividend rate times the par value stated on the preferred stock. The dividends remaining, after the preferred stock dividends have been met, go to the common stockholders.

- There are two types of preferred stock. **Cumulative preferred stock** means the dividend accumulates so that no common stockholder can receive dividends until all past, unpaid dividends (**called dividends in arrears**) have been paid to the cumulative preferred stockholders. **Noncumulative preferred stock** means dividends do not accumulate so that no past, unpaid dividends will be paid, unless the board of directors decides otherwise.

7. A corporation may issue a **stock dividend** instead of a cash dividend. The effect of a stock dividend is:

Assets	Liab.	Shareholders' equity	
		Contributed capital	Retained earnings
		+ Common stock	- Retained Earnings

The purpose of the stock dividend is to give the shareholders more direct claim to equity by converting retained earnings to common stock. A common stockholder's percentage ownership does not increase with a stock dividend because all the other common stockholders receive the same proportion. Since no cash is distributed, the stockholders do not pay taxes on a stock dividend.

8. A **stock split** is the multiplication or division of the current shares of stock by some

factor to increase or decrease the number of shares and decrease or increase the par value by the same multiple or divisor. A 3-for-1 stock split means that the number of shares authorized, issued, and outstanding becomes three times the number before the split and the par value of a single share becomes one-third of the par value before the split. A corporation may "split" its stock if the market price on the stock exchange is perceived as being too expensive. Stock splits have a history of implying future "good news" and thus may cause the price of the stock to increase. There is no effect of a stock split on the accounting equation or the corporation's financial position. The only change is the par value and the number of shares reported parenthetically in the shareholders' equity sections of the financial statements.

9. **Retained earnings,** known as **earned capital** (not contributed capital), is the net income minus dividends declared since the company began. It can be expressed as beginning retained earnings plus net income minus dividends and is typically shown in the statement of changes in shareholders' equity. Some corporations may show changes in retained earnings in a separate statement or at the bottom of the income statement.

10. There are three ratios to help users analyze the shareholders' equity of a corporation. In general, the higher these ratios, the better.

- The **return on equity (ROE)** measures how profitable the company was in using the common stockholders' investment. ROE is calculated as net income (less preferred stock dividends) divided by the average common shareholders' equity.

- **Earnings per share (EPS)** is shown on the income statement and is a popular measure used to evaluate a company's performance. Basic or primary EPS is calculated as net income (less preferred stock dividends) divided by the weighted average number of common shares outstanding. The denominator should be a weighted average since shares may be issued or repurchased during the period. Another type of EPS is called diluted EPS and is calculated as if all convertible securities were converted into common stock. The effect is to dilute or reduce EPS because the larger number of shares in the denominator would make EPS smaller.

- The third ratio is the **book value per (common) share**. It equals total shareholders' equity (minus any preferred stock) divided by the average number of outstanding shares.

11. **Initial public offering (IPO)** is the issuance of a corporation's stock to the public for the first time. In protecting investors, the Securities and Exchange Commission (SEC) requires the corporation to provide it with many reports, such as a prospectus that includes financial statements before "going public." Companies will go public to obtain significant contributed capital. The increase in shareholders' equity helps improve the capital structure (the amount of equity versus debt).

Featured Exercise

Part A: Fill in the accounting equation below for the events of Tim's Ware, Inc. that occurred during 2007.

Tina's Ware, Inc.		Assets =	Liabilities +	Owners' equity
	Beginning balances, January 1, 2007	Cash $ 500 Receivables (net) 6,000 Inventory 10,500 Prepaid insurance 600 Truck (net) 16,000	Accounts payable $5,000 Interest payable 700 Notes payable 7,000	$1 par value common stock $10,000 Additional paid-in capital 5,000 Retained earnings 5,900
a	Received $6,000 by issuing 4,000 shares of its $1 par value common stock.			
b	Purchased $20,000 of inventory on account.			
c	Made sales of $40,000 on account. The cost of the sales was $30,000.			
d	Collected $44,000 of its receivables.			
e	Paid $19,000 of amounts owed to suppliers.			
f	Repurchased 200 shares of treasury stock for $400.			
g	Paid $4,000 for payroll costs.			
h	Adjusting entries are $200 for bad debts expense, $600 for insurance, $4,000 for depreciation, and $700 for interest owed.			
i.	Sold 50 shares of treasury stock for $100.			
j.	Declared a $3,000 dividend payable in 2008.			

Part B: Using Part A, complete the statement of changes in shareholders' equity for Tim's Ware, Inc., for the year ended December 31, 2007.

Tim's Ware, Inc. Statement of Changes in Shareholders' Equity For the Year Ended December 31, 2007					
Description	Common stock, $1 par value	Additional paid-in capital	Treasury stock	Retained earnings	Total
December 31, 2006 balances					
Issued 4,000 shares of common stock for $6,000					
Repurchased 200 shares of treasury stock for $400					
Sold 50 shares of treasury stock for $100.					
Declared a $3,000 dividend payable in 2008.					
Net income					
Total					

Part C: Using Parts A and B, prepare the shareholders' equity section of the balance sheet at December 31, 2007. The number of shares authorized is 100,000 shares.

Part D: Answer the following questions using the information from Parts A, B, and C and assuming the average number of shares outstanding during 2007 is 13,900 shares.

1. How many shares of common stock are issued as of December 31, 2007?

2. How many shares of common stock are outstanding as of December 31, 2007?

3. What was the average selling price of a share of common stock?

4. Calculate the return on equity.

5. Calculate the book value per share.

6. Calculate the earnings per share.

7. If Tim's Ware, Inc., did a 2-for-1 stock split, what would be the number of shares issued and what would be the par value of its common stock?

Solution

Part A: Fill in the accounting equation below for the events of Tim's Ware, Inc., that occurred during 2007.

Tina's Ware, Inc.		Assets =		Liabilities +		Owners' equity	
	Beginning balances, January 1, 2007	Cash	$ 500	Accounts payable $5,000		$1 par value common stock $10,000	
		Receivables (net)	6,000	Interest payable 700		Additional paid-in	
		Inventory	10,500	Notes payable 7,000		capital 5,000	
		Prepaid insurance	600			Retained earnings 5,900	
		Truck (net)	16,000				
a	Received $6,000 by issuing 4,000 shares of its $1 par value common stock.	6,000	Cash			4,000	Common stock
						2,000	Additional paid-in capital
b	Purchased $20,000 of inventory on account.	20,000	Inventory	20,000	Accounts payable		
c	Made sales of $40,000 on account. The cost of the sales was $30,000.	40,000	Receivables			40,000	Sales
		(30,000)	Inventory			(30,000)	Cost of goods sold
d	Collected $44,000 of its receivables.	44,000	Cash				
		(44,000)	Receivables				
e	Paid $19,000 of amounts owed to suppliers.	(19,000)	Cash	(19,000)	Accounts payable		
f	Repurchased 200 shares of treasury stock for $400.	(400)	Cash			(400)	Treasury stock
g	Paid $4,000 for payroll costs.	(4,000)	Cash			(4,000)	Payroll expense
h	Adjusting entries are $200 for bad debts expense, $600 for insurance, $4,000 for depreciation, and $700 for interest owed.	(200)	Allowance for uncollectible accounts	700	Interest payable	(200)	Bad debts expense
						(600)	Insurance expense
		(600)	Prepaid insurance			(4,000)	Depreciation expense
		(4,000)	Accumulated depreciation			(700)	Interest expense
i.	Sold 50 shares of treasury stock for $100.	100	Cash			100	Treasury stock
j.	Declared a $3,000 dividend payable in 2008.			3,000	Dividends payable	(3,000)	Dividends

149

Part B:	Tim's Ware, Inc.				
	Statement of Changes in Shareholders' Equity				
	For the Year Ended December 31, 2007				
Description	Common stock, $1 par value	Additional paid-in capital	Treasury stock	Retained earnings	Total
December 31, 2006 balances	$10,000	$5,000	$0	$5,900	$20,900
Issued 4,000 shares of common stock for $6,000	4,000	2,000			6,000
Repurchased 200 shares of treasury stock for $400			(400)		(400)
Sold 50 shares of treasury stock for $100.			100		100
Declared a $3,000 dividend payable in 2008.				(3,000)	(3,000)
Net income				500	500
Total	$14,000	$7,000	$(300)	$3,400	$24,100

Part C:

December 31, 2007

Shareholders' equity
Common stock, par value $1 per share,
   Authorized 100,000 shares, issued 14,000 shares $14,000
Additional paid-in capital   7,000
Treasury stock: 150 shares   (300)
Retained earnings   3,400
Total shareholders' equity $24,100

Part D:

1. Shares issued equals 14,000 shares.
2. Shares outstanding equals 13,850 (or 14,000 issued minus 150 treasury stock)
3. The average selling price equals $1.50 (or the sum of $14,000 common stock plus $7,000 additional paid in capital divided by 14,000 shares of common stock issued).

4. Return on equity = $\dfrac{\text{net income}}{\text{average shareholders' equity}} = \dfrac{\$500}{(\$24,100 + \$20,900)/2} = 2.2\%$

5. Book value per share = $\dfrac{\text{common shareholders' equity}}{\text{average shares outstanding}} = \dfrac{\$24,100}{13,900 \text{ shares}} = \$1.73$

6. Earnings per share = $\dfrac{\text{net income}}{\text{average shares outstanding}} = \dfrac{\$500}{13,900 \text{ shares}} = \$0.04$

7. The number of shares issued would be 28,000, or double the number of shares issued prior to the split. The par value of its common stock would be $0.50 or one half of the par value prior to the split.

Review Questions and Exercises

Completion Statements

Fill in the blank(s) to complete each statement.

1. The two sources of financing are debt financing (money from creditors), and _____ (money from owners).

2. Shareholders' equity is made up of _____ (owners' contributions) and _____ (earnings kept by the business).

3. When a corporation repurchases its own common stock, the shares are called _____. Since these shares reduce shareholders' equity, the account is called a _____-equity account.

4. The number of shares _____ always equals the number of shares _____ plus the number of shares in the _____.

5. Contributed capital (or paid-in capital) is divided into two parts: _____ and _____.

6. The difference between the market price (the value received from the shareholder) and the par value is called _____ or _____.

7. The _____ date is the date the board of directors decides a dividend will be paid and a legal liability is created. Whoever owns the stock on the _____ date will receive the full dividend. The _____ date is when the cash is actually paid to the shareholders.

8. There are two types of preferred stock: _____ preferred stock, which means that dividends accumulate, and _____ preferred stock, which means dividends do not accumulate.

9. A _____ is the division of the current shares of stock by some factor to increase the number of shares and decrease the par value by the same factor.

10. The _____ measures how profitable the company was in using the common stockholders' investment and is calculated as net income (less preferred stock dividends) divided by the average common shareholders' equity.

True/False

Indicate whether each statement is true (T) or false (F).

_____1. The number of shares outstanding will always equal the number of shares issued minus the number of shares held as treasury stock.

_____2. The earnings per share is the amount of dividends the shareholder will receive.

_____3. The par value per share is the price the shareholders will pay when the shares are issued.

_____4. A reason a company will repurchase its own stock as treasury stock is to have shares it can later give to employees as part of a stock option plan.

_____5. Preferred stockholders do not have voting rights, but do have preference to dividends.

_____6. A stock dividend has the effect of reducing retained earnings and reducing cash.

_____7. Both stock dividends and stock splits increase the actual number of shares a shareholder will own, as well as increase the percentage of the shareholder's ownership.

_____8. The average selling price of common stock can be determined by dividing the sum of the balances in Common Stock and Additional Paid-in Capital by the number of shares issued.

Multiple Choice

Select the best answer for each question.

_____1. The preferred stock dividend amount is calculated by:
   A. dividing the total dividend by the number of shares of preferred stock plus common stock outstanding.
   B. multiplying the dividend rate times the market price per share times the number of preferred stock shares outstanding.
   C. multiplying the dividend rate times the par value per share times the number of preferred stock shares outstanding.
   D. multiplying the total dividend times the percentage of preferred stock to common stock.

_____2. Diluted earnings per share (EPS) is reported on the income statement so that users can see what effect
   A. cumulative preferred stock dividends have on EPS.
   B. contingent liabilities will have on EPS.
   C. treasury stock has on EPS.
   D. the convertible securities would have on EPS if they were converted into common stock.

_____3. Retained earnings is:
   A. net income divided by the average number of shares outstanding.
   B. the amount received in excess of par value.
   C. the net income minus dividends since the inception of the company.
   D. the minimum legal amount of earnings required to be kept by the company.

_____4. The par value of common stock represents the:
   A. amount the stock sold for when it was originally issued.
   B. legal minimum capital that must be retained in the company.
   C. highest price a stock may be sold for.
   D. amount of dividend the shareholder is to receive.

_____5. Stock that has dividends in arrears is called:
   A. cumulative preferred stock.
   B. convertible preferred stock.
   C. cumulative common stock.
   D. noncumulative preferred stock.

_____6. Aria's, Inc., has 1,000 shares of 5%, $100 par value cumulative preferred stock and 10,000 shares of $1 par value common stock outstanding. The company has not paid dividends in two years. In its third year it paid the common stockholders a $2 per share dividend. How much did the preferred stockholders receive per share?
   A. $100
   B. $15
   C. $6
   D. $5

_____7. Aria's, Inc., has 1,000 shares of 5%, $100 par value cumulative preferred stock and 10,000 shares of $1 par value common stock. The company has not paid a dividend in two years. In its third year it paid the common stockholders a $2 per share dividend. What was the total amount of dividends paid?
   A. $35,000
   B. $30,000
   C. $20,000
   D. $20,150

_____8. At the beginning of the year, the balance in retained earnings was $400,000. During the year sales were $1,000,000, of which $800,000 was collected and expenses were $750,000, of which $400,000 had been paid. The company has outstanding 10,000 shares of 6%, $100 par value preferred stock and 100,000 shares of $0.10 par value common stock. The dividend paid to the common stockholders was $1 per share. Calculate the ending retained earnings.
   A. $490,000
   B. $410,000
   C. $240,000
   D. $ 90,000

_____9. Mr. Cello bought 4,000 shares of Ventures, Inc., $1 par value common stock directly from Ventures, Inc. for $80,000. When Mr. Cello sold 1,000 of his shares to Mr. Bilo for $30,000. The result for Ventures, Inc. will be:
   A. shareholders' equity will decrease by $80,000.
   B. net income will increase by $10,000 from the gain on the sale of common stock.
   C. Shareholders' equity will be unaffected by the sale.
   D. Both A and B above are correct.

_____10. A company has treasury stock which cost $50,000. If it resells this stock for $40,000, then:
   A. additional paid-in capital is reduced by $10,000.
   B. additional paid-in capital is reduced by $50,000.
   C. treasury stock is increased by $40,000.
   D. shareholders' equity is increased by $50,000.

Exercises

1. For each event listed below, fill in the correct dollar amounts in the appropriate box(es) to show the effect of the event on shareholders' equity accounts.

Business event	6%, $100 par value preferred stock	$1 par value common stock	Additional paid-in capital	Retained earnings	Treasury stock
January 1, 2006 beginning balances	$50,000	$100,000	$300,000	$400,000	$(10,000)
Sold 10,000 additional shares of $1 par value common stock for $4 per share.					
Purchased 1,000 shares of its own stock for $5,000					
Net income for the year was $50,000					
Declared dividends of $10,000					
December 31, 2006 ending balances					

2. For each of the transactions below, show the effect on the accounting equation by circling one item in each column.

a. On January 1, 2007, Ventures, Inc., declared a $50,000 dividend. The date of record is January 31, 2007 and the date of payment is February 15, 2007.

Total assets	Total liabilities	Total shareholders' equity	
		Contributed capital	Retained earnings
Increase	Increase	Increase	Increase
Decrease	Decrease	Decrease	Decrease
No effect	No effect	No effect	No effect

b. On January 31, 2007, Ventures, Inc., updated its stock records.

Total assets	Total liabilities	Total shareholders' equity	
		Contributed capital	Retained earnings
Increase	Increase	Increase	Increase
Decrease	Decrease	Decrease	Decrease
No effect	No effect	No effect	No effect

154

c. On February 15, 2007, Ventures, Inc., paid the $50,000 dividend in a. above.

Total assets	Total liabilities	Total shareholders' equity	
		Contributed capital	Retained earnings
Increase	Increase	Increase	Increase
Decrease	Decrease	Decrease	Decrease
No effect	No effect	No effect	No effect

d. On February 28, 2007, Ventures, Inc., repurchased $5,000 of its own stock.

Total assets	Total liabilities	Total shareholders' equity
		Contributed capital +Retained earnings
Increase	Increase	Increase
Decrease	Decrease	Decrease
No effect	No effect	No effect

e. On March 31, 2007, Ventures, Inc., paid a $10,000 stock dividend.

Total assets	Total liabilities	Total shareholders' equity	
		Contributed capital	Retained earnings
Increase	Increase	Increase	Increase
Decrease	Decrease	Decrease	Decrease
No effect	No effect	No effect	No effect

f. On May 31, 2007, Ventures, Inc., split its stock 2 for 1.

Total assets	Total liabilities	Total shareholders' equity	
		Contributed capital	Retained earnings
Increase	Increase	Increase	Increase
Decrease	Decrease	Decrease	Decrease
No effect	No effect	No effect	No effect

3. Capital Venture, Inc., began operations in January 2006 by issuing common stock for $10 per share. Net income for 2006 was $500,000 and dividends of $100,000 were declared. Fill in the missing amounts in the spaces provided.

	December 31, 2006
6% preferred stock, $50 par value, 500 shares authorized and issued	(a)
Common stock, $1 par value, 8,000,000 shares authorized, (b)_____ shares issued	$900,000
Additional paid-in capital in excess of par	(c)
Retained earnings	(d)
Treasury stock (1,000 shares at cost)	(25,000)
Total shareholders' equity	(e)

(f) How many shares are outstanding as of December 31, 2006?

4. Tim's Ware's had an initial public offering and sold 200,000 shares of $2 par value common stock for a total of $3,000,000.

a	What was the average selling price for each share of stock?	
b	What amount should be reported for the Common stock?	
c	What amount should be reported for the Additional paid-in capital?	

Completion Statements

1. equity financing
2. contributed capital, retained earnings
3. treasury stock, contra
4. issued, outstanding, treasury
5. paid-in capital, retained earnings
6. paid-in capital in excess of par, additional paid-in capital
7. declaration, record, payment
8. cumulative, noncumulative
9. stock split
10. return on equity

True/False

1. True
2. False EPS is a company's net income (not dividends), less preferred stock dividends if any, on a per share basis.
3. False The par value represents the maximum responsibility of a shareholder and does not have any relationship to the market price of that share.
4. True
5. True
6. False A stock dividend's effect on the accounting equation is to reduce retained earnings and increase common stock. A cash (not stock) dividend reduces cash when it is paid.
7. False Both stock dividends and splits increase the number of shares a shareholder will own. However, since all shareholders receive the same proportion of stock, their ownership percentage remains the same.
8. True

Multiple Choice

1. C Preferred stock typically has a dividend rate and par value stated on the certificate. The preferred stock dividend is the dividend rate times the par value. Common stock does not have a dividend rate and will receive the dividends that are remaining only after the preferred stockholders' dividends have been met.

2. D The diluted EPS assumes that all of the company's convertible securities have been converted into common stock. This makes the denominator larger, causing the EPS to be smaller or diluted.

3. C Retained earnings equals beginning retained earnings plus net income minus dividends.

4. B The par value has no relevance to the market price. Most companies' par value is set well below the selling price of the stock. The lower the par value the less likely a company's equity will fall below this legal minimum capital that must be retained in the company.

5. A Only cumulative preferred stockholders have the right to receive past, unpaid dividends before other shareholders receive any dividends.

6. B The preferred dividend per share is $5 which equals the dividend rate, 5%, times the par value of $100. Since the stock is cumulative, the dividend will equal $15 per share (3 years x $5).

7. A The cumulative preferred shareholders receive $15 per share. The total dividends paid is $35,000 which equals $15,000 to preferred shareholders (or $15 per share times 1,000 shares) plus $20,000 to common shareholders (or $2 per common share times 10,000 shares).

8. A Beginning retained earnings of $400,000 plus net income of $250,000 (or $1,000,000 minus $750,000) minus dividends of $160,000 (6% times $100 par value times 10,000 preferred shares plus $1 times 100,000 common shares) equals ending retained earnings of $490,000.

9. C When the company issued 4,000 shares to Mr. Cello, its contributed capital increased by $80,000. When Mr. Cello sells his shares to another party, there is no effect on Ventures' shareholders' equity.

10. A The reissuance of treasury stock at an amount below cost causes cash to increase by $40,000 and treasury stock to increase by $50,000. Additional paid-in capital is decreased by $10,000 to balance the accounting equation.

Exercises

1. Business event	6%, $100 par value preferred stock	$1 par value common stock	Additional paid-in capital	Retained earnings	Treasury stock
January 1, 2006 beginning balances	$50,000	$100,000	$300,000	$400,000	$(10,000)
Sold 10,000 additional shares of $1 par value common stock for $4 per share.		10,000 $1 x 10,000	30,000 ($4 – 1) x 10,000		
Purchased 1,000 shares of its own stock for $5,000					(5,000)
Net income for the year was $50,000				50,000	
Declared dividends of $10,000				(10,000)	
December 31, 2006 ending balances	$50,000	$110,000	$330,000	$440,000	$(15,000)

2.	Total assets	Total liabilities	Total shareholders' equity	
			Contributed capital	Retained earnings
a	No effect	Increased	No effect	Decreased
b	No effect	No effect	No effect	No effect
c	Decrease	Decrease	No effect	No effect
d	Decrease	No effect	Decrease	
e	No effect	No effect	Increase	Decrease
f	No effect	No effect	No effect	No effect

3.	December 31, 2006
6% preferred stock, $50 par value, 500 shares authorized and issued	(a) $25,000 *$50 par value x 500 shares*
Common stock, $1 par value, 8,000,000 shares authorized, (b) 900,000 shares issued *($900,000/$1 par value)*	$900,000
Additional paid-in capital in excess of par	(c) $8,100,000 *($10 - 1) x 900,000 shares*
Retained earnings	(d) $400,000 *$500,000 – 100,000*
Treasury stock (1,000 shares at cost)	(25,000)
Total shareholders' equity	(e) $9,400,000

(f) 900,000 shares issued minus 1,000 treasury shares equals 899,000 shares outstanding.

4.		
a	What was the average selling price for each share of stock?	$15 *$3,000,000/200,000 shares*
b	What amount should be reported for the common stock?	$400,000 *$2 x 200,000 shares*
c	What amount should be reported for the additional paid-in capital?	$2,600,000 *($15 - $2) x 200,000 shares*

CHAPTER 10
PREPARING THE STATEMENT OF CASH FLOWS

Chapter Overview

Cash may well be a company's most important asset. The statement of cash flows, which describes in detail all of a company's cash receipts and cash payments, is one of the financial statements required by GAAP. In this chapter you will learn to prepare the three sections of the statement of cash flows: 1) cash from operations, which may be prepared using either the direct or the indirect method; 2) cash from investing activities; and 3) cash from financing activities. In learning to prepare the statement of cash flows, you should gain a clearer understanding of the difference between accrual accounting and cash-basis accounting.

Chapter Highlights

1. Cash is a very important asset. It is needed to pay dividends to owners and interest to creditors on a timely basis. Many companies go bankrupt each year because they do not have enough cash at the right time to pay their bills. A cash budget is useful for estimating in advance the cash inflows and outflows that a company expects. If a company expects a shortfall, it can plan ahead of time and secure a line of credit, borrow the money needed, or change the timing of expected cash receipts and payments. At the end of the accounting period, managers can use this same budget to evaluate performance by comparing it with actual events. This year's cash budget is also useful for planning next year's cash activity.

2. GAAP allows two ways of preparing the cash flows from operations section of the statement of cash flows: the **direct method** and the **indirect method**. With the direct method, cash inflows and outflows are shown directly. With the indirect method, the statement begins with net income, an accrual-based number, and adjusts it to cash from operations. Regardless of the method used, net cash flow from operations should be the same dollar amount. The other two sections, cash from investing activities and cash from financing activities, are prepared in the

same way for both the direct and indirect methods.

3. The first section of the statement of cash flows is the operating section, also known as cash from operating activities, where the cash inflows and cash outflows from the normal, day-to-day activities are reported. Typical operating cash inflows are:
- Cash collected from customers
- Cash collected for interest

Typical operating cash outflows are:
- Cash paid to employees
- Cash paid to suppliers for inventory
- Cash paid for operating expenses
- Cash paid for interest
- Cash paid for taxes

4. The second section of the statement of cash flows is the investing section, also known as **cash from investing activities**, where the cash inflows and cash outflows for long-term business assets and from investments are reported. Typical investing cash inflows are:
- Cash received from the sale of property, plant, and equipment
- Cash from the sale of marketable securities
- Cash received when amounts loaned to others are repaid

Typical investing cash outflows are:
- Cash paid to buy property, plant, and equipment
- Cash paid for investments
- Cash loaned to others

5. The third section of the statement of cash flows is the financing section, also known as **cash from financing activities**, where the cash inflows and cash outflows for the principal on loans, contributions from owners, and payments to owners are reported. Typical financing cash inflows are:
- Cash received from the sale of stock
- Cash received from borrowing

Typical financing cash outflows are:
- Cash paid for treasury stock
- Cash paid to retire debt principal
- Cash paid for dividends

6. Most companies keep their accounting records on an accrual basis so that they can easily prepare financial statements in accordance with GAAP. If a company sells goods on account, it will recognize sales revenue for goods that have been sold even if cash has not yet been received. Uncollected accounts receivable represent revenue that has been earned but has not been collected in cash. Moreover, the company may have collected cash during the accounting period from sales on account recorded in a previous accounting period. For both of these reasons, the amount of cash received during an accounting period will not necessarily be the same as the revenue earned during that period.

To convert the accrual-basis sales revenue found on the income statement to cash collected from customers for the statement of cash flows, you must analyze the change in accounts receivable during the accounting period by looking at balance sheets for the beginning and end of the period. If accounts receivable increased during the period, then some of the current period's sales have not yet been collected from customers. This increase in accounts receivable should be subtracted from sales revenue to determine the amount of cash collected.

Every revenue or expense reported on the accrual-basis income statement may be different from the amount of cash actually received or paid. Each income statement line item must be examined along with changes in the related current asset or current liability accounts to determine the amount of cash actually received or paid. For example, a company might show salary expense of $30,000 on its income statement. This represents the cost of services provided by employees during the accounting period, regardless of whether these employees have been paid in cash or not. If the related current liability account, salaries payable, also decreased $400 during the period, then the company must have paid cash for more than just the $30,000 current period's expense. The

decrease in salaries payable should be added to the $30,000 salary expense to determine the amount of cash paid to employees.

7. There are two possible ways to prepare the cash from operations section of the statement of cash flows. The direct method begins with the income statement. Each revenue and expense must be analyzed to determine the amount of cash received or paid. You should look at the income statement in Exhibit 10-3 and the balance sheet in Exhibit 10-4 in your textbook.

- Tom's Wear's income statement shows sales revenue of $2,000 for the month ended March 31, 2001. During the month, accounts receivable grew from $150 at the beginning of the month to $2,000 at the end of the month, an increase of $1,850. This means that none of March's $2,000 in sales revenue has been received in cash yet. Cash collected from customers must be $2,000 in sales revenue minus the $1,850 increase in accounts receivable, or $150.

- Tom's Wear's income statement shows cost of goods sold of $800 for the same month. The first step in calculating cash paid for inventory is to determine how much inventory was purchased during March. Inventory grew from $100 at the beginning of the month to $300 at the end of the month, an increase of $200. Tom's Wear must have purchased enough inventory to cover the $800 in cost of goods sold and to increase its inventory by $200 as well, a total of $1,000 in inventory purchased. However, this does not tell us how much cash the company actually paid for inventory, since often inventory is purchased on account, not for cash. We must also look at changes in accounts payable for the period. Accounts payable went from $800 at the beginning of the month to $0 at the end of the month, a decrease of $800. The company must have paid the full $1,000 for March's purchases plus another $800 for inventory purchased in a previous period, a total of $1,800 cash paid for inventory in March.

- The March income statement for Tom's Wear shows depreciation expense of $100. This represents part of the historical cost of equipment allocated to expense for the current accounting period. No cash is ever paid for depreciation expense.

- The company's income statement shows insurance expense of $50 for the month. During the month, the balance in Prepaid insurance went from $125 at the beginning of the month to $75 at the end of the month, a decrease of $50. Clearly, the $50 in March insurance expense came from a policy purchased in a previous month, not from a current cash payment. No cash was paid for insurance in March.

- Finally, Tom's Wear's income statement shows interest expense of $30. During March, the balance in Interest payable increased from $0 at the beginning of the month to $30 at the end of the month. The company still owes the entire $30 in interest. No cash was paid for interest during the month.

- Although we have covered all of the line items on the income statement, we must look at the balance sheet to make sure that all changes in current assets and current liabilities have been included. The last current asset, prepaid rent, was $0 at the beginning of March and at the end of March as well. Since no rent expense appears on the income statement either, we can be sure that no cash was paid for rent during the month. Property, plant, and equipment, represented by the $3,900 in the Machine account, is not a current asset, so it does not affect cash from operations.

- Among the current liabilities, Other Payables decreased from $50 at the beginning of the month to $0 at the end of the month. Although no other operating expenses appear on the income statement, the company must have paid $50 for other expenses reported during a previous accounting period. Notes payable is a long-term liability, not a current liability, so it does not affect cash from operations.

The cash from operations section for Tom's Wear's statement of cash flows, prepared using the direct method, looks like this:

Cash from operations:

Cash from customers	$ 150
Cash paid to vendors	(1,800)
Cash paid for other expenses	(50)
Net increase (decrease) in cash from operations	$(1,700)

8. The Financial Accounting Standards Board (FASB) prefers that companies use the direct method to prepare the operating activities section of the statement of cash flows. However, the FASB also requires that companies using the direct method must also provide a **reconciliation of net income and cash from operating activities**, which is essentially the same as using the indirect method. Most companies, then, use the indirect method to report cash flows from operations.

Using the indirect method, the operating activities section begins with net income. Any amounts that affect net income but do not affect cash are removed. Then changes in each current asset and current liability account are analyzed to determine the effect on cash. You should look at the income statement in Exhibit 10-3 and the balance sheet in Exhibit 10-4 in your textbook.

- Tom's Wear's income statement shows net income of $1,020. To this amount, add $100 in depreciation expense because this expense decreases income but does not decrease cash.

- Accounts receivable grew from $150 at the beginning of the month to $2,000 at the end of the month, an increase of $1,850. If accounts receivable increase, it means that sales revenue has not been collected in cash. This $1,850 increase in accounts receivable should be subtracted for the calculation of cash from operations.

- Inventory increased from $100 at the beginning of March to $300 at the end of March. This $200 increase in a current asset represents an inventory purchase that might have been paid for in cash, and should be subtracted because it potentially decreases the cash provided by operations.

- Prepaid insurance went from $125 at the beginning of the month to $75 at the end of the month, a decrease of $50. This decrease in a current asset represents an expense on the income statement that decreased income without requiring a decrease in cash as well. The $50 should be added to net income in calculating cash from operations.

- Prepaid rent was $0 at the beginning of March and $0 at the end of March, too. Since it did not change, it did not affect either income or cash for the month, and it can be ignored.

- The change in the Machine account, a long-term asset, does not affect cash from operations because buying and selling property, plant, and equipment is an investing activity, not an operating activity.

- Accounts payable went from $800 at the beginning of March to $0 at the end of March. This decrease in a current liability represents cash paid out by Tom's Wear, and a decrease in cash provided by operations. Similarly, the $50 decrease in other payables decreases the cash provided by operations.

- Interest payable increased from $0 at the beginning of the period to $30 at the end of the period. This means that the $30 expense, which decreased net income on the income statement, did not decrease cash because the company did not pay anything for interest in March. This decrease in a current liability should be added to net income in calculating cash from operations.

- Notes payable is a long-term liability, not a current liability. Increases and decreases in long-term debt are financing, not operating, activities.

The cash from operations section for Tom's Wear's statement of cash flows, prepared using the indirect method, looks like this:

Net income	$ 1,020
+ Depreciation expense	100
- Increase in accounts receivable	(1,850)
- Increase in inventory	(200)
+ Decrease in prepaid insurance	50
- Decrease in payables	
(- 800 – 50 + 30)	(820)
Net cash from operations	$(1,700)

Notice that cash from operations is the same $(1,700) under both the direct and indirect methods.

9. The format of the cash from investing activities section is exactly the same, whether the operating activities are presented under the direct method or indirect method. Analyze changes in non-current assets to determine cash received or paid for investing activities.

- In the month of March, the balance in Tom's Wear's Machine account increased from $0 to $3,900, net of $100 accumulated depreciation. The original cost of the machine must have been $4,000. Since long-term assets are often expensive, it is possible that this entire amount was not paid in cash and we must look further in the company's records. Tom's Wear paid $1,000 in cash and signed a note for the $3,000 remainder. Only the cash paid will appear in the investing activities section of the statement, but the $3,000 note will be shown in a footnote so that the statement includes all major investing activities, even those that did not involve cash.

10. Similarly, the format of the cash from financing activities section is exactly the same, whether the operating activities are presented under the direct method or indirect method. Analyze changes in non-current liabilities and owners' equity accounts for evidence of financing activities.

162

- Notes payable increased from $0 at the beginning of March to $3,000 at the end of March. However, Tom's Wear did not receive cash for the note payable, but instead used it to finance the purchase of equipment. Since no cash was received, the note will not be reported in the financing activities section of the statement, but will be described in a footnote.

- There was no change in Tom's Wear's Common stock account during March. Apparently no cash was received from the sale of stock. Retained earnings went from $1,220 to $2,240 during the month, an increase of $1,020. Since this increase is exactly equal to net income, no dividends were declared or paid.

The investing and financing activities sections of Tom's Wear's statement of cash flows will look like this:

Cash from investing activities:
Purchase of machine*	(1,000)
Net cash from investing activities	(1,000)

Cash from financing activities: 0

* A $4,000 machine was purchased for $1,000 cash and a $3,000 note payable.

11. GAAP requires companies that use the indirect method to disclose cash paid for interest and taxes somewhere in the financial statements.

12. Investors hope to see a positive cash flow from operating activities. In the long run, a company must generate positive operating cash flow or it will not survive. The investing activities section of the statement of cash flows shows the company's future plans. Negative investing cash flow means the company has invested in long-term assets, which may indicate expansion, or at least replacement of aging productive assets. Failure to invest in property, plant and equipment may mean the company has a problem. The financing activities section shows how the company is financed, with debt or with equity.

Financial analysts sometimes calculate **free cash flow**, which is cash flow from operations minus cash paid for dividends and capital expenditures. This is used as a measure of a company's ability to make future investments.

Featured Exercise

Megabucks, Inc.
Income Statement
For the Year Ended December 31, 2005

Sales revenue		$2,000,000
Expenses		
Cost of goods sold	$1,080,000	
Salary expense	572,000	
Depreciation expense	24,000	
Other operating expenses	138,000	
Interest expense	38,800	1,852,800
Net income		$ 147,200

Megabucks, Inc.
Comparative Balance Sheets
At December 31, 2005 and 2004

	2005	2004	Increase (Decrease)
Cash	$ 120,800	$ 40,800	$ 80,000
Accounts receivable	84,000	132,000	(48,000)
Inventory	408,000	384,000	24,000
Equipment (net of depreciation)	480,000	504,000	(24,000)
Total	$1,092,800	$1,060,800	
Accounts payable	$ 98,400	$ 63,200	$ 35,200
Salaries payable	7,600	16,000	(8,400)
Interest payable	9,600	21,600	(12,000)
Bonds payable	400,000	400,000	0
Common stock	104,000	104,000	0
Retained earnings*	473,200	456,000	17,200
Total	$1,092,800	$1,060,800	

*During 2005, Megabucks declared and paid a cash dividend of $130,000.

Part A: Prepare a statement of cash flows for the year ended December 31, 2005, using the direct method.

Megabucks, Inc.
Statement of Cash Flows
For the Year Ended December 31, 2005

Part B: Prepare a statement of cash flows for the year ended December 31, 2005, using the indirect method.

Megabucks, Inc.
Statement of Cash Flows
For the Year Ended December 31, 2005

Solution

Part A

Megabucks, Inc.
Statement of Cash Flows
For the Year Ended December 31, 2005

Cash from operations

Cash from customers	$ 2,048,000	
Cash paid to vendors	(1,068,800)	
Cash paid for salaries	(580,400)	
Cash paid for other operating expenses	(138,000)	
Cash paid for interest	(50,800)	
Net cash from operations		$ 210,000

Cash from investing activities		0

Cash from financing activities

Cash paid for dividends	(130,000)	
Net cash from financing activities		(130,000)
Net increase (decrease) in cash		$ 80,000

Part B

Megabucks, Inc.
Statement of Cash Flows
For the Year Ended December 31, 2005

Cash from operations

Net income	$147,200	
+ Depreciation expense	24,000	
+ Decrease in Accounts receivable	48,000	
- Increase in Inventory	(24,000)	
+ Increase in Accounts payable	35,200	
- Decrease in Salaries payable	(8,400)	
- Decrease in Interest payable	(12,000)	
Net cash from operations		$210,000

Cash from investing activities		0

Cash from financing activities

Cash paid for dividends	(130,000)	
Net cash from financing activities		(130,000)
Net increase (decrease) in cash		$ 80,000

Review Questions and Exercises

Completion Statements

Fill in the blank(s) to complete each statement.

1.   The first section of the statement of cash flows is _____ .

2.   The second section of the statement of cash flows is _____ .

3.   The third section of the statement of cash flows is _____ .

4.   There are two ways to present cash flows from operations: the _____ method and the

       _____ method.

5.   Companies that use the direct method of calculating cash from operations must also provide a

       _____ .

6.   Companies that use the indirect method of calculating cash from operations must also report cash

       paid for _____ and cash paid for _____ somewhere in their
       financial statements.

7.   Investors hope to see _____ cash flow from operations.

8.   Investors look at cash used by _____ for evidence of expansion.

9.   The cash from _____ section shows how a company finances its assets.

10.   A _____ is a detailed plan of a company's estimated cash receipts and
       disbursements.

True/False

Indicate whether each statement is true (T) or false (F).

_____   1.   The Financial Accounting Standards Board prefers that companies use the direct method
                 of reporting cash from operations.

_____   2.   Most companies use the direct method of reporting cash from operations.

_____   3.   Depreciation expense decreases a company's cash.

_____   4.   A company that uses the direct method will show more cash from operations than a
                 company that uses the indirect method.

_____   5.   There are two acceptable ways to report cash from investing activities: the direct method
                 and the indirect method.

_____ 6. Only new companies need to prepare a cash budget to obtain financing.

_____ 7. Negative cash flow from investing activities is usually good.

_____ 8. If a company issues a five-year note payable to buy equipment, the note will not appear on the statement of cash flows because it does not involve receipt or payment of cash.

_____ 9. Only the largest companies are required to prepare a statement of cash flows.

_____ 10. If a company uses the indirect method of calculating cash from operations, its statement of cash flows begins with net income.

Multiple Choice

_____ 1. In the long run, a company must generate positive cash flow from _____ or it will not survive.
A. operations
B. investing activities
C. financing activities
D. operating, investing, or financing activities

_____ 2. Which of the following financial statements explains why a company's cash balance changed over a period of time?
A. Income statement
B. Balance sheet
C. Statement of cash flows
D. Both B and C

Use the following information to answer the next three questions:
Our Feathered Friends, Inc., reported credit sales of $1,500,000 for 2007. Cost of goods sold was $700,000. The following additional information is available from the company's records:

	December 31, 2007	December 31, 2006
Accounts receivable	$50,000	$40,000
Inventory	75,000	80,000
Accounts payable	30,000	25,000

_____ 3. How much cash did the company collect from customers in 2007?
A. $1,500,000
B. $1,510,000
C. $1,490,000
D. $10,000

_____ 4. How much inventory did the company buy from vendors in 2007?
A. $700,000
B. $5,000
C. $705,000
D. $695,000

_____ 5. How much cash was paid to vendors in 2007?
   A. $690,000
   B. $695,000
   C. $700,000
   D. $705,000

Use the following information to answer the next two questions. Both of these companies are merchandisers that began operations this year.

	X Company	Y Company
Cash from operations	$ 20,000	$ 60,000
Cash from investing activities	(200,000)	(100,000)
Cash from financing activities	230,000	90,000
Net increase in cash	$ 50,000	$ 50,000

_____ 6. Which of these two companies appears to have made the larger purchases of property, plant, and equipment during the year?
   A. X Company
   B. Y Company
   C. Both companies have made the same purchases.
   D. Neither company has made any purchases.

_____ 7. Which of these two companies is likely to pay the larger cash dividend per share of stock next month?
   A. X Company
   B. Y Company

_____ 8. Oblique, Inc., prepares its statement of cash flows using the indirect method. In calculating cash from operations, increases in current assets other than Cash should be:
   A. added to net income.
   B. subtracted from net income.
   C. ignored.

_____ 9. Oblique, Inc., prepares its statement of cash flows using the indirect method. In calculating cash from operations, increases in current liabilities should be:
   A. added to net income.
   B. subtracted from net income.
   C. ignored.

_____ 10. Cash flows from investing activities can be discovered by analyzing changes in a company's:
   A. current asset accounts.
   B. current liability accounts.
   C. long-term asset accounts.
   D. long-term liabilities and stockholders' equity accounts.

Exercises

1. Put an X in the appropriate box to identify each of these activities as operating, investing, or financing.

	Activity	Operating	Investing	Financing
a	Cash paid to purchase treasury stock			
b	Cash received for interest			
c	Cash paid to buy machinery			
d	Cash paid to employees			
e	Cash paid for stock of other companies			
f	Cash received from the sale of the company's own stock			
g	Cash paid for interest			
h	Cash paid for dividends			
i	Cash paid for taxes			
j	Cash received from customers			
k	Cash received on loans previously made to other companies			
l	Cash received from selling equipment			
m	Cash paid for rent on warehouse			
n	Cash paid to retire the principal on debt			
o	Cash collected on accounts receivable			
p	Cash received from selling investments in stock of other companies			
q	Cash paid to buy land that will be used for the company's new store			
r	Cash paid for utilities used in one of the company's stores			
s	Cash paid for inventory			
t	Cash received from borrowing			
u	Cash loaned to other companies			

2. The column below on the left lists line items from the income statement. The column on the right lists current assets and current liabilities. Match each income statement item with the related balance sheet account(s) used for preparing the statement of cash flows.

_____ 1. Sales	A. Interest payable
_____ 2. Salary expense	B. Other payables
_____ 3. Cost of goods sold	C. Inventory and Accounts payable
_____ 4. Interest expense	D. Interest receivable
_____ 5 Interest revenue	E. Salaries payable
_____ 6. Insurance expense	F. Accounts receivable
_____ 7. Operating expenses	G. Prepaid rent
_____ 8. Rent expense	H. Prepaid insurance

3. Use the information below to prepare the cash flows from investing activities and cash flows from financing activities sections of the statement of cash flows. Some of the items listed are not investing or financing activities.

a. Sold equipment for $6,000 cash that had a book value of $8,000.

b. Paid $50,000 cash to retire bonds payable.

c. Bought an $80,000 building by making an $8,000 cash down payment and signing a 20-year mortgage note for the remainder.

d. Made a $4,000 payment on an installment note. $600 of this payment was interest and the rest was principal.

e. Issued 5,000 shares of $1 par value common stock for $20 per share.

f. The company had 500 shares of treasury stock that cost $8,000. It sold these shares for $10,000.

g. Declared and paid a cash dividend of $40,000.

h. Paid $12,000 for the bonds of another company to be held as a long-term investment.

i. Received $1,000 interest from the investment in bonds of another company.

Completion Statements

1. cash from operations (or cash from operating activities)
2. cash from investing activities
3. cash from financing activities
4. direct, indirect
5. reconciliation of net income and cash from operating activities
6. interest, income taxes
7. positive
8. investing activities
9. financing activities
10. cash budget

True/False

1. True
2. False   Around 90% of companies use the indirect method.
3. False   The entry to record depreciation expense decreases the book value of the asset and decreases owners' equity. Cash is never paid for depreciation expense.
4. False   Cash from operations should be the same regardless of the method used.
5. False   There is only one acceptable way to report cash from investing activities. There are two acceptable ways to report cash from operations.
6. False   Lenders expect to see a cash budget from all borrowers.
7. True
8. False   Noncash investing and financing activities are described in footnotes to the statement of cash flows, so that the statement summarizes all important investing and financing activities.
9. False   The statement of cash flows is one of the financial statements required by GAAP.
10. True

Multiple Choice

1. A   In the long run, a business must be able to generate enough cash from normal, day-to-day activities to pay for its operations, investments in long-term assets, loans from creditors, and dividends to owners. In the short run, a company can raise cash by borrowing or by selling stock. However, if it can't generate a positive cash flow from operations to pay back the loans, eventually creditors will be unwilling to lend the company any more money. Similarly, it will become very difficult to raise additional cash by issuing more shares of stock, since investors will be unwilling to buy more shares.

2. C   A. is wrong because the income statement shows revenues earned and expenses incurred, not cash received and cash paid. B. is wrong because the balance sheet shows the cash balance at a single point in time, not the detailed activities that caused changes in cash during the accounting period. Only the statement of cash flows shows the sources and applications of cash during an accounting period.

3. C   The $10,000 increase in Accounts Receivable ($50,000 – 40,000) means that some customers who purchased merchandise on account in 2007 have not yet paid the company. Credit sales of $1,500,000 minus the $10,000 increase in Accounts Receivable equals $1,490,000. Or, $40,000 beginning A/R, plus $1,500,000 in additional A/R from sales during the year, minus $50,000 ending A/R equals $1,490,000.

4. D   The $5,000 decrease in Inventory ($75,000 – 80,000) means that some of the merchandise sold came from beginning inventory. Cost of goods sold of $700,000, minus the $5,000 decrease in inventory, equals $695,000. Or $700,000 in cost of goods sold, plus $75,000 in ending inventory,

means that the company had $775,000 of merchandise available for sale during the year. If $80,000 of this merchandise came from beginning inventory, the remaining $695,000 must have been purchased during the year. ($700,000 + 75,000 – 80,000 = $695,000)

5. A The $5,000 increase in Accounts Payable ($30,000 – 25,000) means that the company did not pay for all of the inventory it purchased in 2007. Purchases of $695,000, minus the $5,000 increase in Accounts Payable, equals $690,000. Or, beginning Accounts Payable of $25,000, plus $695,000 in additional accounts payable during the year, minus $30,000 in ending Accounts Payable, equals $690,000 paid in cash.

6. A Company X has paid more cash for investing activities. Purchases of property, plant, and equipment are investing activities.

7. B Y Company has generated more cash from operations than X Company and is in a better position for paying dividends. Also, Y Company, with less cash coming in from financing activities, probably has less debt, so it doesn't need to worry as much about cash for future interest payments. Furthermore, less cash from financing activities probably means that Y Company issued fewer shares of stock than X Company. Each share of Y Company stock can receive a larger cash dividend without requiring as much total cash as X Company would need for the same dividend per share.

8. B Increases in current assets such as inventory or prepaid rent represent purchases of goods or services that might have required a payment of cash. An increase in the current asset Accounts Receivable means that some of the current period's sales have not been collected in cash yet.

9. A Increases in current liabilities such as Accounts Payable or Salaries Payable represent purchases of goods or services that were not paid for in cash. They are associated with expenses that decreased net income, but did not decrease cash.

10. C Typical investing activities are purchases or sales of stock in another company or property, plant, and equipment. These are long-term assets. A. and B. are wrong because changes in current assets and current liabilities are used to analyze cash from operations. D. is wrong because changes in long-term liabilities and stockholders' equity accounts are indicators of financing activities.

Exercises

1.	Activity	Operating	Investing	Financing
a	Cash paid to purchase treasury stock			X
b	Cash received for interest	X		
c	Cash paid to buy machinery		X	
d	Cash paid to employees	X		
e	Cash paid for stock of other companies		X	
f	Cash received from the sale of the company's own stock			X
g	Cash paid for interest	X		
h	Cash paid for dividends			X
i	Cash paid for taxes	X		
j	Cash received from customers	X		
k	Cash received on loans previously made to other companies		X	
l	Cash received from selling equipment		X	
m	Cash paid for rent on warehouse	X		
n	Cash paid to retire the principal on debt			X
o	Cash collected on accounts receivable	X		
p	Cash received from selling investments in stock of other companies		X	
q	Cash paid to buy land that will be used for the company's new store		X	
r	Cash paid for utilities used in one of the company's stores	X		

173

s	Cash paid for inventory	X			
t	Cash received from borrowing				X
u	Cash loaned to other companies		X		

2.

F   1.   Sales/ Accounts receivable
E   2.   Salary expense/ Salaries payable
C   3.   Cost of goods sold/ Inventory and Accounts payable
A   4.   Interest expense/ Interest payable
D   5   Interest revenue/ Interest receivable
H   6.   Insurance expense/ Prepaid insurance
B   7.   Operating expenses/ Other payables
G   8.   Rent expense/ Prepaid rent

3.

Cash from investing activities

Sale of equipment	$ 6,000	
Purchase of building*	(8,000)	
Purchased bonds of another company	(12,000)	
Net cash from investing activities		$(14,000)

Cash from financing activities

Retired bonds payable	$(50,000)	
Made payment on loan	(3,400)	
Issued common stock	100,000	
Sold treasury stock	10,000	
Paid dividends	(40,000)	
Net cash from financing activities		$ 16,600

* An $80,000 building was purchased by making an $8,000 down payment and signing a 20-year mortgage note for the remainder.

CHAPTER 11
FINANCIAL STATEMENT ANALYSIS

Chapter Overview

This chapter introduces accounting for several new items that are often found on the income statement and discusses accounting for certain types of investments, too. The concept of comprehensive income is introduced. Techniques for analyzing financial statements are illustrated and discussed as well. Vertical and horizontal analysis are introduced, and ratios that were presented in previous chapters are revisited.

Chapter Highlights

1. Because the earnings a company reports are so important, the Financial Accounting Standards Board (FASB) requires that three particular items be presented separately on the income statement and not be included with income from continuing operations. They are 1) discontinued operations, 2) extraordinary items, and 3) the cumulative effect of a change in accounting principle. Each of these is shown net of tax, that is, the tax expense or tax benefit is combined with the dollar amount of the gain or loss to show the effect of the item on earnings after taxes. You can remember the order in which they are presented by the letters **C-D-E-F**: income from **C**ontinuing operations, **D**iscontinued operations, **E**xtraordinary items, and the cumulative e**F**fect of a change in accounting principle. If a company had all three of these items, its income statement would look something like this:

Revenues
- Expenses
  Income before taxes
- Income tax expense
  Income from continuing operations
  Discontinued operations:
+/- Income or loss from discontinued
    operations, net of tax
+/- Gain or loss on disposal, net of tax
    Income before extraordinary item and
    cumulative effect of a change in accounting
    principle

+/- Extraordinary item, net of tax
+/- Cumulative effect of a change in accounting
    principle, net of tax
    Net income

2. **Discontinued operations** are a part of a company's past activities that will not be continued in the future. They represent a major portion of the business, usually a segment or an entire division, that will no longer earn profits (or incur losses) for the company. The actual disposal of the segment will happen only once and will not affect future earnings either, so the impact on income must be shown separately in the financial statements. Then analysts can better predict the company's future earnings.

If a company has discontinued operations, the first part of its income statement will show revenue, expenses, and income taxes for continuing operations. Then, under a heading called "Discontinued operations," it will show the after-tax income or loss from operating the discontinued segment during the accounting period. A second line item, still under "Discontinued operations," shows the after-tax gain or loss from the actual sale or disposal of the segment.

3. **Extraordinary items** are events that are both unusual in nature and infrequent in occurrence. Accountants must use professional judgment to decide if an item should be reported as extraordinary. Natural disasters, for example, will sometimes be considered extraordinary and sometimes not, depending upon how frequently they occur in a particular area. Other possible extraordinary items are the one-time cost of complying with new laws or the loss of assets in a foreign country seized by that country's government. The FASB has decided that losses from the September 11, 2001 terrorist attack should not be reported as extraordinary because it is too difficult to separate the amount of loss directly caused by the event from losses due to the general economic downturn.

If any event qualifies as an extraordinary item, it will be shown on the income statement net of tax after income from continuing operations and any discontinued operations.

4. Sometimes a company will change from one generally-accepted accounting principle to another. For example, a company might decide to change from using straight-line depreciation to using declining-balance depreciation for its equipment. The company must go back to the original purchase of the equipment and recalculate depreciation expense as if it had been using the new method from the beginning. The difference in depreciation expense under the new method and depreciation expense under the old method is shown net of tax on the income statement as the **cumulative effect of a change in accounting principle**. This prevents a company from manipulating earnings, or "cooking the books" by changing accounting methods and hiding the effect on net income from financial statement users.

5. There are several events that have a direct effect on owners' equity that are not reported on the income statement. Two of them are owner contributions (which increase contributed capital) and dividends to corporate owners (which decrease retained earnings). However, there are two other items, known as part of **other comprehensive income**, which are not shown on the income statement because they are unrealized. The company has not yet fully completed a transaction and the resulting gain or loss has not been "locked in" through collection or payment of cash. The first item is unrealized gains and losses from foreign currency translations and the second is unrealized gains and losses on certain types of investments. Neither of these items appears on the income statement. Both of them are treated as direct additions to (if gains) or subtractions from (if losses) retained earnings. However, so that financial statement users will not overlook these items, the FASB requires that companies show **comprehensive income**, which is equal to net income (shown on the income statement) plus other comprehensive income. Comprehensive income, then, is the total of all items that affect shareholders' equity except for transactions with

stockholders (such as issuing or repurchasing the company's stock or declaring dividends.)

6. Companies will often invest surplus cash in the stocks and bonds of other companies. Management's plans to sell or hold these securities determine how they should be treated.

- **Held-to-maturity securities** are debt securities that the company plans to keep until they mature. Equity securities (stocks) cannot be held-to-maturity securities because they do not have maturity dates. These debt securities are recorded at cost and shown as assets on the balance sheet at historical cost, (plus any unamortized premium or minus any unamortized discount). Changes in market value do not affect the recorded value of held-to-maturity securities.

- **Trading securities** are either debt or equity securities that the company has purchased in hope of making a short-term profit. These securities are first recorded at cost. However, before the company issues financial statements, it must revalue these securities and show them as current assets on the balance sheet at their market values, known as marking-to-market. If the market value is higher than cost, the company has an **unrealized gain**, (holding gain) and if the market value is lower than cost, the company has an **unrealized loss** (holding loss). Unrealized gains and losses on trading securities appear on the company's income statement.

- **Available-for-sale securities** are either debt or equity securities that the company does not plan to sell in the short-run, but does not intend to hold to maturity, either. These securities are initially recorded at cost and revalued to market value at the balance sheet date. Any unrealized gain or loss does not appear on the income statement, however. Instead it is shown after retained earnings in the owners' equity section of the balance sheet. Unrealized gains and losses on available-for-sale securities are part of other comprehensive income.

7. **Horizontal analysis** is a technique used to evaluate individual financial statement line items over a period of time. A specific past year is chosen as a base year. The increase or decrease in the same line item for other years is then expressed as a percentage of the base year. For example:

Property, plant and equipment		
2005	2004	2003
$130,000	$120,000	$100,000
30%	20%	100%

In this example, 2003 is the base year. In 2004, property, plant and equipment has increased $120,000 minus $100,000, or $20,000. This $20,000 increase divided by the $100,000 base year equals 20%. During 2004, property, plant and equipment increased 20%.

8. **Vertical analysis** expresses each item on a particular year's financial statement as a percentage of a single item on that financial statement. The most common vertical analysis is performed on the income statement, where each line item on the statement is expressed as a percentage of sales for the period. This technique is more useful if two or more periods are available for comparison.

9. Ratio analysis uses information on the financial statements to calculate specific values, which can then be used to determine a company's financial condition. Ratios for a particular accounting period are more useful when compared with ratios from other periods or with industry averages or other companies in the same industry. Chapter 11 summarizes the ratios discussed in previous chapters and introduces a few new ratios as well. Some analysts will use variations of the formulas presented in this book.

10. **Liquidity ratios** measure a firm's ability to meet its short-term debt obligations when they fall due.

- The **current ratio** measures a company's ability to cover its current liabilities (due within the next year) with its current assets, which are cash and items that will be converted to cash or used in the business during the next year. The current ratio is calculated as:

$$\frac{\text{Total Current Assets}}{\text{Total Current Liabilities}}$$

A current ratio of 2.0 or more is considered good. It means that current assets are at least twice the amount of current liabilities and the company should have no trouble paying its short-term debts.

- The **acid-test ratio** (also called the **quick ratio**) is similar to the current ratio, but it is a more stringent test of a company's short-term debt-paying ability. The numerator uses only the most liquid current assets: cash, short-term investments, and net accounts receivable. Since inventory must first be sold, and the related account receivable must then be collected, it is two steps away from cash and it is not used in the acid-test ratio. The formula is:

$$\frac{\text{Cash} + \text{Short-term Investments} + \text{Net Current Receivables}}{\text{Total Current Liabilities}}$$

An acid-test ratio of 1.0 or more is considered good.

- **Working capital**, current assets minus current liabilities, is not actually a ratio, but it too is an indication of a company's ability to pay its short-term debts. It should be a positive number. If it is negative, a company's current liabilities are larger than its current assets and it will probably have trouble paying its short-term debts.

- The **inventory turnover ratio** measures how quickly a company turns over (or sells) its inventory. It is calculated as:

$$\frac{\text{Cost of Goods Sold}}{\text{Average Inventory}}$$

- The **accounts receivable turnover ratio** measures how quickly a company turns over (or collects) its accounts receivable. It is calculated as:

$$\frac{\text{Net Sales}}{\text{Average Net Accounts Receivable}}$$

11. **Solvency ratios** are a measure of a company's ability to pay its long-term obligations and survive over time.

- The **debt to equity ratio** shows how much of a company's financing is provided by creditors and how much is provided by owners. The formula is:

$$\frac{\text{Total Liabilities}}{\text{Total Equity}}$$

- **Times interest earned** shows how easily a company can handle the debt it already has. It compares a company's earnings with its interest:

$$\frac{\text{Net Income} + \text{Interest Expense}}{\text{Interest Expense}}$$

12. **Profitability ratios** evaluate a company's earnings for a period of time.

- **Return on assets** compares a company's earnings with the assets invested to generate those earnings:

$$\frac{\text{Net Income} + \text{Interest}}{\text{Average Total Assets}}$$

- **Return on equity** compares a company's earnings with the investment made by the common stockholders:

$$\frac{\text{Net Income} - \text{Preferred Dividends}}{\text{Average Common Stockholders' Equity}}$$

- **Gross margin on sales** measures the percentage of each dollar of sales that is left over after covering the cost of the merchandise:

$$\frac{\text{Gross Margin}}{\text{Sales}}$$

A small decrease in the gross margin percentage can make a big difference in a company's profitability.

- **Earnings per share** expresses the company's income on a per-share basis:

$$\frac{\text{Net Income} - \text{Preferred Dividends}}{\text{Number of Shares of Common Stock Outstanding}}$$

Market indicators are of interest to stockholders because they look at the current market price of the stock, the amount a new investor would pay for a share.

- The **price-earnings ratio** compares the market price of a share of stock with the earnings that share generates:

$$\frac{\text{Market Price per Common Share}}{\text{Earnings per Share}}$$

A high price-earnings ratio shows that investors believe the company has potential for future growth. A price-earnings ratio above 50, however, is considered to be an indicator of an over-valued stock.

- **Dividend yield** compares the dividend paid on a single share of stock with the market price of that share:

$$\frac{\text{Dividends per Share}}{\text{Market Price per Share}}$$

Dividend yields may be quite low, since many investors expect to profit from increases in the market price of the stock rather than dividends. However, some investors are dependent on dividend income and prefer stocks with a high dividend yield.

Featured Exercise

Virtual Company
Consolidated Balance Sheet
At December 31,

millions, except share data	2005	2004	2003
Current assets			
Cash and cash equivalents	$ 5.6	$ 16.2	$ 14.9
Accounts receivable, less allowances	18.9	17.5	20.4
Inventories	32.4	39.4	38.6
Other current assets	3.8	1.2	2.3
Total current assets	60.7	74.3	76.2
Property, plant & equipment, net	145.7	135.8	122.4
Other assets	1.4	2.1	1.1
Total assets	207.8	212.2	199.7
Current liabilities			
Accounts payable	2.5	13.4	15.2
Current portion of long-term debt	24.3	22.9	21.5
Other current liabilities	1.9	2.1	0.7
Total current liabilities	28.7	38.4	37.4
Long-term debt	126.0	118.6	115.8
Other liabilities	1.6	1.4	1.2
Shareholders' equity			
Common stock, $0.10 par, 20,000,000 shares authorized.			
Issued 14,000,000 shares in 2005, 13,700,000 in 2004			
and 13,650,000 in 2003	1.4	1.4	1.4
Capital in excess of par value	36.3	35.2	34.7
Retained earnings	25.9	22.1	18.7
Treasury stock at cost	(9.7)	(8.2)	(7.8)
Currency translation adjustment	(1.5)	1.9	(1.3)
Unrealized gain (loss) on available-for-sale securities	(0.9)	1.4	(0.4)
Total shareholders' equity	51.5	53.8	45.3
Total liabilities and shareholders' equity	$ 207.8	$ 212.2	$ 199.7

Virtual Company
Consolidated Statement of Earnings
For the Year Ended December 31,

millions, except share data	2005	2004	2003
Net sales	$ 120.8	$ 140.4	$ 109.5
Cost of goods sold	65.7	82.5	58.3
Selling and administrative expense	39.7	37.3	32.8
Operating profit	15.4	20.6	18.4
Interest expense	1.1	0.7	1.0
Earnings before income taxes	14.3	19.9	17.4
Income taxes	5.0	7.0	6.1
Net earnings	$ 9.3	$ 12.9	$ 11.3

Part A: Use the financial statements for Virtual Company to complete the following chart:

		2005	2004	2003
1	Net income			
2	Other comprehensive income			
3	Comprehensive income			

Part B: Use the financial statements for Virtual Company to complete the ratios in the chart below. If you cannot calculate a ratio, explain why. The following additional information may be helpful:

	2005	2004	2003
Market price per share	$9.00	$13.00	$12.80
Dividend per common share	$0.60	$0.60	$0.58
Weighted average number of common shares outstanding during the year	13,800,000	13,680,000	13,600,000

		2005	2004	2003
1	Current ratio			
2	Acid-test ratio (quick ratio)			
3	Working capital			
4	Inventory turnover ratio			
5	Accounts receivable turnover ratio			
6	Debt to equity			
7	Times interest earned			
8	Return on assets			

9	Return on equity			
10	Gross margin on sales			
11	Earnings per share			
12	Price-earnings ratio			
13	Dividend yield			

Part C: Prepare a vertical analysis of Virtual Company's income statements for all three years.

	2005		**2004**		**2003**	
Net sales	$ 120.8		$ 140.4		$ 109.5	
Cost of goods sold	65.7		82.5		58.3	
Selling and administrative expense	39.7		37.3		32.8	
Operating profit	15.4		20.6		18.4	
Interest expense	1.1		0.7		1.0	
Earnings before income taxes	14.3		19.9		17.4	
Income taxes	5.0		7.0		6.1	
Net earnings	$ 9.3		$ 12.9		$ 11.3	

Part D: Prepare a horizontal analysis of the following selected items for Virtual Company. Use 2003 as the base year.

1		**2005**	**2004**	**2003**
	Accounts receivable	$18.9	$17.5	$20.4

2		**2005**	**2004**	**2003**
	Property, plant & equipment, net	$145.7	$135.8	$122.4

3		**2005**	**2004**	**2003**
	Net sales	$120.8	$140.4	$109.5

4		**2005**	**2004**	**2003**
	Net earnings	$9.3	$12.9	$11.3

Solution

	Part A	**2005**	**2004**	**2003**
1	Net income *Net income is the same as net earnings.*	$9.3	$12.9	$11.3
2	Other comprehensive income *unrealized gains & losses from foreign currency translation + unrealized gains & losses from available-for-sale securities*	$ (1.5) loss + (0.9) loss $ (2.4) loss	$ 1.9 gain + 1.4 gain $ 3.3 gain	$ (1.3) loss + (0.4) loss $ (1.7) loss
3	Comprehensive income *net income + other comprehensive income*	$9.3 – 2.4 = $6.9	$12.9 + 3.3 = $16.2	$11.3 – 1.7 = $9.6

	Part B	**2005**	**2004**	**2003**
1	Current ratio	$\frac{\$60.7}{\$28.7} = 2.12$	$\frac{\$74.3}{\$38.4} = 1.93$	$\frac{\$76.2}{\$37.4} = 2.04$
2	Acid-test ratio (quick ratio)	$\frac{\$5.6 + 18.9}{\$28.7} = .85$	$\frac{\$16.2 + 17.5}{\$38.4} = .88$	$\frac{\$14.9 + 20.4}{\$37.4} = .94$
3	Working capital	$60.7 – 28.7 = $32.0	$74.3 – 38.4 = $35.9	$76.2 – 37.4 = $38.8
4	Inventory turnover ratio	$\frac{\$65.7}{(\$32.4+39.4)/2} = 1.83$	$\frac{\$82.5}{(\$39.4+38.6)/2} = 2.1$	*Can't calculate average inventory for 2003*
5	Accounts receivable turnover ratio	$\frac{\$120.8}{(\$18.9+17.5)/2} = 6.6$	$\frac{\$140.4}{(\$17.5+20.4)/2} = 7.4$	*Can't calculate average A/R for 2003*
6	Debt to equity	$\frac{\$28.7+126.0+1.6}{\$51.5} = 3.0$	$\frac{\$38.4+118.6+1.4}{\$53.8} = 2.9$	$\frac{\$37.4+115.8+1.2}{\$45.3} = 3.4$
7	Times interest earned	$\frac{\$9.3 + 1.1}{\$1.1} = 9.5$	$\frac{\$12.9 + 0.7}{\$0.7} = 19.4$	$\frac{\$11.3 + 1.0}{\$1.0} = 12.3$
8	Return on assets	$\frac{\$9.3+1.1}{(\$207.8 + 212.2)/2} =$ $0.0495 = 5\%$	$\frac{\$12.9 + 0.7}{(\$212.2 + 199.7)/2} =$ $.066 = 6.6\%$	*Can't calculate average assets for 2003*

9	Return on equity	$\dfrac{\$9.3-0}{(\$51.5+53.8)/2} =$ $0.177 = 17.7\%$	$\dfrac{\$12.9-0}{(\$53.8+45.3)/2} =$ $0.260 = 26.0\%$	*Can't calculate average shareholders' equity for 2003*
10	Gross margin on sales	$\dfrac{\$120.8\text{-}65.7}{\$120.8} = 45.6\%$	$\dfrac{\$140.4-82.5}{\$140.4} = 41.2\%$	$\dfrac{\$109.5-58.3}{\$109.5} = 46.8\%$
11	Earnings per share	$\dfrac{\$\,9,300,000}{13,800,000} = \$0.67$	$\dfrac{\$12,900,000}{13,680,000} = \$0.94$	$\dfrac{\$11,300,000}{13,600,000} = \$0.83$
12	Price-earnings ratio	$\dfrac{\$9.00}{\$0.67} = 13.4$	$\dfrac{\$13.00}{\$0.94} = 13.8$	$\dfrac{\$12.80}{\$0.83} = 15.4$
13	Dividend yield	$\dfrac{\$0.60}{\$9.00} = .067 = 6.7\%$	$\dfrac{\$\,0.60}{\$13.00} = .046 = 4.6\%$	$\dfrac{\$\,0.58}{\$12.80} = .045 = 4.5\%$

	2005		2004		2003	
Net sales	$ 120.8	100.0%	$ 140.4	100.0%	$ 109.5	100.0%
Cost of goods sold	65.7	54.4%	82.5	58.8%	58.3	53.2%
Selling and administrative expense	39.7	32.9%	37.3	26.6%	32.8	30.0%
Operating profit	15.4	12.7%	20.6	14.7%	18.4	16.8%
Interest expense	1.1	0.9%	0.7	0.5%	1.0	0.9%
Earnings before income taxes	14.3	11.8%	19.9	14.2%	17.4	15.9%
Income taxes	5.0	4.1%	7.0	5.0%	6.1	5.6%
Net earnings	$ 9.3	7.7%	$ 12.9	9.2%	$ 11.3	10.3%

		2005	2004	2003
a	Accounts receivable	$18.9	$17.5	$20.4
		$\dfrac{\$18.9-20.4}{\$20.4} = (7.4)\%$	$\dfrac{\$17.5-20.4}{\$20.4} = (14.2)\%$	100%

		2005	2004	2003
b	Property, plant & equipment, net	$145.7	$135.8	$122.4
		$\dfrac{\$145.7-122.4}{\$122.4} = 19.0\%$	$\dfrac{\$135.8-122.4}{\$122.4} = 11.0\%$	100%

		2005	2004	2003
c	Net sales	$120.8	$140.4	$109.5
		$\dfrac{\$120.8-109.5}{\$109.5} = 10.3\%$	$\dfrac{\$140.4-109.5}{\$109.5} = 28.2\%$	100%

		2005	2004	2003
d	Net earnings	$9.3	$12.9	$11.3
		$\dfrac{\$9.3\text{-}11.3}{\$11.3} = -17.7\%$	$\dfrac{\$12.9\text{-}11.3}{\$11.3} = 14.2\%$	100%

Review Questions and Exercises

Completion Statements

Fill in the blank(s) to complete each statement.

1. _____ are events that are both unusual in nature and infrequent in occurrence.

2. _____ measures the percentage of each dollar of sales that is left over after covering the cost of the merchandise.

3. The _____ ratio shows how much of a company's financing is provided by creditors and how much is provided by owner.

4. _____ are a part of a company's past activities that will not be continued in the future.

5. _____ expresses each item on a particular year's financial statement as a percentage of a single item on that financial statement.

6. _____ is a technique used to evaluate individual financial statement line items over a period of time. A specific past year is chosen as a base year.

7. _____ are debt securities that the company plans to keep until they mature.

8. _____ are either debt or equity securities that the company has purchased in hope of making a short-term profit.

9. _____ are either debt or equity securities that the company does not plan to sell in the short-run, but does not intend to hold to maturity, either.

10. _____ is the total of all items that affect shareholders' equity except for transactions with stockholders.

True/False

Indicate whether each statement is true (T) or false (F).

_____ 1. The current ratio will always be greater than 1.0.

_____ 2. Comprehensive income will always be greater than net income.

_____ 3. Trading securities are shown on the balance sheet at historical cost.

_____ 4. Held-to-maturity securities are shown on the balance sheet at historical cost, plus any unamortized premium minus any unamortized discount.

_____ 5. Available-for-sale securities are shown on the balance sheet at historical cost.

_____ 6. Ratios are more meaningful when they are compared with other companies in the same industry or with industry averages.

_____ 7. Investors should buy stocks with the highest possible price-earnings ratio.

_____ 8. Stock with a high dividend yield is a good investment.

_____ 9. To be classified as an extraordinary item, an event must be both unusual in nature and infrequent in occurrence.

_____ 10. Gains and losses from discontinued operations are shown separately on a company's income statement.

Multiple Choice

Select the best answer for each question.

_____ 1. Beta Business has total current assets of $1,000,000 and total current liabilities of $400,000. Its current ratio is:
A. 2.00.
B. 2.25.
C. 2.50.
D. 0.40.

_____ 2. Beta Business has total current assets of $1,000,000 and total current liabilities of $400,000. If the company collects $100,000 of its accounts receivable, its current ratio will:
A. increase.
B. decrease.
C. stay the same.
D. The answer cannot be determined from the information given.

_____ 3. Beta Business has total current assets of $1,000,000 and total current liabilities of $400,000. If the company purchases $100,000 of inventory for cash, its acid-test ratio will:
A. increase.
B. decrease.
C. stay the same.
D. The answer cannot be determined from the information given.

_____ 4. Beta Business has total current assets of $1,000,000 and total current liabilities of $400,000. If the company purchases $100,000 of inventory and promises to pay for it in the next two weeks, its current ratio will:
A. increase.
B. decrease.
C. stay the same.
D. The answer cannot be determined from the information given.

5. Last year Iota, Inc., had earnings per share of $1.95. In December this year, Iota repurchased some of its own common stock. Assume that net income this year is exactly the same as it was last year. This purchase of treasury stock will _____ the number of shares of common stock outstanding and _____ earnings per share.
   A. increase   increase
   B. increase   decrease
   C. decrease   decrease
   D. decrease   increase

6. Last year Madd Hatter, Inc., bought baseball caps for $3 each and sold them for $9. This year the company's supplier is charging $4 for each cap, but Madd Hatter can not raise its prices because competition is too tough. If Madd Hatter continues to sell caps for $9, its gross margin will _____ and its gross margin percentage will _____.
   A. increase   increase
   B. increase   decrease
   C. decrease   decrease
   D. decrease   increase

7. Nu News, Inc., has total current assets of $1,000,000 and total current liabilities of $500,000. If the company pays $100,000 of accounts payable, its current ratio will:
   A. increase.
   B. decrease.
   C. stay the same.
   D. The answer cannot be determined from the information given.

8. If a company increases its collection effort, it hopes to see its accounts receivable turnover ratio _____, because the average amount of accounts receivable will _____.
   A. increase   increase
   B. increase   decrease
   C. decrease   decrease
   D. decrease   increase

9. One of Caribbean Cruises' ships hit an iceberg just off Miami and sank. Icebergs in the Caribbean are both unusual and infrequent, so the company plans to treat the $10,000,000 uninsured loss as an extraordinary item. The company's tax rate is 35%. What effect will this event have on net income for the year?
   A. Net income will decrease $3,500,000.
   B. Net income will decrease $6,500,000.
   C. No effect. Extraordinary items appear on the balance sheet as a direct increase or decrease to retained earnings.
   D. No effect. Companies are not required to report extraordinary items because they will have no effect on future earnings.

10. Which of the following ratios would most interest a banker who is thinking about making a long-term loan to a company?
    A. Return on equity
    B. Return on assets
    C. Dividend yield
    D. Debt to equity

Exercises

1. Classify each of the ratios listed in the table below by putting an X in the appropriate box.

		Liquidity	Solvency	Profitability	Market indicators
a	Return on assets				
b	Times interest earned				
c	Current ratio				
d	Return on equity				
e	Debt to equity				
f	Working capital				
g	Gross margin on sales				
h	Accounts receivable turnover ratio				
i	Dividend yield				
j	Inventory turnover ratio				
k	Acid-test ratio				
l	Earnings per share				
m	Price-earnings ratio				

2. 2005 was a very complicated year for Buck's Better Bacon.
*   In December, 2005 Buck's decided to change the depreciation method it uses for its delivery equipment. The company owns one truck, purchased in January of 2002 for $24,000 with an estimated useful life of eight years and no salvage value. So far, Buck's has recorded three years of straight-line depreciation on the truck. However, the company has decided to switch to double declining-balance depreciation.
*   Buck's decided to discontinue its manure processing division, which wasn't very profitable even in good years. On October 31, Buck's sold the division for a small gain of $10,000. Up to the date of sale, the division earned revenues of $50,000 and had expenses of $45,000.
*   In August, Buck's Iowa research farm was leveled by an earthquake. Uninsured damages amounted to $300,000. Buck's will treat this disaster as an extraordinary loss, since earthquakes in Iowa are both unusual and infrequent.
*   Normal continuing operations earned revenues of $900,000. Expenses were $600,000, including double-declining balance on the delivery truck for 2005. Buck's has a 30% tax rate that applies to all income.

Complete the chart that shows depreciation expense for the delivery truck under both the straight-line and double declining-balance methods. Then prepare an income statement for the year ended December 31, 2005, in good form.

Year	Straight-line depreciation expense	Double declining-balance depreciation expense
2002		
2003		
2004		
Total		

Buck's Better Bacon, Inc.
Income Statement
For the Year Ended December 31, 2005

Completion Statements

1. Extraordinary items
2. Gross margin on sales
3. debt to equity
4. Discontinued operations
5. Vertical analysis
6. Horizontal analysis
7. Held-to-maturity securities
8. Trading securities
9. Available-for-sale securities
10. Comprehensive income

True/False

1. False A company's current ratio will be greater than 1.0 only when its current assets are greater than its current liabilities.
2. False Comprehensive income is net income plus other comprehensive income. The elements of other comprehensive income include losses as well as gains, so it's possible that comprehensive income will be smaller than net income.
3. False Trading securities are shown at their market value as of the balance sheet date.
4. True
5. False Available-for-sale securities are shown at their market value as of the balance sheet date.
6. True
7. False Although a high price-earnings ratio may indicate that investors expect future growth, an extremely high price-earnings ratio may be the sign of an over-valued stock.
8. False Some investors are dependent on dividend income and prefer stocks with a high dividend yield. However, many investors expect to profit from increases in the market price of the stock rather than dividends. For them, a low dividend yield is fine.
9. True
10. True

Multiple Choice

1. C $1,000,000/$400,000 = 2.5
2. C If Beta collects $100,000 of accounts receivable, its cash will increase $100,000 while its accounts receivable decrease $100,000. Total current assets will still be $1,000,000.
3. B The acid-test ratio includes only cash, short-term investments, and accounts receivable in the numerator. Beta is decreasing cash with this purchase of inventory, so its acid-test ratio will decrease, even though its total current assets remain the same.
4. B Both current assets and current liabilities increase by $100,000. $1,100,000/$500,000 = 2.2
5. D Treasury stock is subtracted from stockholders' equity and reduces the number of shares held by those outside the company. With fewer shares outstanding, the denominator of the EPS calculation will be smaller, and earnings for each outstanding common share will be larger.
6. C Last year the company's gross margin was $6, which is 67% of sales. This year, gross margin will be only $5, or 56%.
7. A Right now the company's current ratio is $1,000,000/$500,000, or 2.0. If it pays $100,000 of accounts payable, both current assets and current liabilities will decrease by $100,000. $900,000/$400,000 = 2.25
8. B If a company collects its receivables more quickly, fewer dollars will remain uncollected in accounts receivable at any given point in time. The denominator of the accounts receivable turnover ratio will decrease, which increases the ratio itself.
9. B. Extraordinary items appear on the income statement after discontinued operations and before the cumulative effect of a change in accounting principle. They are shown net of tax. The $10,000,000 loss will result in a tax savings of 35% times $10,000,000, or $3,500,000. The overall impact of the extraordinary loss is to reduce income by $10,000,000 − 3,500,000 = $6,500,000.
10. D The debt to equity ratio compares the amount of debt financing the company already has to the amount of financing provided by its shareholders. A banker would look at this ratio to determine if a company could take on additional debt. The other ratios listed in this question are of more interest to shareholders than creditors.

Exercises

1.		Liquidity	Solvency	Profitability	Market indicators
a	Return on assets			X	
b	Times interest earned		X		
c	Current ratio	X			
d	Return on equity			X	
e	Debt to equity		X		
f	Working capital	X			
g	Gross margin on sales			X	
h	Accounts receivable turnover ratio	X			
i	Dividend yield				X
j	Inventory turnover ratio	X			
k	Acid-test ratio	X			
l	Earnings per share			X	
m	Price-earnings ratio				X

2.	Straight-line depreciation expense $24,000/8 years = $3,000 per year	Double declining-balance depreciation expense
2002	$3,000	$24,000 x 2/8 years = $ 6,000
2003	$3,000	($24,000 – 6,000) x 2/8 years = $ 4,500
2004	$3,000	($24,000 – 6,000 – 4,500) x 2/8 years = $ 3,375
Total	$9,000	$13,875

Buck's Better Bacon, Inc.
Income Statement
For the Year Ended December 31, 2005

Revenues		$900,000
Expenses		600,000
Income before taxes		300,000
Income tax expense		90,000
Income from continuing operations		210,000
Discontinued operations		
Income from discontinued operations, net of $1,500 tax	$3,500 [1]	
Gain or loss on disposal, net of $3,000 tax	7,000 [2]	10,500
Income before extraordinary item and cumulative effect of a change in accounting principle		220,500
Extraordinary loss from earthquake, net of $90,000 tax savings [3]		(210,000)
Cumulative effect of a change in accounting principle, net of $1,463 tax savings [4]		(3,412)
Net income		$ 7,088

---

[1]

Revenue	$50,000
Expenses	45,000
Income before tax	5,000
Taxes (30%)	1,500
Net income	$ 3,500

[2] $10,000 gain x 30% = $3,000 tax

[3] The loss is tax deductible, so Buck's will save 30% times $300,000, or $90,000 in taxes. The $300,000 loss decreases income, but the $90,000 saved in taxes increases income, so the overall effect on profits is a decrease of $210,000.

[4] Buck's has previously reported $9,000 in straight-line depreciation expense on the truck. If Buck's had used double declining-balance method instead, depreciation expense would have been $13,875, or $4,875 more. However, the extra $4,875 in depreciation expense is partially offset by $1,463 less tax expense. 30% x $4,875 = $1,463, rounded

FINANCIAL
ACCOUNTING
A Business Process Approach

Chapter 1

Business: What's it all About?

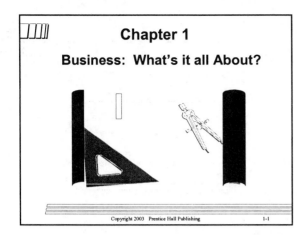

1-1

_____

_____

_____

_____

_____

_____

_____

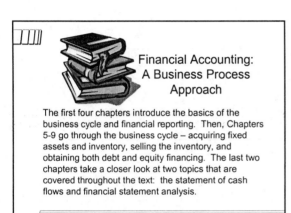

Financial Accounting: A Business Process Approach

The first four chapters introduce the basics of the business cycle and financial reporting. Then, Chapters 5-9 go through the business cycle – acquiring fixed assets and inventory, selling the inventory, and obtaining both debt and equity financing. The last two chapters take a closer look at two topics that are covered throughout the text: the statement of cash flows and financial statement analysis.

1-2

_____

_____

_____

_____

_____

_____

Purpose of a Business

Add Value → Make a Profit

1-3

_____

_____

_____

_____

_____

_____

_____

Simple Model of a Business

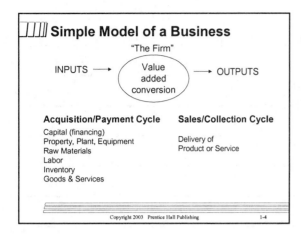

"The Firm"

INPUTS → Value added conversion → OUTPUTS

Acquisition/Payment Cycle

Capital (financing)
Property, Plant, Equipment
Raw Materials
Labor
Inventory
Goods & Services

Sales/Collection Cycle

Delivery of
Product or Service

What are Business Processes?

- **Series of activities that a company performs to achieve its goals.**
  - » **ACQUISITION / PAYMENT: acquire, maintain, and pay for the resources needed by the organization.**
  - » **CONVERSION: convert the resources acquired into goods and/or services.**
  - » **SALES / COLLECTIONS: sell and deliver goods and/or services to customers and to collect payment.**

Types of Businesses

- ❖ **Service company**
  - ▪ provides a service for customers
- ❖ **Sales company**
  - » **Special case: financial services**
  - ▪ **Merchandising--**buys goods and resells them to other businesses (wholesale) or to final customers (retail)
  - ▪ **Manufacturing--**makes a product and sells it to other businesses (wholesale) or to final consumers (retail)

Examples:

- Service
  - accountants, attorneys, physicians
- Financial Service
  - Citicorp, Merrill Lynch, American Express
- Merchandising
  - Wal-Mart, Safeway, The Gap
- Manufacturing
  - General Motors, 3M, Reynolds Metals

[Obviously, some businesses provide more than one of the functions listed above]

1-7

Ownership Structure of Businesses

Sole Proprietorship--a single owner business

Partnership--a multiple-owner business

Corporation--a business whose ownership is divided into "shares" and may be owned by a large number of people

1-8

Corporations

- A corporation is a popular form of business because . . .
  - It is simple for individuals to **purchase** small amounts of stock.
  - It allows for an easy **transfer of ownership** through established markets, like the New York Stock Exchange.
  - It provides stockholders with **limited liability**.

1-9

Corporations

- Because a corporation is a separate legal entity, it can . . .
  - Own assets.
  - Incur liabilities.
  - Sue and be sued.
  - Enter into contracts independent of the stockholder owners.
- Many Americans own stock through a mutual fund or pension program.

Characteristics of Different Forms of Business Organization

Issues in deciding between sole proprietorship, partnership, or corporation

- Personal liability
- Taxation
- Transfer of ownership
- Ability to raise capital
- Government regulation

Ownership of a Corporation

- Owners of common stock generally receive the following rights:
  - Voting (in person or by **proxy**).
  - Distributions of profits.
  - Distributions of assets in a liquidation.
  - Offers to purchase shares of a new stock issue (**pro rata basis**).

Creating a Corporation

- State laws govern the creation of corporations.
- An application for a charter (or articles of incorporation) must include the corporation's name and purpose, kinds and amounts of capital stock authorized, and other detailed information.

1-13

Creating a Corporation

Once the state issues a charter, the stockholders elect a board of directors.

1-14

What Do All Business have in Common?

- No matter what the ownership structure of a business, they all have at least two main business processes:

☐ Acquisition/Payment
☐ Sales/Collection

1-15

Acquisition/payment process

Activity	Possible Document(s)
Identify need for good/services	→ Purchase Requisition
Identify vendor	
Order goods/services	→ Purchase Order
Receive and Inspect Goods	→ Receiving Report
Pay for Goods and/or Services	→ Check Requisition / Check

Sales/collection process

- Customer places an order *(Customer order)*
- Customer's credit is approved
- Warehouse selects goods for shipment *(Picking slip)*
- Goods are shipped *(Packing slip and Shipping notice)*
- Customer is billed for goods *(Invoice)*
- Payment for goods is received *(Check)*

Business Transactions

- Business transactions are exchanges.
- The two transactions that make up an "exchange" are the GIVE part and the GET part.
- The exchange occurs between the business entity and a person or business external to the entity.
- The business gives something and then gets something in return.

Resources, Events, and Agents

- We can model an exchange with these three components:
  - the **resources** are the things being exchanged (goods or services for money)
  - the **event** describes the business action (e.g. cash disbursement, sale, etc.)
  - the **agents** are the people involved in the exchange (e.g., the customer)

Acquisition and Payment for T-shirts

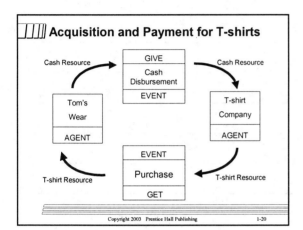

Acquisition and Payment for a Service

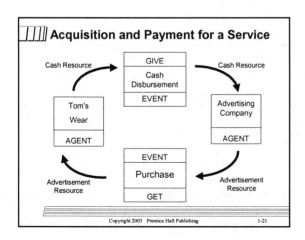

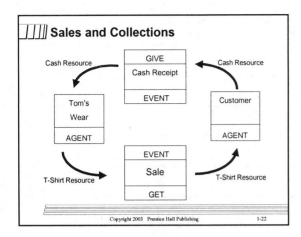

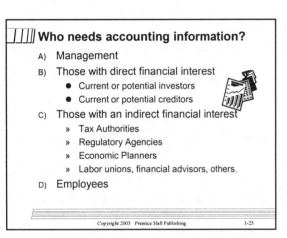

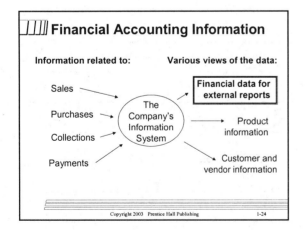

The Accounting Equation

> Assets = Claims
> Assets = Liabilities + Equity

- Asset: something of value
- Liability: something owed (creditors' share of the assets)
- Equity: what remains (owner's share of the assets)

Equity: The Owner's Share

- There are two sources of equity
  - equity "contributed" by owners
  - equity "earned" by operations

- Expanded accounting equation:

$$ASSETS = LIABILITIES + \underset{\text{CAPITAL}}{\text{CONTRIBUTED}} + \underset{\text{EARNINGS}}{\text{RETAINED}}$$

Equity: The Owner's Share

Expanded accounting equation:

$$ASSETS = LIABILITIES + \boxed{\underset{\text{CAPITAL}}{\text{CONTRIBUTED}} + \underset{\text{EARNINGS}}{\text{RETAINED}}}$$

Together, these are called Shareholders' Equity, Stockholders' Equity, or Owners' Equity. They are all names for the same thing--the owners' claims to the firm's assets.

Four Basic Financial Statements

- **Balance Sheet**
  Assets = Liabilities + Equity
- **Income Statement**
  Revenues - Expenses = Net income
- **Statement of Changes in Owner's Equity**
  Beginning equity + Contributions + Net income - Distributions = Ending equity
- **Statement of Cash Flows**
  Cash inflow - Cash outflow = Net cash flow

Dates of Financial Statements are Important!

- **Balance sheet** is "AS OF…" or "AT" a particular date, sometimes called a "snapshot" in time.
- **Income statement**
- **Statement of changes in owner's equity**
- **Statement of cash flows**
  - These last three cover a period of time, and thus are "FOR THE PERIOD ENDING"

1-29

Acquiring Financing for a Business

Date	Transactions
Jan. 1	• Tom contributes $5,000 of his own money to the business.

Assets = Liabilities + <u>Owner's Equity</u>

Contributed Capital + Retained Earnings

+5,000 cash	+5,000 common stock

1-30

Acquiring Financing for a Business

Date	Transactions
Jan. 1	• Tom's Wear borrows $500 from Tom's mom.

Assets	=	Liabilities	+	CC	+	Retained Earnings
+500 cash		+ 500 N/P				

Acquiring Financing for a Business

Date	Transactions
Jan. 1	• Tom contributes $5,000 of his own money to start the business. • Tom's Wear borrows $500 from Tom's mom.

Assets	=	Liabilities	+	CC	+	Retained Earnings
+5,000 cash				+5,000 common stock		
+500 cash		+ 500 N/P				

Acquiring Inventory

Date	Transactions
Jan. 5	• Tom's Wear buys 100 T-shirts for $400 cash.

Acquiring Inventory

Date	Transactions
Jan. 5	• Tom's Wear buys 100 T-shirts for $400 cash.

Assets = Liabilities + CC + RE

(400) cash

+400 inventory

Acquiring a Service

Date	Transactions
Jan. 10	• Tom's Wear pays $50 for advertising.

Assets = Liabilities + CC + RE

(50) cash   (50) expenses

Sales and Collection

Date	Transactions
Jan. 20	• Tom's Wear sells 90 of the T-shirts to friends for cash, $10 each.

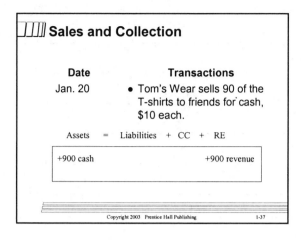

Sales and Collection

Date	Transactions
Jan. 20	• Tom's Wear sells 90 of the T-shirts to friends for cash, $10 each.

Assets = Liabilities + CC + RE

+900 cash	+900 revenue

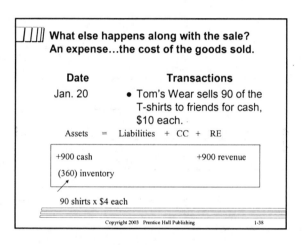

**What else happens along with the sale?
An expense...the cost of the goods sold.**

Date	Transactions
Jan. 20	• Tom's Wear sells 90 of the T-shirts to friends for cash, $10 each.

Assets = Liabilities + CC + RE

+900 cash	+900 revenue
(360) inventory	

90 shirts x $4 each

**What else happens along with the sale?
An expense...the cost of the goods sold.**

Date	Transactions
Jan. 20	• Tom's Wear sells 90 of the T-shirts to friends for cash, $10 each.

Assets = Liabilities + CC + RE

+900 cash	+900 revenue
(360) inventory	(360) expense

90 shirts x $4 each   Special expense called **cost of goods sold**

Payment for the acquired financing

Date	Transactions
Jan. 30	• Tom's Wear repays the debt of $500 plus $5 interest.

1-40

Payment for the acquired financing

Date	Transactions
Jan. 30	• Tom's Wear repays the debt of $500 plus $5 interest.

Assets   =   Liabilities   +   CC   +   RE

(505) cash

1-41

Payment for the acquired financing

Date	Transactions
Jan. 30	• Tom's Wear repays the debt of $500 plus $5 interest.

Assets   =   Liabilities   +   CC   +   RE

(505) cash   (500) N/P

1-42

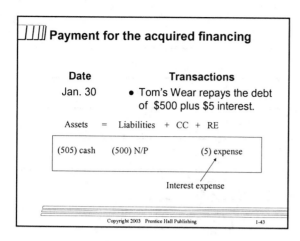

Payment for the acquired financing

Date	Transactions
Jan. 30	• Tom's Wear repays the debt of $500 plus $5 interest.

Assets = Liabilities + CC + RE

(505) cash	(500) N/P	(5) expense

Interest expense

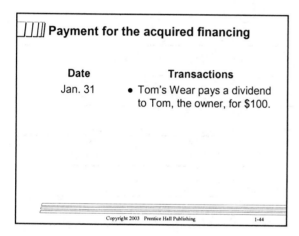

Payment for the acquired financing

Date	Transactions
Jan. 31	• Tom's Wear pays a dividend to Tom, the owner, for $100.

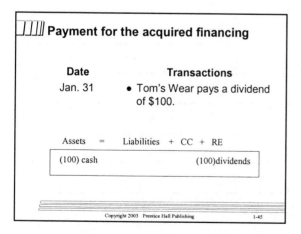

Payment for the acquired financing

Date	Transactions
Jan. 31	• Tom's Wear pays a dividend of $100.

Assets = Liabilities + CC + RE

(100) cash		(100)dividends

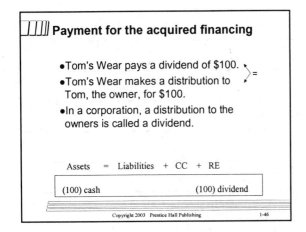

Payment for the acquired financing

- Tom's Wear pays a dividend of $100.
- Tom's Wear makes a distribution to Tom, the owner, for $100.
- In a corporation, a distribution to the owners is called a dividend.

Assets	=	Liabilities	+ CC	+ RE
(100) cash				(100) dividend

1-46

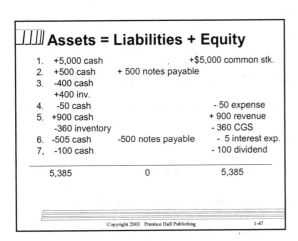

Assets = Liabilities + Equity

1.	+5,000 cash			+$5,000 common stk.
2.	+500 cash	+ 500 notes payable		
3.	-400 cash			
	+400 inv.			
4.	-50 cash			- 50 expense
5.	+900 cash			+ 900 revenue
	-360 inventory			- 360 CGS
6.	-505 cash	-500 notes payable		- 5 interest exp.
7,	-100 cash			- 100 dividend

5,385	0	5,385

1-47

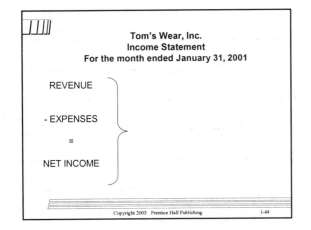

Tom's Wear, Inc.
Income Statement
For the month ended January 31, 2001

REVENUE

- EXPENSES

=

NET INCOME

1-48

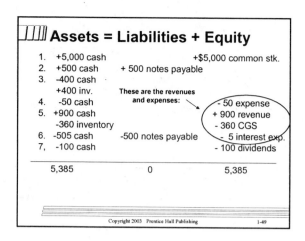

Assets = Liabilities + Equity

1. +5,000 cash   +$5,000 common stk.
2. +500 cash   + 500 notes payable
3. -400 cash
    +400 inv.   **These are the revenues**
               and expenses: - 50 expense
4.   -50 cash   + 900 revenue
5. +900 cash
    -360 inventory   - 360 CGS
6. -505 cash   -500 notes payable   - 5 interest exp.
7,   -100 cash   - 100 dividends

      5,385   0   5,385

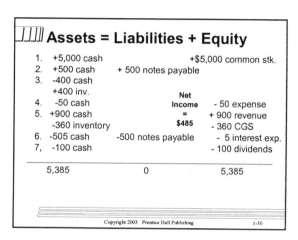

Assets = Liabilities + Equity

1. +5,000 cash   +$5,000 common stk.
2. +500 cash   + 500 notes payable
3. -400 cash
    +400 inv.   **Net**
4.   -50 cash   **Income**   - 50 expense
5. +900 cash   **=**   + 900 revenue
    -360 inventory   **$485**   - 360 CGS
6. -505 cash   -500 notes payable   - 5 interest exp.
7,   -100 cash   - 100 dividends

      5,385   0   5,385

Tom's Wear, Inc.
Income Statement
For the Month Ended Jan. 31, 2001

Revenue
     Sales $900
Expenses
      Cost of sales   360
      Advertising   50
      Interest   5
Total expenses   415
Net income $485

Tom's Wear, Inc.
Statement of Changes in Owner's Equity
For the month ended Jan. 31, 2001

Beginning CC	$ 0	
Common stock issued	5,000	
Total Contributed Capital		$ 5,000
Beginning RE	$ 0	
Net income		
Dividends		
Ending RE		
Total Owners' Equity		

1-52

Tom's Wear, Inc.
Statement of Changes in Owner's Equity
For the month ended Jan. 31, 2001

Beginning CC	$ 0	
Common stock issued	5,000	
Total Contributed Capital		$ 5,000
Beginning RE	$ 0	
Net income	485	
Dividends	(100)	
Ending RE		$ 385
Total Owners' Equity		$5,385

1-53

Assets = Liabilities + Equity

1.	+5,000 cash		+$5,000 common stk.
2.	+500 cash	+ 500 notes payable	
3.	-400 cash		
	+400 inv.		
4.	-50 cash	Net Income	- 50 expense
5.	+900 cash	=	+ 900 revenue
	-360 inventory	$485	- 360 CGS
6.	-505 cash	-500 notes payable	- 5 interest exp.
7.	-100 cash		- 100 dividends
	5,385	0	5,385

1-54

1-18

Slide 1-55

Tom's Wear
Balance Sheet
At Jan. 31,2001

Assets   *Liabilities + Shareholder's Equity*

_____   _____

1-55

Slide 1-56

Tom's Wear
Balance Sheet
At Jan. 31, 2001

Assets   *Liabilities + SHs Equity*

Cash $ 5,345
Inventory $ 40

_____   _____

Total Assets $ 5,385

1-56

Slide 1-57

Tom's Wear
Balance Sheet
At Jan. 31, 2001

Assets   *Liabilities + Shareholder's Equity*

Cash $5,345   Note Payable   -0-
Inventory   40

_____   _____

Total Assets $5,385

1-57

Tom's Wear
Balance Sheet
At Jan. 31, 2001

Assets		Liabilities + Shareholder's Equity	
Cash	$5,345	Note payable	-0-
Inventory	$ 40		
		Common stock, T. Phillips	$5,000
Total assets	$ 5,385	Retained earnings	385
		Total liabilities + SH's Equity	$ 5,385

1-58

Tom's Wear, Inc.
Statement of Cash Flows
For the month ending Jan. 31, 2001

Cash from Operating Activities

Cash from Investing Activities

Cash from Financing Activities

1-59

Assets = Liabilities + Equity

**Look at every CASH transaction and classify it as operating, investing, or financing.**

1.	+5,000 cash		+$5,000 common stk.
2.	+500 cash	+ 500 notes payable	
3.	-400 cash +400 inv.		
4.	-50 cash	Net Income = $485	- 50 expense
5.	+900 cash -360 inventory		+ 900 revenue - 360 CGS
6.	-505 cash	-500 notes payable	- 5 interest exp.
7.	-100 cash		- 100 dividends
	5,385	0	5,385

1-60

1-20

Tom's Wear, Inc.
Statement of Cash Flows
For the month ended Jan. 31,2001

Cash from operating activities

Cash from customers	$ 900
Cash paid to vendor for T-shirts	(400)
Cash paid for advertising	(50)
Interest paid	(5)
Total cash from operations	$445

1-61

Tom's Wear, Inc.
Statement of Cash Flows
For the month ended Jan. 31, 2001

Cash from operating activities

Cash from customers	$ 900
Cash paid to vendor for T-shirts	(400)
Cash paid for advertising	(50)
Cash paid for interest	(5)
Total cash from operations	$445
Cash from investing activities	-0-

1-62

Tom's Wear, Inc.
Statement of Cash Flows
For the month ended Jan. 31, 2001

Cash from operating activities

Cash from customers	$ 900
Cash paid to vendor for T-shirts	(400)
Cash paid for advertising	(50)
Cash paid for interest	(5)
Total cash from operations	$445
Cash from investing activities	-0-
Cash from financing activities	

1-63

Tom's Wear, Inc.
Statement of Cash Flows
For the month ended Jan. 31, 2001

Cash from operating activities		
Cash from customers	$ 900	
Cash paid to vendor for T-shirts	(400)	
Cash paid for advertising	(50)	
Cash paid for interest	(5)	
Total cash from operations		$445
Cash from investing activities		-0-
Cash from financing activities		
Owner's contributions	5,000	
Dividends	(100)	
Total Cash from Financing		4,900

1-64

Tom's Wear, Inc.
Statement of Cash Flows
For the month ended Jan. 31, 2001

Cash from operating activities		
Cash from customers	$ 900	
Cash paid to vendor for T-shirts	(400)	
Cash paid for advertising	(50)	
Cash paid for interest	(5)	
Total cash from operations		$445
Cash from investing activities		-0-
Cash from financing activities		
Owner's contributions	5,000	
Dividends	(100)	
Total Cash from Financing		4,900
Net Increase in Cash		$ 5,345

1-65

Chapter 2

Qualities of Accounting Information

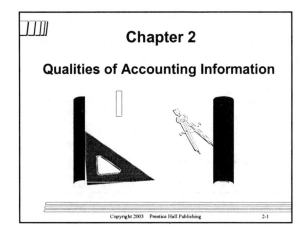

2-1

Who Sets the Rules?

- Securities and Exchange Commission has the legal authority to set the accounting rules for companies that are publicly traded.
- The SEC has delegated that responsibility to the accounting profession.
- Currently, the Financial Accounting Standards Board is the standards-setting body.

2-2

GAAP (not a clothes store)

- Generally Accepted Accounting Principles (GAAP) are the rules that most companies follow in preparing their financial reports.
- GAAP are not exact rules: professional judgment is needed.
- Statements of Financial Accounting Concepts provide the basis and guidance for establishing accounting standards.

2-3

Statements of Financial Accounting Concepts

- Objectives of accounting information
- Qualitative characteristics of accounting information
- Elements of financial statements
- Recognition and measurement in financial statements

GAAP

Objectives ⟶ *Qualities*

- To provide useful information for decision-making.
  - *Relevant:*
    - » specific to a business entity,
    - » timely,
    - » simplified and condensed,
    - » focus on earnings,
    - » all within a cost-benefit framework.

Objectives ⟶ *Qualities*

- To provide useful information for decision-making.
  - *Reliable*:
    - » representational faithfulness
    - » verifiable
    - » unbiased

Objectives ⟶ *Qualities*

- To provide useful information for decision-making.
  - *Comparable*:
    - » from year to year for one company,
    - » across companies for a single year,
    - » to industry averages,
    - » estimates.

Objectives ⟶ *Qualities*

- To provide useful information for decision-making.
  - *Consistent*:
    - » same rules used each time

Additional Concepts/Constraints

- Cost/benefit
- Materiality
- Full disclosure

Elements of Financial Statements

- Assets
- Liabilities
- Equity
- Revenue
- Expenses

Elements of Financial Statements

Next to each item, indicate whether it is an
Asset, **L**iability, **E**quity, **R**evenue or **E**xpense.

_____	Cash
_____	Common Stock ($1 par)
_____	Depreciation Expense
_____	Insurance Expense
_____	Interest Receivable
_____	Interest Earned
_____	Investment in U.S. Bonds

Elements of Financial Statements

_____	Cash	Asset
_____	Common Stock ($1 par)	Equity
_____	Depreciation Expense	Expense
_____	Insurance Expense	Expense
_____	Interest Receivable	Asset
_____	Interest Earned	Revenue
_____	Investment in U.S. Bonds	Asset

More elements of financial statements

_____	Miscellaneous Expense
_____	Prepaid Insurance
_____	Rent Revenue
_____	Retained Earnings
_____	Salaries Expense
_____	Salaries Payable
_____	Service Revenue
_____	Supplies Used
_____	Unearned Rent

2-13

More elements of financial statements

_____	Miscellaneous Expense	Expense
_____	Prepaid Insurance	Asset
_____	Rent Revenue	Revenue
_____	Retained Earnings	Equity
_____	Salaries Expense	Expense
_____	Salaries Payable	Liability
_____	Service Revenue	Revenue
_____	Supplies Used	Expense
_____	Unearned Rent	Liability

2-14

Recognition and Measurement in Financial Statements

- Transactions are measured and recorded at COST.
- Revenue is recognized--included on the income statement--when it is EARNED.
- Expenses are recognized in the period in which the related revenue is recognized: MATCHING CONCEPT.
- This is ACCRUAL ACCOUNTING.

2-15

Accruals and Deferrals

- ACCRUALS:
  - Action first, dollars later
  - E.g., services are performed, payment to be received later

- DEFERRALS:
  - Dollars first, action later
  - E.g., payment is made in advance for insurance or rent, the action of using it comes later

Both types of transactions and adjustments are part of ACCRUAL ACCOUNTING.

2-16

Tom's Wear: February 2001

- Let's look at each of the transactions that took place during February, Tom's second month of business.
- We'll show how each affects the accounting equations, and then we'll prepare the four basic financial statements.

2-17

Acquisition of Inventory

Date	Transactions
February 1	• Tom's Wear purchases 200 T-shirts at $4 each on account.

Assets   =   Liabilities + CC + RE

2-18

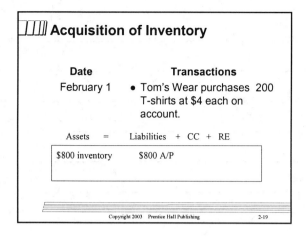

Acquisition of Inventory

Date	Transactions
February 1	• Tom's Wear purchases 200 T-shirts at $4 each on account.

Assets = Liabilities + CC + RE

$800 inventory	$800 A/P

2-19

Acquisition of a Service

Date	Transactions
February 5	• Tom's Wear hires a company to advertise his business for $150--$100 cash and $50 on account.

Assets = Liabilities + CC + RE

2-20

Acquisition of a Service

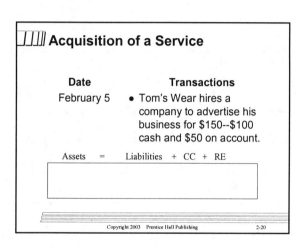

Date	Transactions
February 5	• Tom's Wear hires a company to advertise his business for $150--$100 cash and $50 on account.

Assets = Liabilities + CC + RE

(100) cash	50 other payables	(150) expenses

2-21

Sales and Collection Cycle

Date	Transactions
February 14	• Tom's Wear pays for 3 month's worth of insurance for $150.

Assets =   Liabilities + CC + RE

Sales and Collection Cycle

Date	Transactions
February 14	• Tom's Wear pays for 3 month's worth of insurance for $150.

Assets =   Liabilities + CC + RE

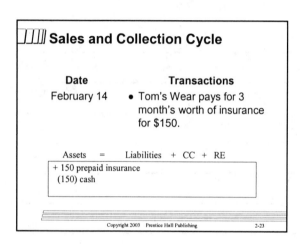

+ 150 prepaid insurance
(150) cash

Sales and Collection Cycle

Date	Transactions
February 20	• Tom's Wear sells 185 T-shirts for $10 each. 170 shirts were cash sales and the other sales were on account.

Assets =   Liabilities + CC + RE

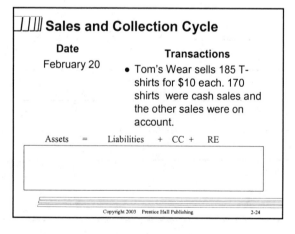

Sales and Collection Cycle

Date
February 20

Transactions
- Tom's Wear sells 185 T-shirts for $10 each. 170 shirts were cash sales and the other sales were on account.

Assets	=	Liabilities	+	CC +	RE
+1,700 cash					+1,850 sales
+ 150 A/R					

Sales and Collection Cycle

Date
February 20

Transactions
- Tom's Wear sells 185 T-shirts for $10 each. 170 shirts were cash sales and the other sales were on account.

Assets	=	Liabilities	+	CC +	RE
+1,700 cash					+1,850 sales
+ 150 A/R					
(740) inventory					(740) cost of goods sold

Note: Recall that the *cost* of shirts was $4 each.

Acquisition/Payment Cycle

Date
February 28

Transactions
- Tom's Wear pays dividends of $100.

Assets	=	Liabilities	+	CC	+	RE

Acquisition/Payment Cycle

Date	Transactions
February 28	• Tom's Wear pays dividends of $100.

Assets   =   Liabilities + CC + RE

(100) cash	(100) dividends

Adjustment for Year-end Financial Statements

Date	
February 28	Prepaid insurance that has been used needs to be recorded as an expense. Only the unused portion remains on the balance sheet as an asset.

Assets   =   Liabilities + CC + RE

(25) prepaid insurance	(25) insurance expense

Tom's Wear, Inc.
Income Statement
For the month ended February 28, 2001

Tom's Wear, Inc.
Income Statement
For the month ended February 28, 2001

Revenue

    Sales $1,850

2-31

Tom's Wear, Inc.
Income Statement
For the month ended February 28, 2001

Revenue

    Sales $1,850

Expenses

    Cost of sales $

    Total Expenses

Net Income

2-32

Tom's Wear, Inc.
Income Statement
For the month ended February 28, 2001

Revenue

    Sales $1,850

Expenses

    Cost of sales $ 740

    Other expenses   175   915

Net income $ 935

2-33

Tom's Wear, Inc.
Statement of Changes in
Shareholder's Equity
For the month ending 2/28/01

Beginning contributed capital	$5,000
Contributions during the year	-0-
Ending contributed capital	5,000

2-34

Tom's Wear, Inc.
Statement of Changes in
Shareholder's Equity
For the month ending 2/28/01

Beginning contributed capital	$5,000
Contributions during the year	-0-
Ending contributed capital	5,000
Beginning retained earnings	**$ 385**
Net income for the year	**935**

2-35

Tom's Wear, Inc.
Statement of Changes in
Shareholder's Equity
For the month ending 2/28/01

Beginning contributed capital	$5,000
Contributions during the year	-0-
Ending contributed capital	5,000
Beginning retained earnings	**$ 385**
Net income for the year	**935**
Dividends	**(100)**
Ending retained earnings	**$1,220**

2-36

Tom's Wear, Inc.
Statement of Changes in
Shareholder's Equity
For the month ending 2/28/01

Beginning contributed capital	$5,000
Contributions during the year	-0-
Ending contributed capital	5,000
Beginning retained earnings	$ 385
Net Income for the year	935
Dividends	(100)
Ending Retained earning	$1,220
Total shareholders's equity	$6,220

2-37

Tom's Wear, Inc.
Balance Sheet
At 2/28/01

Assets

Cash	$6,695
Accounts Receivable	150
Inventory	100
Prepaid Insurance	125
Total Assets	$7,070

2-38

Tom's Wear, Inc.
Balance Sheet
At 2/28/01

Assets		Liabilities + Shareholders' Equity	
Cash	$6,695	Accounts Payable	$800
Accounts Receivable	150	Other Payables	50
Inventory	100	Common Stock	5,000
Prepaid Insurance	125	Retained Earnings	1,220
		Total Liabilities +	
Total Assets	$7,070	Shareholders' Equity	$7,070

2-39

2-13

Tom's Wear
Statement of Cash Flows
For the year ending 2/28/01

Cash from Operating Activities
Cash collected from customers	$1,700	
Cash paid for advertising	(100)	
Cash paid for insurance	(150)	
Total Cash from Operations		$1,450

2-40

Tom's Wear
Statement of Cash Flows
For the year ending 2/28/01

Cash from Operating Activities
Cash collected from customers	$1,700	
Cash paid for advertising	(100)	
Cash paid for insurance	(150)	
Total Cash from Operations		$1,450

Cash from Investing Activities   -0-

Cash from Financing Activities

2-41

Tom's Wear
Statement of Cash Flows
For the year ending 2/28/01

Cash from Operating Activities
Cash collected from customers	$1,700	
Cash paid for advertising	(100)	
Cash paid for insurance	(150)	
Total Cash from Operations		$1,450

Cash from Investing Activities   -0-

Cash from Financing Activities
Cash paid for dividends	(100)	
Total Cash from Financing		(100)

Net Increase in Cash $1,350

2-42

Chapter 3

**Accruals and Deferrals:
Timing is Everything in Accounting**

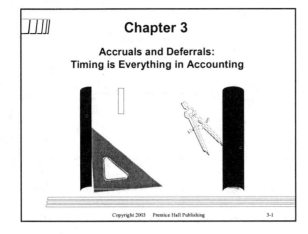

3-1

More About Accruals

Accrual Accounting: Recording the financial transactions of a business in the period in which they occur, rather than in the period in which cash is exchanged.

The *economic substance* of the transaction signals the recording...not disbursing or receiving cash.

3-2

Examples of Accrual Events

- Sales made "on account"
- Purchases made "on credit"
- Wages expense for employees
  - » when they've worked but you haven't yet paid them
- Interest on money borrowed or lent
  - » when time has passed (so interest has been earned by the lender) but the actual cash for the interest has not changed hands
- Income tax expense
  - » when you owe it but haven't yet paid the IRS

3-3

Accounts Receivable:
Amounts owed by customers
for goods and services received

- **Recognition of event *versus* realization of cash**
  - recognizing a revenue or expense means to record it in the accounting records so that it shows up on the *income statement*
- **When is revenue recognized?**
  - when the amounts are earned (required activities are complete)
- **Realization means you actually get the cash.**

Accounts Payable:
Amounts you owe creditors
for the purchase of goods and services

When are costs **recognized** as **expenses**?
- when the "matching" revenue is recognized, or
- when the benefits of the expenditures are received

INVOICE

Accruals that need to be made before the financial statements are prepared -- adjustments to the "books"

1. Any revenue earned that has not been billed (no receivable has been recorded)
2. Any interest revenue that has been earned on investments that has not been recorded
3. Any expense that has been incurred (used) but has not been recorded (a common one is salary expense)
4. Income tax expense incurred but not recorded

Revenue that needs to be accrued

- Work that has been completed -- but nothing has been recorded for the financial statements.
  - This situation arises when a customer has not been billed yet has not paid
  - Computerization of record-keeping has made this situation less frequent

Example:
1. Revenue to be accrued

- An employee of Maids-R-Us finished cleaning a house on January 31, but didn't get the paperwork into the office in time to get it included in the January records.
- An income statement for January must include the revenue because it has been earned.

Accruing Revenue

- Accruing revenue affects the accounting equation in the following way:

Assets = Liab. + Cont. Cap. + Retained Earnings

+ A/R			+ Revenue

- Income Statement: Increases income
- Statement of Changes in Equity: Increases equity
- Statement of Cash Flows: No effect on cash flows

What happens when the customer pays?

- When the customer pays, the accounting equation is affected on the asset side only.
  - A/R is decreased by the amount of the payment
  - Cash is increased by the amount of the payment
- The revenue has already been recognized.

2. Accruing Interest
(Revenue or expense)

- The most common accrual is for interest-- the cost of borrowing money.
  - **If you loaned the money or purchased a CD, you'd be dealing with interest revenue.**
  - If you borrowed the money, you'd be dealing with interest expense.

Interest Revenue

- You have a 6-month, $100 CD that earns 12%, (always given as an annual rate), purchased on January 1.
- The natural recording of this interest revenue will happen when you receive the money.
- An income statement for January needs to show the amount of interest revenue for January.

Accruing Interest Revenue

- Interest = principal x rate x time
- Interest = $100 x .12 x 1/12 = $1
    - Since the rate is "per year," the time has to be given in terms of a year.
- Interest receivable and interest revenue will each be $1. Show how that keeps the accounting equation in balance.

3-13

Accruing Interest Revenue

Assets   =   Liab.   + Cont. Cap. + Retained Earnings

+1 interest receivable	+1 interest revenue

Income Statement: Increases income

Statement of Changes in Equity: Increases equity

Statement of Cash Flows: No effect on cash flow

3-14

---

3. An Expense to be Accrued

- Salary expense is a common expense that needs to be accrued before financial statements are prepared.
- Suppose employees work five days per week and are paid every Friday, but January 31 falls on a Tuesday.
- The salary expense for the week from January 30 to February 3 will not be paid until Friday, February 3.

3-15

Accruing Salary Expense

- The income statement for January should have the expense for January 30 and 31, while the February income statement will have the expense for February 1, 2, and 3.

Accruing Salary Expense

- Suppose a week's payroll is $5,000.
- On January 31, the company should accrue $2,000 worth of salary expense.
- i.e., 2 out of 5 days' worth of the salary must be a January expense.
- How is this reflected in the accounting equation?

Accruing Salary Expense

Assets	=	Liab.	+	Cont. Cap.	+	Retained Earnings
		+ 2,000 salaries payable				(2,000) salary expense

- Income Statement (Jan.): Decreases income
- Statement of Changes in Equity: Decreases equity
- Statement of Cash Flows: No effect on cash flows

What happens when the salaries are actually paid to the employees on Friday, February 3?

Assets = Liab. + Cont. Cap. + Retained Earnings

(5,000) cash	(2000) salaries payable		(3000) salary expense

- Income Statement (for Feb!): Decreases income
- Statement of Changes in Equity: Decreases equity
- Statement of Cash Flows: Operating cash outflow

3-19

---

4. Taxes to be accrued

- Tax expense is a common expense that needs to be accrued when financial statements are prepared.
- The income statement for January needs to include the income taxes for January, even though they will not be paid until several months later.
- WHY??

3-20

What is a Deferral?

- **A deferral event occurs when cash is received or paid before revenue is earned or an expense is incurred.**

- **Deferral events are a part of the accrual basis of accounting**

3-21

Deferred Revenue

- You've **received** payment for something you have NOT yet provided.
- Dollars first, action later.
- Revenue is not **recognized** until the service is performed or the goods are delivered...but you have to **record** the fact that you have received the cash.

$

Example of deferred revenue:

A publishing company collects money for magazine subscriptions before the magazines are actually delivered.

- What is exchanged? Cash is received but the *give* part will come later.
- In the meantime, the company has an obligation--a liability. (The company gives a promise of future delivery of magazines.)

How does receiving a payment in advance affect the accounting equation?

Assets =	Liab. +	Cont. Cap. +	Retained Earnings
+ cash	+ unearned revenue		

Income Statement: No effect

Statement of Changes in Equity: No effect

Statement of Cash Flows: Operating cash flows

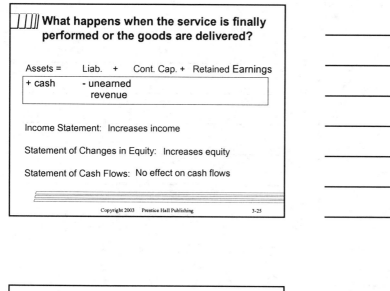

What happens when the service is finally performed or the goods are delivered?

Assets =   Liab.   +   Cont. Cap. +   Retained Earnings

+ cash	- unearned revenue

Income Statement: Increases income

Statement of Changes in Equity: Increases equity

Statement of Cash Flows: No effect on cash flows

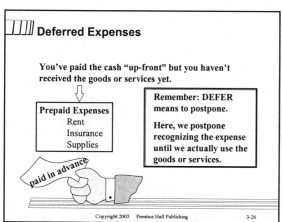

Deferred Expenses

You've paid the cash "up-front" but you haven't received the goods or services yet.

Prepaid Expenses
Rent
Insurance
Supplies

Remember: DEFER means to postpone.

Here, we postpone recognizing the expense until we actually use the goods or services.

paid in advance

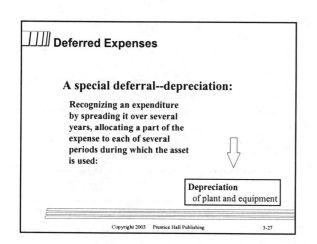

Deferred Expenses

A special deferral--depreciation:

Recognizing an expenditure by spreading it over several years, allocating a part of the expense to each of several periods during which the asset is used:

Depreciation
of plant and equipment

PREPAID RENT

- Often companies pay rent in advance.
- When the cash is paid, the company has purchased an asset called **prepaid rent.**
- Dollars first--action later.
- What's the action that triggers recognition of the expense?
    - Passing of the time to which the rent applies.

How does paying the rent in advance affect the accounting equation?

Assets =   Liab.   +   Cont. Cap. + Retained Earnings

+ prepaid rent

+ cash

Income Statement: Decreases income

Statement of Changes in Equity: Decreases equity

Statement of Cash Flows: Operating Cash Outflows

The expense is recorded when the time of the rent has passed – when it's been used up.
Usually it's an adjustment, made when the financial statements are being prepared.

Assets =   Liab.   +   Cont. Cap. + Retained Earnings

- Prepaid rent   - rent expense

Income Statement: Decreases income

Statement of Changes in Equity: Decreases equity

Statement of Cash Flows: No effect on cash flow

PREPAID INSURANCE

- Often companies pay insurance in advance.
- When the cash is paid, the company has purchased an asset called **prepaid insurance.**
- Dollars first--action later.
- What's the action that triggers recognition of the expense?

    Passing of the time to which the insurance applies.

How does paying for the insurance in advance affect the accounting equation?

Assets = Liab. + Cont. Cap. + Retained Earnings

| + prepaid insurance |
| - cash |

Income Statement: No effect

Statement of Changes in Equity: No effect

Statement of Cash Flows: Operating cash outflow

The expense is recorded when the time to which the insurance applies has passed--when it's been used up.

Usually it's an adjustment, made when the financial statements are being prepared.

Assets = Liab. + Cont. Cap. + Retained Earnings

| - prepaid insurance | - insurance expense |

Income Statement: Decreases income

Statement of Changes in Equity: Decreases equity

Statement of Cash Flows: No effect on cash flow

BUYING SUPPLIES

- Companies purchase supplies to be used later.
- When the cash is paid, the company has purchased an asset called *supplies.* Sometimes they are called **supplies-on-hand** to differentiate them from supplies expense (used).
- Dollars first--action later.
- What's the action that triggers recognition of the expense?
  - Actually <u>using</u> the supplies.

3-34

How does buying the supplies in advance affect the accounting equation?

Assets	=	Liab.	+	Cont. Cap.	+	Retained Earnings
+ supplies						
- cash						

Income Statement: No effect

Statement of Changes in Equity: No effect

Statement of Cash Flows: Operating cash outflow

3-35

The expense is recorded when supplies are used.

Usually, supplies-on-hand are counted at the end of the period, and an adjustment is made to get the amount of the remaining asset correct for the balance sheet.

Assets	=	Liab.	+	Cont. Cap.	+	Retained Earnings
- supplies						- supplies expense

Income Statement: Decreases income

Statement of Changes in Equity: Decreases equity

Statement of Cash Flows: No effect on cash flow

3-36

DEPRECIATION

- When a company buys an asset that is used up in the business (i.e., they didn't buy it to resell it) AND it will be useful for more than one year, GAAP says that the expense must be spread over the accounting periods during the useful life of the asset.

DEPRECIATION

- The portion of the cost of an asset allocated to any one accounting period-- **DEPRECIATION EXPENSE**
- Depreciation of an asset is an allocation process--spreading the cost of an asset that benefits more than one accounting period over the estimated useful life of the asset.

Example of Depreciation

- ABC Co. bought a satellite dish for $5,000. The asset is expected to last five years and have no salvage value at the end of its useful life. How will the purchase and use of the asset affect the financial statements?

Purchase of the asset:
How does it affect the financial statements?

Assets	=	Liabilities	+	CC	+	RE

+5,000 satellite dish
(5,000) cash

ᵡ Income Statement: no effect

ᵡ Statement of Changes in Equity: no effect

ᵡ Statement of Cash Flows: $5,000 investing activity cash outflow

---

USE OF THE ASSET

- We want to *allocate* the cost of the asset to the income statement as an expense during the time period we use the asset.

- If we depreciate the asset using the STRAIGHT LINE method, we will divide the cost of the asset (minus any estimated salvage value) by the useful life: $5,000/5 = $1,000 each year.

Use of the asset:
How does it affect the financial statements?

Assets	=	Liabilities	+	CC	+	RE
(1,000)						(1,000)
reduces the asset						expense

Income Statement: Reduces income

Statement of Changes in Equity: Reduces equity

Statement of Cash Flows: No effect on cash flow

Use of the asset: How does it affect the financial statements?

- Each year for five years, we will reduce the asset's value on the balance sheet by $1,000.
- Each year for five years, we will have an expense of $1,000 on the income statement.
- Instead of netting out the subtracted amount on the balance sheet, we will always show the original cost and then the amount of the total reduction. That amount is called **accumulated depreciation** and it is a **contra-asset**.
- The **expense** is called **depreciation expense**.

 3-43

Chapter 4
Keeping the Books:
The Mechanics of an
Accounting System

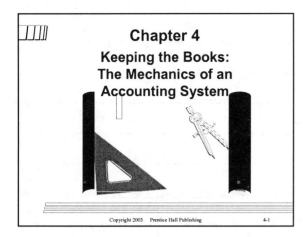

The Traditional Way to Keep the Books: The General Ledger System

THE ACCOUNTING CYCLE:

- Transactions occur in the normal course of business. We record them in our records with a **JOURNAL ENTRY**.
- Journal entries are **posted** to the **GENERAL LEDGER**.
- **ADJUSTING ENTRIES** are made and posted.

Transactions →   **Financial Statements**

Accounting cycle continued...

- A **trial balance** can be prepared at any time to make sure we haven't made an error with the debit-credit part of the accounting system. More about that after we learn the nuts and bolts about DEBITS and CREDITS...
- **Financial statements** are written.
- **Closing journal entries** are made and posted (and a post-closing trial balance may be prepared).

▥ Terminology

- What's a general ledger?
  - A big book of accounting records in which every page is an "account."
- What's an account?
  - A page in the general ledger that is devoted to keeping track of an individual asset or liability or type of owners' equity.
  - How many are there? As many as the business find necessary for its record keeping.

▥ Accounts…debits and credits

- Each account can be increased or decreased.
- For example, CASH can be increased (when it is collected) and decreased (when it is disbursed).
- Each item on the balance sheet is either an account or a composite of several accounts.

▥ How this debit/credit stuff works:
DEBIT means LEFT side
CREDIT means RIGHT side

We can represent an account with a **T**, where one side is the place where we put the increases and the other side is for decreases.

The **left** side is always called the **debit** side.
When we put something on the left side of an account, we are debiting the account.
The **right** side is always called the **credit** side.
When we put something on the right side of an account, we are crediting the account.

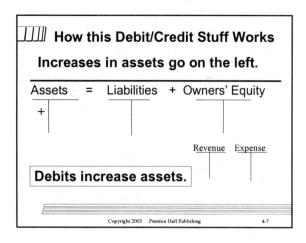

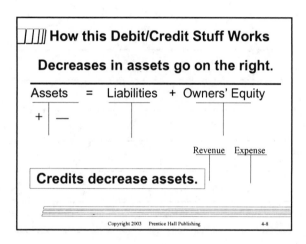

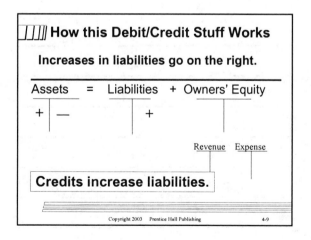

|||| How this Debit/Credit Stuff Works

Decreases in liabilities go on the left

Assets = Liabilities + Owners' Equity

+ | —   — | +

Revenue   Expense

Debits decrease liabilities.

|||| Owner's Equity Accounts

Contributed Capital and Retained Earnings) are increased with credits and decreased with debits.

Assets= Liabilities + Owners' Equity

+ | —   — | +   — | +

Expense   Revenue

|||| Revenue and Expense Accounts

- Revenue and expense accounts are not considered "owners' equity" accounts--even though they effectively increase or decrease equity!
- They are called income statement accounts, often called temporary or nominal accounts.

Revenue Accounts

Revenue accounts keep track of all the company's earnings from sales and services.

- An increase in a revenue causes an increase in owners' equity--so the debits and credits will be the same for revenue accounts as they are for owners' equity: Credits increase revenue accounts and debits decrease revenue accounts.

Revenues are increased with credits and decreased with debits.

Assets=   Liabilities   + Owners' Equity

+ | −   − | +   − | +

Expense   Revenue

− | +

Expenses reduce owners' equity, so the debits and credits are opposite of those for the OE accounts: debits increase expenses, credits decrease expenses.

Assets=   Liabilities   + Owners' Equity

+ | −   − | +   − | +

Expense   Revenue

+ | −   − | +

SUMMARY: DOUBLE-ENTRY ACCOUNTING

- Each account can be increased or decreased.
- Debit means "left side"
- Credit means "right side"
- Asset and expense accounts are increased with debits and decreased with credits.
- Liability, equity, and revenue accounts are increased with credits and decreased with debits.

T-Accounts

ASSETS

| + Increase | |

- In a transaction that increases an asset, put that amount on the left.

T-Accounts

ASSETS

| + Increase | - Decrease |

- In a transaction that increases an asset, put that amount on the left.

- In a transaction that decreases an asset, put that amount on the right.

T-Accounts

- In a transaction that increases an asset, put that amount on the left.

- In a transaction that decreases an asset, put that amount on the right.

ASSETS

+ Increase	- Decrease

In our accounting records, we never cross out or subtract or change a number. Instead, we use debits and credits to change the balance in an account.

T-Accounts

- In a transaction that increases an asset, put that amount on the left.

- In a transaction that decreases an asset, put that amount on the right.

ASSETS

+ Increase	- Decrease

Calculate the balance in an asset account at any time by adding the amounts on the left and subtracting the amounts on the right.

T-Accounts: Assets

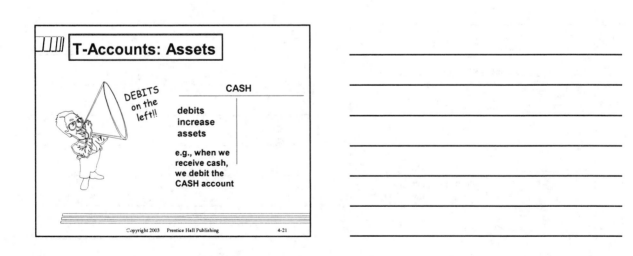

DEBITS on the left!!

CASH

debits increase assets

e.g., when we receive cash, we debit the CASH account

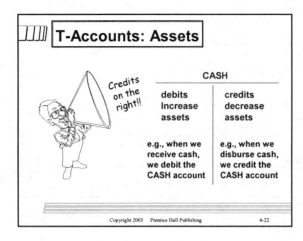

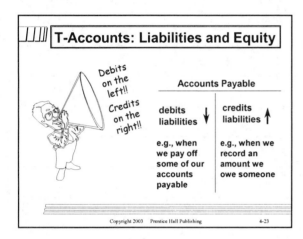

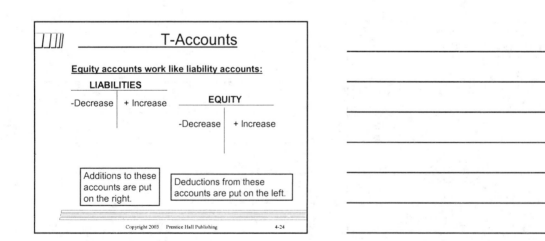

What about Revenue and Expense Accounts?

Since **revenues** increase owners' equity, they are increased with credits---just like owners' equity accounts.

Service Revenue

+

Revenue accounts are rarely debited..

4-25

What about Revenue and Expense Accounts?

Since **expenses** decrease owners' equity, they are increased with debits---just the opposite of owners' equity accounts.

Expenses

+

Expense accounts are rarely credited.

4-26

What about Revenue and Expense Accounts?

Since **expenses** decrease owners' equity, they are increased with debits---just the opposite of owners' equity accounts.

Expenses

+

Expense accounts are rarely credited..

Remember, an expense account is simply a list of the company's expenses. So as we incur expenses, we increase the expense account. That is, we are adding to our list of expenses.

4-27

What is a journal and a journal entry?

- A journal is a book where a chronological record of transactions is recorded.
- Only basic information is contained in the journal.
- A "journal entry" is just a recorded transaction.
- Because of the design of the debit/credit system to go with the accounting equation, in every journal entry there are equal dollar amounts of debits and credits.

How do journal entries relate to T-Accounts?

- Journal entries are recorded chronologically as the transactions occur:

e.g., Services are rendered for $100 cash:

Cash	100	
Service Revenue		100
An explanation goes here.		

- Journal entries are written in a journal and then posted to the general ledger accounts (our t-accounts)

They are then posted to the General Ledger (our t-accounts)

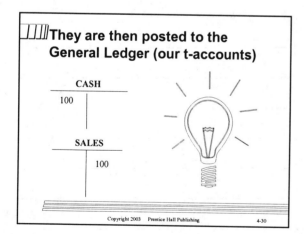

CASH

100

SALES

100

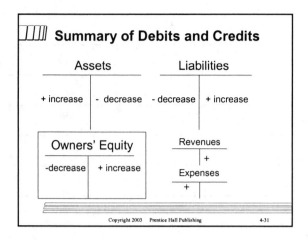

Summary of Debits and Credits

Assets

+ increase	- decrease

Liabilities

- decrease	+ increase

Owners' Equity

-decrease	+ increase

Revenues

+

Expenses

+

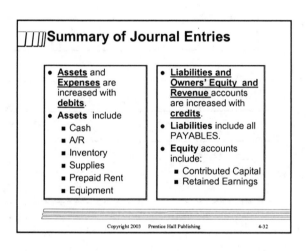

Summary of Journal Entries

- **Assets** and **Expenses** are increased with **debits**.
- **Assets** include
  - Cash
  - A/R
  - Inventory
  - Supplies
  - Prepaid Rent
  - Equipment

- **Liabilities and Owners' Equity and Revenue** accounts are increased with **credits**.
- **Liabilities** include all PAYABLES.
- **Equity** accounts include:
  - Contributed Capital
  - Retained Earnings

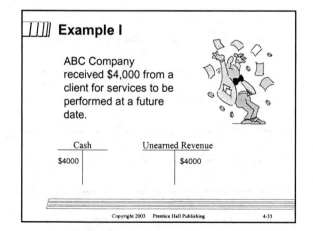

Example I

ABC Company received $4,000 from a client for services to be performed at a future date.

Cash		Unearned Revenue	
$4000			$4000

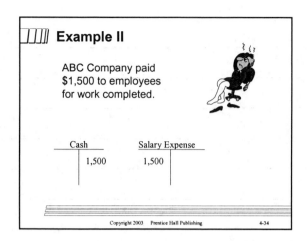

Example II

ABC Company paid $1,500 to employees for work completed.

Cash		Salary Expense	
1,500		1,500	

4-34

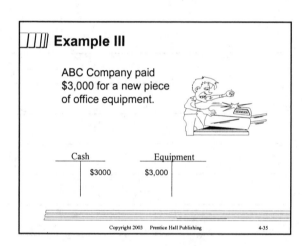

Example III

ABC Company paid $3,000 for a new piece of office equipment.

Cash		Equipment	
$3000		$3,000	

4-35

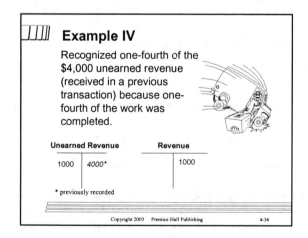

Example IV

Recognized one-fourth of the $4,000 unearned revenue (received in a previous transaction) because one-fourth of the work was completed.

Unearned Revenue		Revenue	
1000	4000*		1000

* previously recorded

4-36

Trial Balance: a list of each account and its debit or credit balance.

Since debits = credits in all journal entries, at any point in time we should be able to take the balances in all of our general ledger accounts and confirm that DEBITS = CREDITS for all accounts together.

Adjusting Entries

- Before financial statements are prepared, adjusting entries must be recorded to make sure that all accounts are properly stated and that nothing has been omitted.

- Adjustments need to be made for
  - Accruals
  - Deferrals

Adjusting for Accruals

- ACCRUALS--actions that have been completed but for which the cash has not changed hands (and the events are not yet recorded)
  - ABC Company has a CD on which $500 of interest had been earned during the year but not yet received (or recorded).

Interest receivable	Interest revenue
500	500

Adjusting for Deferrals

- Deferrals--dollars have been exchanged and recorded before the action is completed
  - ABC Company paid $600 for rent on December 1. The rent was for three months, beginning in December. When they paid it, ABC recorded it as Prepaid Rent. Now, on 12/31, one month's worth of rent has been used.

Prepaid Rent	Rent Expense
600*	200	200

* previously recorded

The Goal of the Whole Process

- **_Financial Statements_** that reflect the financial condition and transactions of the company
  - Balance Sheet
  - Income Statement
  - Statement of Changes in Owners' Equity
  - Statement of Cash Flows

Communicating Information to Users

Closing Entries

- All temporary accounts (income statement accounts and distributions) are closed at the end of the accounting period, after the statements are prepared.
- Their balances are brought to ZERO, and the balancing entry is made to the retained earnings account.

Closing Entries

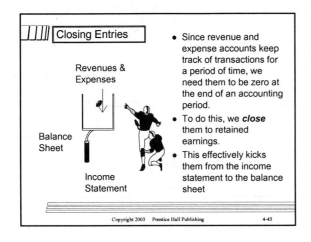

Revenues & Expenses

Balance Sheet

Income Statement

- Since revenue and expense accounts keep track of transactions for a period of time, we need them to be zero at the end of an accounting period.
- To do this, we **close** them to retained earnings.
- This effectively kicks them from the income statement to the balance sheet

4-43

Journal Entries to Close Revenue and Expense Accounts: Closing Entries

- Revenue accounts have credit balances, so we must **DEBIT** them to close them (to get a zero balance)
- What should we credit?

  RETAINED EARNINGS

4-44

Closing continued...

- To close expense accounts, we should **credit** the expense account and **debit** the Retained Earnings account.

- We are emptying the revenue and expense accounts...

- All revenue and expense accounts will have a balance of ZERO after we close them.

4-45

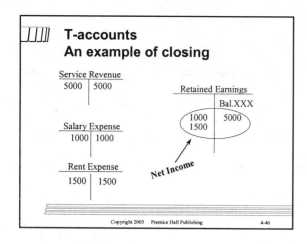

T-accounts
An example of closing

Service Revenue
5000 | 5000

Retained Earnings
Bal.XXX

1000 | 5000
1500

Salary Expense
1000 | 1000

Rent Expense
1500 | 1500

Net Income

4-46

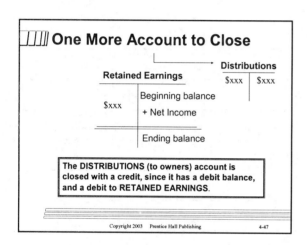

One More Account to Close

Retained Earnings

Distributions
$xxx | $xxx

$xxx

Beginning balance
+ Net Income

Ending balance

The DISTRIBUTIONS (to owners) account is
closed with a credit, since it has a debit balance,
and a debit to RETAINED EARNINGS.

4-47

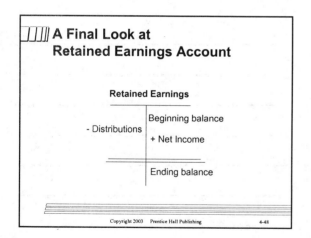

A Final Look at
Retained Earnings Account

Retained Earnings

- Distributions

Beginning balance
+ Net Income

Ending balance

4-48

The Post-closing Trial Balance:

A trial balance written after closing the books is called a *post-closing* trial balance sheet.

What accounts will be on this trial balance?

ONLY the BALANCE SHEET ACCOUNTS

-- the revenue and expense accounts have zero balances.

4-49

Chapter 5

Acquisitions: Purchase and Use of Business Assets

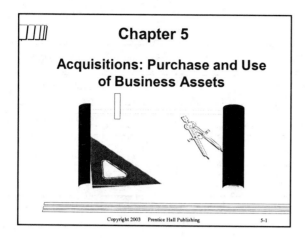

Classification of Operational Assets

- Operational assets are *used* by a business to generate revenue.

- Tangible operational assets have physical substance.
  - Land, buildings, fixtures, and equipment
  - Natural resources

Long-term Operational Assets...

- Long-term assets will be used more than one year.
- Tangible operational assets are reported on the balance sheet in a classification called **Property, Plant, and Equipment.**

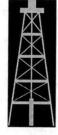

Classification of Operational Assets

- **_Intangible_** operational assets lack physical substance and confer specific use rights on the owner.
  - Patents
  - Copyrights
  - Franchises
  - Licenses
  - Trademarks

Measuring and Recording Acquisition Cost

Purchased operational assets are **recorded at cost**, an amount that includes all normal and reasonable expenditures necessary to get the asset in place and ready for its intended use.

Invoice price
- Sales taxes
- Transportation costs
- Installation costs
- Renovation and repair cost incurred prior to use.

Measuring Acquisition Cost

- Acquisition cost is the net cash equivalent amount paid for the asset.

- Financing charges are excluded from the acquisition cost but should be reported as interest expense.

Measuring Acquisition Cost

- The cost of land includes:
  - Acquisition price
  - Real estate commissions
  - Title search and transfer fees
  - Title insurance premiums
  - Delinquent taxes
  - Surveying fees
- Land is **not** depreciated.

Basket Purchase of Acquisitions

When land and building are purchased together, the land cost and the building cost are placed in separate accounts.

The total cost of the purchase is separated on the basis of relative market values.

Basket Purchase of Acquisitions

Example: On March 1, Arco Co. purchased land and building for $200,000 cash. The appraised value of the building was $172,500, and the land was appraised at $57,500. How much of the $200,000 purchase price will be allocated to each account?

Basket Purchase of Acquisitions

Fair Market Values:

Building	$ 172,500
Land	$ 57,500
Total market value	$ 230,000

Allocation of cost:

Building	*	$200,000 =
Land	*	$200,000 =

5-10

Basket Purchase of Acquisitions

Fair Market Values:

Building	$ 172,500
Land	$ 57,500
Total market value	$ 230,000

Allocation of cost:

Building	172,500/230,000 *	$200,000 =
Land	57,500/230,000 *	$200,000 =

5-11

Basket Purchase of Acquisitions

Fair Market Values:

Building	$ 172,500
Land	$ 57,500
Total market value	$ 230,000

Allocation of cost:

Building	.75	*	$200,000 = 150,000
Land	.25	*	$200,000 = 50,000

5-12

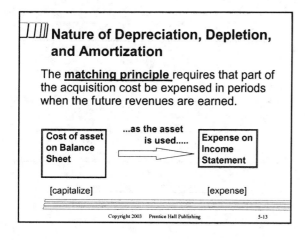

Nature of Depreciation, Depletion, and Amortization

The **matching principle** requires that part of the acquisition cost be expensed in periods when the future revenues are earned.

| Cost of asset on Balance Sheet | ...as the asset is used..... → | Expense on Income Statement |

[capitalize]   [expense]

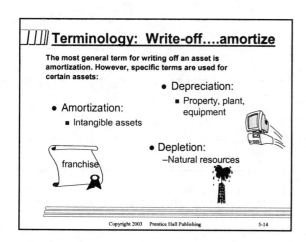

Terminology: Write-off....amortize

The most general term for writing off an asset is amortization. However, specific terms are used for certain assets:

- Amortization:
  - Intangible assets

  franchise

- Depreciation:
  - Property, plant, equipment

- Depletion:
  - Natural resources

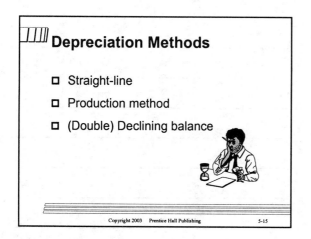

Depreciation Methods

- ☐ Straight-line
- ☐ Production method
- ☐ (Double) Declining balance

Straight-Line Method

$$\text{Depreciation Expense per Year} = \frac{\text{Cost - Residual Value}}{\text{Life in Years}}$$

Straight-Line Method: Example

On January 1, 2003, equipment was purchased for $55,000 cash. The equipment has an estimated useful life of 5 years and an estimated residual value of $10,000.

What is the annual straight-line depreciation expense?

Straight-Line Method: Example

$$\text{Depreciation Expense per Year} = \frac{\text{Cost - Residual Value}}{\text{Life in Years}}$$

$$\text{Depreciation Expense per Year} = \underline{\hspace{3cm}}$$

$$\text{Depreciation Expense per Year} =$$

Straight-Line Method: Example

$$\text{Depreciation Expense per Year} = \frac{\text{Cost} - \text{Residual Value}}{\text{Life in Years}}$$

$$\text{Depreciation Expense per Year} = \frac{55{,}000 - 10{,}000}{5}$$

$$\text{Depreciation Expense per Year} =$$

5-19

Straight-Line Method: Example

$$\text{Depreciation Expense per Year} = \frac{\text{Cost} - \text{Residual Value}}{\text{Life in Years}}$$

$$\text{Depreciation Expense per Year} = \frac{55{,}000 - 10{,}000}{5}$$

$$\text{Depreciation Expense per Year} = \boxed{9{,}000}$$

5-20

Straight-Line Method: Example

Calculate depreciation expense for the fourth year of the asset's life.

$$\boxed{\$9000}$$

Depreciation expense is the same amount each year of the asset's life using the straight-line method.

5-21

Units-of-Production Method

Step 1:

$$\text{Depreciation Rate} = \frac{\text{Cost - Residual Value}}{\text{Estimated units of useful life}}$$

Units-of-Production Method

Step 1:

$$\text{Depreciation Rate} = \frac{\text{Cost - Residual Value}}{\text{Estimated units of useful life}}$$

Step 2:

$$\text{Depreciation Expense} = \text{Depreciation Rate} \times \text{Number of Units Produced for the Year}$$

Units of Production Method: Example

Given the same information [asset cost $55,000, a residual value of $10,000, and a useful life of five years] plus the asset is estimated to have a total productive capacity of 100,000 units during the useful life:

If 22,000 units were produced this year, what is the amount of depreciation expense?

Production Method: Example

Step 1:

$$\text{Depreciation Rate} = \frac{\text{Cost - salvage value}}{\text{Productive output}} = \frac{45,000}{100,000}$$

Step 2:

Depreciation Expense =

5-25

Production Method: Example

Step 1:

$$\text{Depreciation Rate} = \frac{\text{Cost - salvage value}}{\text{Productive output}} = \frac{45,000}{100,000}$$

Step 2:

Depreciation Expense = Dep. rate * units produced
= $ .45/unit   *   22,000   = $\boxed{9,900}$

5-26

Production Method: Example

- If 15,000 units are produced during the second year of the asset's life, what is the amount of depreciation expense?

.45   *   15000 = $\boxed{6750}$

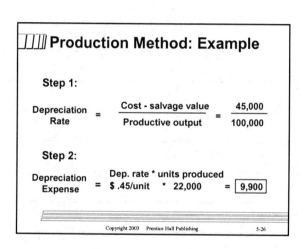

5-27

Accelerated Depreciation

- Accelerated depreciation methods result in **more** depreciation expense in the early years of an asset's useful life and **less** depreciation expense in later years of the an asset's useful life.

5-28

Double-Declining Balance Method

- Declining-balance depreciation is based on the straight-line rate multiplied by an acceleration factor.
    - For example, when the acceleration factor is 200 percent, the method is referred to as **double-declining balance depreciation**.
- Declining-balance depreciation computations <u>ignore residual value</u>, although the asset can't be depreciated below the residual value.

5-29

Double-Declining Balance Method

First, calculate a rate by dividing 2 by the number of years of useful life.

=

The annual depreciation amount is calculated with the following formula:

Book Value × (2 × Straight-Line Rate)

5-30

Double-Declining Balance Method

Annual depreciation expense is
calculated with
the following formula:

$$\text{Book Value} \times \left(\frac{2}{\text{Useful Life in Years}} \right)$$

Double-Declining-Balance Example

Using the same information from our
earlier example [asset cost $55,000,
residual value is $10,000, and useful life
is 5 years]:

Calculate the depreciation expense
for the first two years of the asset's life.

Double-Declining Balance Method

Rate = 2/5 = 40%

First year's depreciation:

Second year's depreciation:

Double-Declining-Balance Example

Rate = 2/5 = 40%

First year's depreciation:

$$55,000 * .40 = \boxed{22,000}$$

Double-Declining-Balance Example

Rate = 2/5 = 40%

First year's depreciation:

$$55,000 * .40 = \boxed{22,000}$$

Second year's depreciation:

$$33,000 * .40 = \boxed{13,200}$$

Comparison of Methods

- The total amount of depreciation recorded over the useful life of an asset is the same regardless of the method used.
- Depreciation expense recorded in any one period will vary according to method used.
- The straight-line method is used by about 95 percent of companies because it is easy to use and to explain.

Depreciation and Federal Income Tax

- Most corporations use the Modified Accelerated Cost Recovery System (MACRS) for tax purposes.

- MACRS provides for rapid write-off of an asset's cost in order to stimulate investment in modern facilities.

Revising Estimates of Salvage Value or of Useful Life

- When an estimate is revised, no changes are made to amounts reported in the past.
- The new estimates are incorporated into the **present** and **future** calculations only.
- Depreciation amounts are revised using the book value and the estimated useful life and salvage value at beginning of the year of the revision.

Continuing Expenditures for Plant Assets

- Expenditures made to keep an asset in good working order are **expensed** in the period in which they are incurred.
- Substantial costs spent to improve the quality or extend the life of an asset are **capitalized**.

Accounting for Capital Expenditures

- Extend the life?
  - viewed as canceling some of the previous depreciation
  - journal entry to reduce (debit) accumulated depreciation
  - new depreciation amount will be calculated

- Improve the quality?
  - viewed as an additional cost of the equipment
  - journal entry to increase (debit) the cost of the asset
  - new depreciation amount will be calculated

5-40

Disposal of Operational Assets

- Voluntary disposal refers to situations where a business gives up ownership of an asset by:
  - Sale
  - Trade-in
  - Retirement
- Involuntary disposal results because of a casualty such as a fire or an accident.

5-41

Disposal of Operational Assets

1. Update the depreciation on the asset to the date of disposal.
2. Compare the book value of the asset to the cash proceeds from the disposal. If the proceeds > book value, there is a gain on the disposal. If the book value > proceeds, then there is a loss on the sale.
3. Gains and losses go on the income statement.

5-42

Asset Disposal: Example

- Truck which was purchased for $10,000 and with accumulated depreciation of $8,000 was sold for $3,000.

- Compare the Book Value (10,000-8,000) to the cash proceeds (3,000).
- The difference is a gain or loss on the sale.
- Here it is a gain:
  Proceeds of $3,000 > BV of $2,000
- Gain of $1,000 goes to the income statement.

Asset Disposal: Example

- Truck which was purchased for $10,000 and with accumulated depreciation of $8,000 was sold for $1,000.

||||

- Compare the Book Value (10,000-8,000) to the cash proceeds (1,000).
- The difference is a gain or loss on the sale.
- Here it is a loss:
  Book value of $2,000 > Proceeds of $1,000
- Loss on disposal of $1,000 goes to the income statement.

|||| Disposal of Operational Assets

Compare cash received for the asset with the asset's book value (BV).

- If cash greater than BV, record a gain.
- If cash less than BV, record a loss.
- If cash equals BV, no gain or loss.

asset for sale

|||| Natural Resources

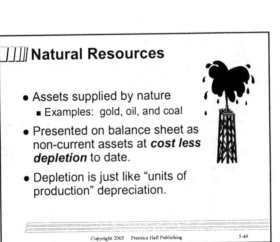

- Assets supplied by nature
  - Examples: gold, oil, and coal
- Presented on balance sheet as non-current assets at *cost less depletion* to date.
- Depletion is just like "units of production" depreciation.

Natural Resources

- Total cost of the asset is the cost of acquisition, exploration and development.
- Total cost is apportioned by means of **depletion** over periods in which resulting revenues are earned.

5-49

Natural Resources

A depletion rate is calculated using the units-of-production method.

Depletion Cost Per Unit Is Calculated As Follows:

$$\frac{\text{Total Cost of Natural Resource}}{\text{Estimated Number of Available Units of Natural Resource}}$$

5-50

Intangible Assets

- Noncurrent assets without physical substance that confer certain rights and privileges on the owner of the asset.
  - Examples: patents, copyrights, franchises and licenses, leaseholds, leasehold improvements, trademarks, and goodwill.
- Purchased intangible assets are recorded at cost.

5-51

Intangible Assets

- Purchased intangible assets are ***amortized*** over the shorter of their economic life or legal life, subject to a maximum of 40 years.
- Normally the straight-line method is used and the asset is reported in the balance sheet at book value without a related accumulated amortization account.

 5-52

Intangible Assets: Patents

- A patent is an exclusive right granted by federal government to sell or manufacture an invention.

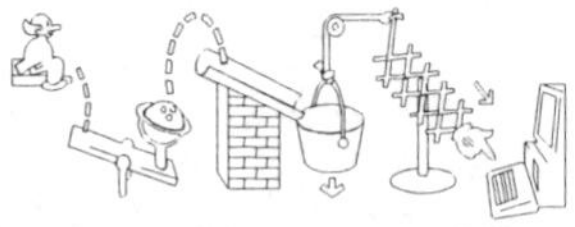

- A patent is amortized over the shorter of its useful life or 17-year legal life.

 5-53

Chapter 6

Acquisitions/Payment:
Inventory and Liabilities

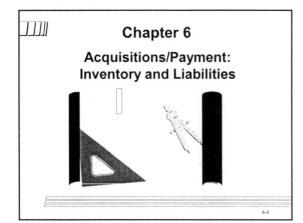

6-1

Questions we will answer in this chapter

- How does a firm account for inventory?
- How are financial statements affected by the purchase of merchandise inventory?
- What kinds of liabilities result from the acquisition of inventory and other resources?
- How does a firm account for payroll?

6-2

Inventory Cost

Inventory is recorded at the price paid for it.

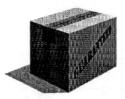

6-3

▯▯▯ Inventory Cost

- The amount recorded for inventory should include:
  - Invoice price, freight charges, inspection costs, and preparation costs.

- Inventory may be tracked with either a periodic or a perpetual inventory system.

6-4

▯▯▯ Cost of Goods Sold

Beginning inventory
Add: Purchases (net)
Goods available for sale
Deduct: Ending inventory
Cost of goods sold

6-5

▯▯▯ Inventory

- Inventory is tangible property that is held for resale or will be used in producing goods or services.
- Inventory is reported on the balance sheet as a current asset.
- Types of inventory:
  - Merchandise inventory
  - Raw materials inventory ⎫
  - Work in process inventory ⎬ These 3 will be studied in managerial accounting.
  - Finished goods inventory ⎭

6-6

Shipping Terms (Sales & Purchases)

- F.O.B. shipping point or destination
  - tells who pays shipping
- *F.O.B shipping* indicates that the title to the goods changes hands at shipping.
- *F.O.B. destination* indicates that the title to the goods changes hands at destination.

6-7

Shipping Costs

- Whoever owns the goods while they are in-transit pays for the shipping.
- Shipping costs to get the inventory IN are included as part of the cost of the inventory.
- Shipping costs for a sale are part of operating expenses.

6-8

Alternative Inventory Cost Flow Methods

FIFO

LIFO

Weighted Average

Specific Identification

6-9

Inventory Cost Flow Methods

These four inventory costing methods are used to assign the total dollar amount of goods available for sale between ending inventory and cost of goods sold.

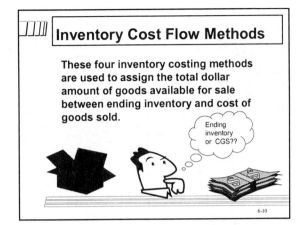

Ending inventory or CGS??

6-10

First-In, First-Out

- The cost of the **oldest** inventory items are charged to cost of goods sold when goods are sold.

- The cost of the **newest** inventory items remain in ending inventory.

- The actual physical flow of inventory items may differ from the FIFO cost flow assumptions.

6-11

Last-In, First-Out

- The cost of the newest inventory items are charged to cost of goods sold when goods are sold.

- The cost of the oldest inventory items remain in ending inventory.

- The actual physical flow of inventory items may differ from the LIFO cost flow assumptions.

6-12

⌿⌿⌿ Weighted-Average

- Take the average cost of all goods available for sale to value both CGS and Ending Inventory.
- BE SURE IT'S WEIGHTED!

6-13

⌿⌿⌿ Specific Identification

- Specific cost of each inventory item is known.

- Used with small volume, high dollar inventory.

6-14

⌿⌿⌿ Example

Date	Event	Units	Price	Total
3/1	Beg. Inv.	10	$ 6	$ 60
3/10	Purchase	12	7	84
3/15	Purchase	11	8	88
3/27	Sale	18	15	270

6-15

FIFO

● Cost of Goods Sold:

From	Units	Price	Cost

● Ending Inventory:

From	Units	Price	Cost

6-16

FIFO

Cost of Goods Sold:

From	Units	Price	Cost
3/1	10	$ 6	$ 60
3/10	8	7	56
Totals	18		$116

● Ending Inventory:

From	Units	Price	Cost
3/10	4	$ 7	$ 28
3/15	11	8	88
Totals	15		$116

6-17

LIFO

● Cost of Goods Sold:

From	Units	Price	Cost

● Ending Inventory:

From	Units	Price	Cost

6-18

LIFO

- **Cost of Goods Sold:**

From	Units	Price	Cost
3/15	11	$ 8	$ 88
3/10	7	7	49
Totals	18		$137

- **Ending Inventory:**

From	Units	Price	Cost
3/10	5	$ 7	$ 35
3/1	10	6	60
Totals	15		$ 95

6-19

Weighted Average

Average cost per unit:

$$\frac{\text{Cost of GAFS}}{\text{\# of units GAFS}} \Longrightarrow \boxed{}$$

6-20

Weighted Average

Average cost per unit:

$$\frac{\text{Cost of GAFS} \quad \$\ 232}{\text{\# of units GAFS} \Longrightarrow \quad 33} = \$7.03$$

Cost of Goods Sold:

Ending Inventory:

6-21

⫿⫿⫿ Weighted Average

Average cost per unit:

$$\frac{\text{Cost of GAFS} \qquad \$\,232}{\text{\# of units GAFS} \implies 33} = \$7.03$$

Cost of Goods Sold:

    18 units @ $7.03 = $127 (rounded)

Ending Inventory:

6-22

⫿⫿⫿ Weighted Average

Average cost per unit:

$$\frac{\text{Cost of GAFS} \qquad \$\,232}{\text{\# of units GAFS} \implies 33} = \$7.03$$

Cost of Goods Sold:

    18 units @ $7.03 = $127 (rounded)

Ending Inventory:

    15 units @ $7.03 = $105 (rounded)

6-23

⫿⫿⫿ Income Statements

[Given operating expenses of $50 and a 40% tax rate]

	FIFO	LIFO	Wt. Avg.
Sales			
CGS			
GM			
Oper. exp.			
Pretax inc.			
Taxes (40%)			
Net Income			

6-24

Income Statements

[Given operating expenses of $50 and a 40% tax rate]

	FIFO	LIFO	Wt. Avg.
Sales	$270	$270	$ 270
CGS	116	137	127
GM	154	133	143
Oper. exp.	50	50	50
Pretax inc.	104	83	93
Taxes (40%)	42	33	37
Net Income	$ 62	$ 50	$ 56

6-25

Cash Flow from Operations

	FIFO	LIFO	Wt. Avg.
Inflows:			
Sales	$270	$270	$270
Outflows:			
Purchases	172	172	172
Oper. exp.	50	50	50
Taxes (40%)	42	33	37
Net cash flow	$ 6	$ 15	$ 11

6-26

Summary:
Effects of Cost Flow Assumptions

- Effects on financial statements
  - cost of goods sold & gross profit
  - taxes
  - net earnings
  - inventory
- Effects on cash flows
  - cash flows are affected only because of taxes

6-27

Comparison of Methods

- Each of the four methods is acceptable, and an argument can be made for using each.

- The choice of an inventory method will depend on management's incentives, the tax laws, and the reporting company's particular economic circumstances.

6-28

Consistency Principle

Because the choice of an inventory method can significantly affect the financial statements, a company might be inclined to select a new method each year that would result in the most favorable financial statements. However . . .

6-29

Consistency Principle

. . . the consistency principle requires that companies use the same accounting methods period after period so the financial statements of succeeding periods will be comparable.

6-30

Alternative Inventory Costing Methods in Practice

The LIFO conformity rule states that if LIFO is used for taxes, then LIFO must also be used for financial reporting.

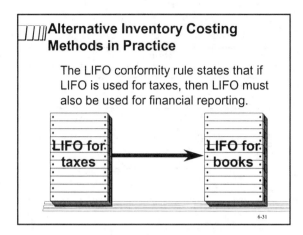

LIFO for taxes → LIFO for books

6-31

Terms of Sale and Purchases

- 2/10, n/30 (for example)
  - 2% discount if invoice paid in ten days
  - tells when and how much must be paid
  - high interest cost of not taking purchase discounts

6-32

Income Statements

Revenues
− Expenses
Net Income

Multistep Income Statement

Sales
− Cost of Goods Sold

Gross margin
− **Operating Expenses**

Income before taxes
− **Income Taxes**

Net income

6-33

Costs of Goods Sold

- Cost of goods sold is calculated as the number of units sold during the period multiplied by their unit costs.
- Cost of goods sold is a major expense item for most nonservice businesses.
- The measurement of cost of goods sold is an excellent example of the application of the matching principle.

6-34

Perpetual Inventory Systems

- The inventory account is continuously updated for the following items:
  - Purchases
  - Returns & Allowances
  - Sales
- Detailed record-keeping has become much easier with current technology.
- A physical count of the inventory is still required at the end of the accounting period to assure accurate inventory records in case of errors or theft.

6-35

Periodic Inventory Systems

- The ending inventory is determined at the end of the period by taking a physical count of the goods remaining on hand.
- Cost of goods sold is calculated at the end of the accounting period using the ending inventory count.

6-36

Periodic Inventory Systems

- Because entries are not made to the inventory account during the accounting period, the amount of inventory is not known until the end of the period, when the inventory count is done.
- This system is being used less and less due to advancements in technology.

6-37

Accounting and Inventory Management

The accounting system plays three roles in inventory management:

- Provides accurate information for financial statements and tax reports.
- Provides up-to-date information on inventory quantities and cost.
- Provides information necessary to protect inventory from theft and misuse.

6-38

Financial Statement Analysis

- Inventory Turnover

$$\text{Inventory Turnover} = \frac{\text{Cost of Goods Sold}}{\text{Average Inventory}}$$

This ratio is often used to measure the liquidity (nearness to cash) of the inventory.

6-39

Gross Profit Method of Estimating Inventory

- Provides an <u>estimate</u>
- Not acceptable for GAAP
- When to use
  - for interim reporting purposes
  - when physical inventory not possible

6-40

Example

Given the following:

Beginning Inventory	$ 1,000	(cost)
Purchases	9,000	(cost)
Sales	12,000	(retail)

Historically, gross margin has been 40% of sales. Estimate the cost of inventory and CGS for the period.

6-41

<u>First</u> estimate cost of goods sold:

Sales have been $12,000, and the gross margin has been 40%. If the gross margin is $4,800 (40% of $12,000), then the cost of goods sold must be the remainder, $7,200.

6-42

Next estimate ending inventory:
Goods avail. (1,000 + 9,000)
- Cost of goods sold
Ending inventory

$10,000 minus $7,200 =
$2,800

6-43

Recap

First estimate cost of goods sold:

Sales	12,000
x CGS % (1.0 - GM %)	60%
Estimated CGS	7,200

Next estimate ending inventory:

Goods avail. (1,000 + 9,000)	10,000
- Cost of goods sold	7,200
Estimated ending inventory	2,800

6-44

Lower of Cost or Market

- Ending inventory is reported at the lower of cost or market (LCM).

- Market refers to the replacement cost of the merchandise.

- This practice is in keeping with the generally accepted accounting principle of conservatism.

6-45

║║║║ Errors in Measuring Ending Inventory

- Misstatements in inventory may cause errors in the following areas:
  - Income Statement
    - » **Cost of Goods Sold, Gross Profit, Net Income**
  - Balance Sheet
    - » **Inventory, Payables, Retained Earnings**
- Because the ending inventory of one period becomes the beginning inventory of the next period, ending inventory errors affect two accounting periods.

6-46

║║║║ Inventory Errors

The ending inventory for CBCR Co. was overstated by $2000 for the year 2002. What effect did the error have on

- Beginning inventory 2002:
- Purchases in 2002:
- Goods available for sale in 2002:
- Cost of Goods Sold in 2002:
- Gross margin in 2002:
- Net income in 2002:

6-47

║║║║ Inventory Errors

The ending inventory for CBCR Co. was overstated by $2000 for the year 2002. What effect did the error have on

- Beginning inventory 2002: **no effect**
- Purchases in 2002: **no effect**
- Goods available for sale in 2002: **no effect**
- Cost of Goods Sold in 2002: **understated**
- Gross margin in 2002: **overstated**
- Net income in 2002: **overstated**

6-48

The Next Year

- Beginning inventory 2003:
- Purchases for 2003:
- Goods available for sale in 2003:
- Cost of Goods Sold for 2003:
- Gross margin for 2003:
- Net income for 2003:

6-49

The Next Year

- Beginning inventory 2003: **overstated**
- Purchases for 2003: **no effect**
- Goods available for sale in 2003: **overstated**
- Cost of Goods Sold for 2003: **overstated**
- Gross margin for 2003: **understated**
- Net income for 2003: **understated**

6-50

Example: Periodic vs. Perpetual

- BI   15 units @ $20 each
- 1/5/95 purchased   20 units @ $21 each
- 3/6/95 sold   10 units
- 5/16/95 purchased   30 units @ $22 each
- 7/5/95 sold   20 units
- 9/3/95 purchased   10 units @ $23 each

Calculate Ending Inventory and Cost of Goods
Sold under
  1-FIFO perpetual
  2-FIFO periodic
  3-LIFO perpetual
  4-LIFO periodic

6-51

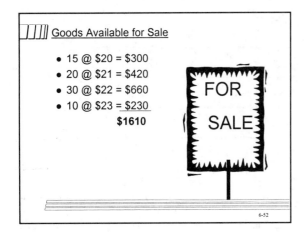

Goods Available for Sale

- 15 @ $20 = $300
- 20 @ $21 = $420
- 30 @ $22 = $660
- 10 @ $23 = $230
  $1610

FOR SALE

6-52

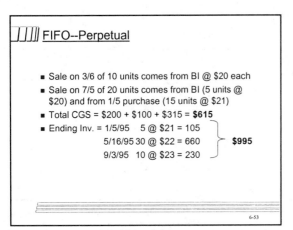

FIFO--Perpetual

- Sale on 3/6 of 10 units comes from BI @ $20 each
- Sale on 7/5 of 20 units comes from BI (5 units @ $20) and from 1/5 purchase (15 units @ $21)
- Total CGS = $200 + $100 + $315 = **$615**
- Ending Inv. = 1/5/95   5 @ $21 = 105
  5/16/95 30 @ $22 = 660   } **$995**
  9/3/95   10 @ $23 = 230

6-53

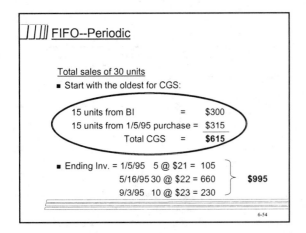

FIFO--Periodic

Total sales of 30 units
- Start with the oldest for CGS:

  15 units from BI   = $300
  15 units from 1/5/95 purchase = $315
           Total CGS   =   **$615**

- Ending Inv. = 1/5/95   5 @ $21 = 105
  5/16/95 30 @ $22 = 660   } **$995**
  9/3/95   10 @ $23 = 230

6-54

⫽⫽⫽ LIFO--Perpetual

- Sale on 3/6 of 10 units comes from 1/5 purchase (the most recent one at the time of the sale): **$210**
- Sale on 7/5 of 20 units comes from 5/16 purchase: **$440**
- Total CGS = $210 + $440 = **$650**
- Ending Inv. = BI   15 @ $20 = $300
           1/5/95   10 @ $21 =   210
           5/16/95 10 @ $22 =   220   **$960**
           9/3/95   10 @ $23 =   230

6-55

⫽⫽⫽ LIFO--Periodic

Total sales of 30 units
- Start with the latest purchases for CGS:

     10 units from 9/3/95 purchase   = $230
     20 units from 5/16/95 purchase = $440
             Total CGS   =   **$670**

- Ending Inv. =   BI   15 @ $20 = $300
           1/5/95   20 @ $21 = $420
           5/16/95   10 @ $22 = $220
                        $940

6-56

⫽⫽⫽ Ratios: Gross Margin Percentage

- Gross margin %:

  - *gross margin as a percent of sales*

  - Net sales - CGS (=gross margin)
               Net sales

6-57

Ratios: Return on Sales

- Return on sales =

$$\frac{\text{Net income}}{\text{Net sales}} =$$

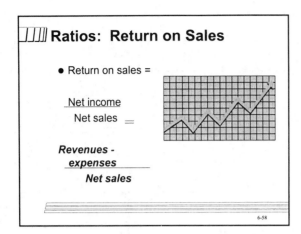

$$\frac{\text{Revenues -}}{\text{expenses}}$$

$$\frac{}{\text{Net sales}}$$

6-58

Ratios: Return on Assets

$$\text{Return on Assets} = \frac{\text{Net Income}}{\text{Assets}}$$

6-59

Chapter 7
Sales and Collection Cycle

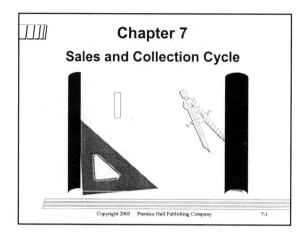

7-1

Sales And Services Are The Backbone Of Any Business

- Sales forecasts are the starting point for making any plans for the business.

- New ways of making sales are becoming very important to businesses.

7-2

Receiving Orders

- In person
- By mail
- By phone
- By fax
- By computer
  - Ordering merchandise over the internet is becoming a very significant portion of many businesses.

7-3

Selecting And Preparing Goods For Delivery

- Increasing automation is reducing inventory costs and decreasing delivery time.
- Have you benefited from these trends?
- How does a business benefit?

Receiving Payment For Goods And Services

- Cash (includes checks): control is the biggest issue
- Credit card sales
- Credit: accounts receivable
  - Bad debts

Controlling CASH

- Cash has universal appeal and ownership is difficult to prove.
- Both cash receipts and cash payments should be recorded immediately when received and made.
- Checks should be prenumbered and kept secure.

Safeguarding Cash

- Separation of duties
  - Different people receive and disburse the cash.
  - Procedures for the record keeping of cash receipts and disbursements are separate.
  - Handling the cash and record keeping are completely separate.

Procedures To Have In Place

- Both cash receipts and cash payments should be recorded immediately when received and made.
- Keep cash under strict physical control, and deposit cash receipts daily.
- Have separate approvals for purchases and the payment for those purchases.

Procedures

- Use pre-numbered checks, and keep a log of electronic transfers.
- Payment approval, check signing, and electronic funds transfer should be assigned to different individuals.
- Bank accounts and cash balances should be reconciled monthly.

Accounting For Cash:
Reconciling The Bank Statement

- An important part of internal control
- Need for calculating a *true* cash balance
- Two "sides" to be reconciled
  - balance per bank
  - balance per books
- If there are any mistakes or transactions that have not been recorded in the company's books, the company's records should be updated.

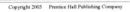

Terminology

Bank statement

Monthly report prepared by bank that contains details of a company's deposits, disbursements, and bank charges.

Bank reconciliation

Report prepared by the company after receiving the bank statement that compares the bank statement with the company's records to verify the accuracy of both.

More Terminology

Outstanding check

A check written by the company that has been recorded on the company's records but has not yet cleared the bank

Deposit in transit

A deposit that the company has made and recorded, but it has not reached the bank's record keeping system yet.

More Terminology

NSF check

A "bad" check written by a customer that must be deducted from the company's records. The company recorded the check as a cash receipt (and then deposited it), but the check writer didn't have the money in his or her account to cover it. The bank will have already deducted it from the company's balance (in the bank's records), but the company will have to make an adjustment to their records.

7-13

More Terminology

Credit memo

An addition to the company's balance in the bank's records for a reason such as the bank having collected a note for the company (from a third party who owed the company).

Debit memo

A deduction from the company's balance in the bank's records for a reason such as a bank service charge.

7-14

An Example Of A Reconciliation

Given the following information:

Balance per bank at 4/30	$8,750
Balance per books at 4/30	6,900
Outstanding checks at 4/30	1,380
Bank service charge for April	30
Deposit in transit at 4/30	400
Customer's NSF check	100
(returned with bank statement)	
Bank collected note receivable	1,000 for
company	

7-15

Balance Per Bank Section Of The Reconciliation

Balance per bank	$8,750
Plus: Deposit in transit	400
Less: Outstanding checks	(1,380)
Cash Balance at 4/30	$7,770

7-16

Balance Per Books Section Of The Reconciliation

Balance per books	$6,900
Plus: Note collected by bank	1,000
Less: NSF check returned	(100)
Service charge	(30)
Cash balance at 4/30	$7,770

7-17

There Is One True Cash Balance

- Bank balance per statement is reconciled to the TRUE cash balance
- Book balance (company's records) is reconciled to the TRUE cash balance

7-18

Cash (Bank) Reconciliation Has Two "Independent" Parts

Balance per bank	Balance per books
++ deposits in transit	++ collections for us made by the bank
++	++
-- outstanding checks	-- NSF checks (from customers)
--	-- Service charges
True cash balance	True cash balance

Accounts And Notes Receivable

- A/R are the expected future cash receipts of a company. They are typically small and are expected to be received within 30 days.
- N/R are used when longer credit terms are necessary. The note specifies the maturity date, the rate of interest, and other credit terms.

Value Of Receivables

- Receivables are reported at their face value less an allowance for accounts which are likely to be uncollectible.
- The amount which is actually expected to be collected is called the net realizable value (NRV).
- GAAP requires that A/R be reported at NRV.

Two Methods

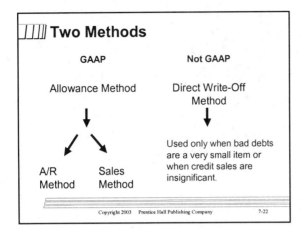

GAAP | Not GAAP

Allowance Method | Direct Write-Off Method

A/R Method   Sales Method | Used only when bad debts are a very small item or when credit sales are insignificant.

7-22

The Most Common Method

Allowance method

- Estimate the bad debt expense as an adjustment when it is time to prepare the financial statements.
- Record the amount as a reduction in ACCOUNTS RECEIVABLE, even though you don't know whose accounts will be "bad."

7-23

Allowance Method, continued

- We will base the estimate on:
  » Sales, or
  » Accounts Receivable
- This method attempts to match the expense (bad debt) with the revenue (sale) by recording the expense in the same period as the sale even though the company has not specifically identified which accounts will go unpaid.

7-24

⊞ The Other Method

Direct Write-Off

- No estimates of bad debts are made.
- Only when a specific account is known to be uncollectible (customer files bankruptcy, for example) is bad debt expense recorded.
- This doesn't do a very good job of matching the revenue (sale) with the expense (bad debt), because a company often discovers an account is uncollectible in a period subsequent to the one in which the sale was made.

⊞ Transaction Analysis

- Assume the following selected events occurred at Cell-It. For each event:
  - Determine how the accounting equation was affected.
  - Determine the effect on the financial statements.

⊞ 1. Provided services to customers for $9,000, on account.

Assets	=	Liab.	+	Cont. Cap.	+	Ret. Earnings
+9000						+9000

- Income Statement: Increases income
- Statement of Changes in Equity: Increases equity
- Statement of Cash Flows: No effect on cash flow

2. Collected $6,000 Cash From Account Receivable.

Assets	=	Liab.	+	Cont. Cap.	+	Ret. Earnings

+6000
(6000)

- Income Statement: **no effect on income**
- Statement of Changes in Equity: **no effect on equity**
- Statement of Cash Flows: **increases cash flow**

Copyright 2003   Prentice Hall Publishing Company   7-28

---

3. At year-end it was estimated that $200 of accounts receivable will never be collected.

Assets	=	Liab.	+	Cont. Cap.	+	Ret. Earnings

(200)   (200)

- Income Statement: **Decreases income**
- Statement of Changes in Equity: **Decreases equity**
- Statement of Cash Flows: **No effect on cash flow**

Copyright 2003   Prentice Hall Publishing Company   7-29

How Do We Report AR On The Balance Sheet?

Net Realizable Value of AR = what we expect to collect

On the balance sheet:

Accounts Receivable	$3,000
less allowance for uncollectible accounts	(200)
Net AR	$2,800

Copyright 2003   Prentice Hall Publishing Company   7-30

7-10

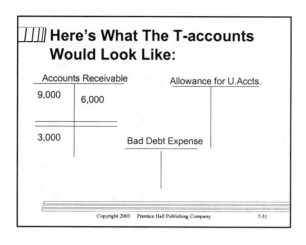

Here's What The T-accounts Would Look Like:

Accounts Receivable

9,000	6,000
3,000	

Allowance for U.Accts.

Bad Debt Expense

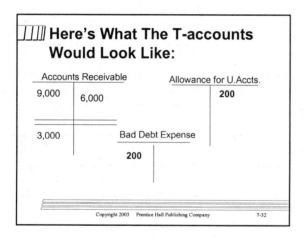

Here's What The T-accounts Would Look Like:

Accounts Receivable

9,000	6,000
3,000	

Allowance for U.Accts.

| | 200 |

Bad Debt Expense

| 200 | |

4. The $50 account receivable of Jane Doe was written-off as uncollectible.

Assets	=	Liab.	+	Cont. Cap.	+	Ret. Earnings
+50						
(50)						

- Income Statement: **no effect on income**
- Statement of Changes in Equity: **no effect on equity**
- Statement of Cash Flows: **no effect on cash flow**

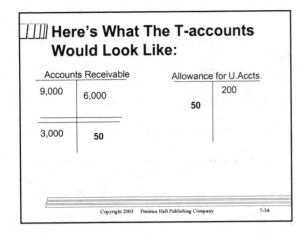

Here's What The T-accounts Would Look Like:

Accounts Receivable		Allowance for U.Accts.
9,000	6,000	200
		50
3,000	50	

Effect of Transaction 4 on
AR Net Realizable Value

Before Event 4		After Event 4	
AR	$3,000	AR	$2,950
Allow.	200	Allow.	150
N.R.V.	$2,800	N.R.V.	$2,800

Net realizable value of accounts receivable did not change as a result of the write-off.

An Example

- Two years of transactions
  - Effect on accounting equation
  - Financial statements

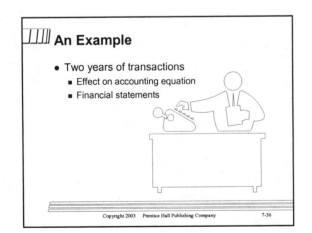

1. Provided $5,000 Services On Account.

Assets = Liab. + Cont. Cap. + Ret. Earnings

+5000 A/R	+5000 Sales Revenue

- Income Statement: **Increases income**
- Statement of Changes in Equity: **Increases equity**
- Statement of Cash Flows: **No effect on cash flow**

2. Collected $4,000 Cash From Accounts Receivable.

Assets = Liab. + Cont. Cap. + Ret. Earnings

+4000 cash
(4000) A/R

- Income Statement: **No effect**
- Statement of Changes in Equity: **No effect**
- Statement of Cash Flows: **Increases cash flow**

3. Adjusting Entry Booked To Reflect The Estimate Of 5% Of Ending A/R To Be Uncollectible.

Assets = Liab. + C C. + Ret. Earnings

(50) Allowance	(50) Bad Debt Expense

- Income Statement: **Decreases income**
- Statement of Changes in Equity: **Decreases equity**
- Statement of Cash Flows: **No effect on cash flow**

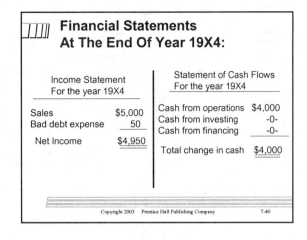

Financial Statements
At The End Of Year 19X4:

Income Statement For the year 19X4		Statement of Cash Flows For the year 19X4	
Sales	$5,000	Cash from operations	$4,000
Bad debt expense	50	Cash from investing	-0-
		Cash from financing	-0-
Net Income	$4,950		
		Total change in cash	$4,000

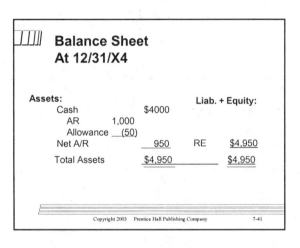

Balance Sheet
At 12/31/X4

Assets:			Liab. + Equity:	
Cash		$4000		
AR	1,000			
Allowance	(50)			
Net A/R		950	RE	$4,950
Total Assets		$4,950		$4,950

1-b. Wrote Off A $40 A/R
That Was Determined To
Be Uncollectible

Assets = Liab. + Cont. Cap. + Ret. Earnings

| (40) AR |
| +40 Allowance |

- Income Statement: **No effect**
- Statement of Changes in Equity: **No effect**
- Statement of Cash Flows: **No effect**

2-b. Provided $6,000 Worth Of Services On Account.

Assets = Liab. + Cont. Cap. + Ret. Earnings

| +6000 AR | | | +6000 revenue |

- Income Statement: **Increases incomes**
- Statement of Changes in Equity: **Increases equity**
- Statement of Cash Flows: **No effect on cash flow**

    7-43

3-b. Collected $4,500 Cash From Accounts Receivable.

Assets = Liab. + Cont. Cap. + Ret. Earnings

| +4500 Cash |
| (4500) AR |

- Income Statement: No effect
- Statement of Changes in Equity: No effect
- Statement of Cash Flows: Increases cash flow

    7-44

4-b. Adjusted the accounting records to reflect the expectation that 5% of the ending AR balance would be uncollectible. (Balance is $2460.)

Assets = Liab. + Cont. Cap. + Ret. Earnings

- Income Statement:
- Statement of Changes in Equity:
- Statement of Cash Flows:

    7-45

⫿⫿⫿ Where Do We Stand?

We overestimated bad debts by $10--we estimated $50 but we only wrote off $40 in the subsequent year.

This year our estimate is 5% of $2460 (BB 1,000 + 6,000 credit sales - $4,500 collections -$40 accounts written off)= **$123**. But since we overestimated last year, we only need to record **$113** this year.

⫿⫿⫿ 4.b Adjusted The Accounting Records To Reflect the Expectation That 5% Of The Ending AR Balance Would Be Uncollectible.

Assets	=	Liab.	+	Cont. Cap.	+	Ret. Earnings
(113) allowance for doubtful accounts						(113) bad debt expense

- Income Statement: **Decreases incomes**
- Statement of Changes in Equity: **Decreases equity**
- Statement of Cash Flows: **No effect on cash flow**

⫿⫿⫿ To summarize:

- Two methods:
  - the allowance method
  - the direct write-off method
- Which one involves estimating future uncollectibles?

Summary Of The Allowance Method Continued

- One way to estimate bad debt expense is to use a percentage of ending A/R (or an aging schedule)
- When an actual account is written off as uncollectible, it is credited out of A/R and debited out of the Allowance. **THERE IS NO NET EFFECT ON ASSETS** and **NO EXPENSE** at the time of the write-off.

Other Accounting Issues Related to Sales: Warranty Costs

- Why give warranties?
- *When* should expense be recognized?

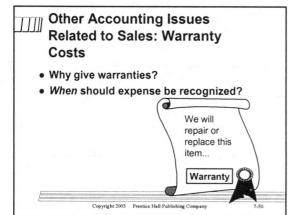

We will repair or replace this item...

Warranty

Warranties

- How is the warranty obligation met and subsequently removed from the balance sheet?
- How do all of the above affect financial statements?
- What other issues are similar to warranties?

Transaction Analysis

- Assume the following selected events occurred at Cell-It. For each event:
  - Determine how the accounting equation was affected.
  - Determine the effect on the financial statements.
  - Record the event in t-accounts.

---

1. Sold Merchandise For $5,000 Cash That Had Originally Cost $4,000. These Goods Were Sold With A Two-year Warranty.

Assets	=	Liab.	+	Cont. Cap.	+	Ret. Earnings
+5000						+5000
(4000)						(4000)

- Income Statement: **Increases incomes**
- Statement of Changes in Equity: **Increases equity**
- Statement of Cash Flows: **No effect on cash flow**

---

2. Estimated That $100 Of Warranty Cost Will Be Incurred Over The Next Two Years On The Goods Sold In Transaction 1.

Assets	=	Liab.	+	Cont. Cap.	+	Ret. Earnings
		+100				(100)

- Income Statement: **Decreases incomes**
- Statement of Changes in Equity: **Decreases equity**
- Statement of Cash Flows: **No effect on cash flow**

3. A Customer Returned Goods Under Warranty For Repair. The Cost Of The Repair Was $30 Cash.

Assets = Liab. + Cont. Cap. + Ret. Earnings

(30)	(30)

- Income Statement: **No effect on income**
- Statement of Changes in Equity: **No effect on equity**
- Statement of Cash Flows: **Decreases cash flow**

7-55

Chapter 8

Special Acquisitions:
Financing A Business with Debt

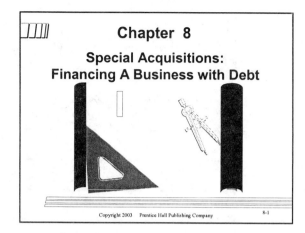

8-1

Business Background

Capital structure is the mix of debt and equity used to finance a company.

DEBT:

Loans from banks, insurance companies, or pension funds are often used when borrowing small amounts of capital.

Bonds are debt securities issued when borrowing large amounts of money.

> **Can be issued by either corporations or governmental units.**

8-2

Notes Payable and Mortgages

- When a company borrows money from the bank for longer than a year, the obligation is called a long-term note payable.
- A mortgage is a special kind of "note" payable--one issued for property.
- These obligations are frequently repaid in equal installments, part of which are repayment of **principal** and part of which are **interest**.

8-3

How Borrowing Money With A Long-term Note Affects The Accounting Equation

When the note is issued (when the money is borrowed):

Assets	=	Liabilities + OE
+ cash	=	+ N/P

How Borrowing Money With A Long-term Note Affects The Accounting Equation

When a payment (that is MORE than the interest) is made:

Assets = Liabilities + OE

-cash	-N/P	- interest expense
	(a little part)	(for the period)

Example: Borrowing To Buy Land By Using A Mortgage

- ABC Co. signed a $100,000, 3 yr. mortgage (for a piece of land) which carried an 8% annual interest rate. Payments are to be made annually on December 31 of each year for $38,803.35.
- What is the amount of the liability (**mortgage payable**) *after* the first payment is made?

Example continued...

- For Yr.1, the outstanding amount borrowed is $100,000 (at 8%), so the interest is:
  - **$8,000**
- Payment is $38,803.35, so the amount that will reduce the principal is
  - **$30,803.35**
- New outstanding principal amount is
  - $100,000 - 30,803.35 = **$69,196.65**

8-7

Amortization Schedule

Principle Balance	Payment	Interest	Reduction in Principle
100,000.00	38,803.35	8,000.00	38,803.35
69,196.65	38,803.35	5,535.73*	33,267.62
35,929.03	38,803.35	2,874.32**	35,929.03

*69,196.65 x .08   **35,929.03 x .08   = 2,874.32

8-8

Time Value of Money

- The example of the mortgage demonstrates that money has value over time.
- When you borrow $100,000 and pay it back over three years, you have to pay back MORE than $100,000.
- Your repayment includes interest--the cost of using someone else's money.
- A dollar received today is worth more than a dollar received in the future.
- The sooner your money can earn interest, the faster the interest can earn interest.

8-9

Interest and Compound Interest

- **Interest** is the return you receive for investing your money. You are actually "lending" your money, so you are paid for letting someone else use your money.
- **Compound interest** -- is the interest that your investment earns on the interest that your investment previously earned.

8-10

Future Value of a Single Amount

How much will today's dollar be worth in the future?

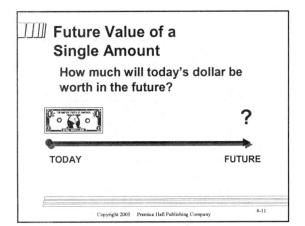

TODAY   FUTURE

8-11

If You Deposit $100 In An Account Earning 6%, How Much Would You Have In The Account After 1 Year?

PV = [100]   FV = [106]

0   1

| $\underline{n}$:i% = 6 | PV = 100 |
| N = 1 | FV = 100 * 1.06 |

8-12

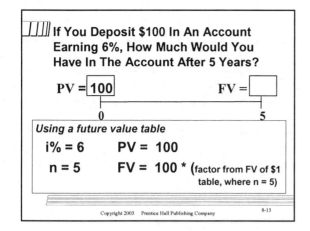

If You Deposit $100 In An Account Earning 6%, How Much Would You Have In The Account After 5 Years?

PV = 100   FV = [ ]

0   5

Using a future value table

i% = 6   PV = 100

n = 5   FV = 100 * (factor from FV of $1 table, where n = 5)

8-13

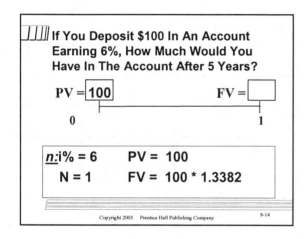

If You Deposit $100 In An Account Earning 6%, How Much Would You Have In The Account After 5 Years?

PV = 100   FV = [ ]

0   1

*n:*i% = 6   PV = 100

N = 1   FV = 100 * 1.3382

8-14

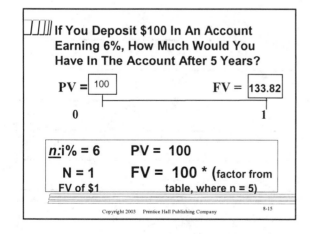

If You Deposit $100 In An Account Earning 6%, How Much Would You Have In The Account After 5 Years?

PV = 100   FV = 133.82

0   1

*n:*i% = 6   PV = 100

N = 1   FV = 100 * (factor from

FV of $1   table, where n = 5)

8-15

The Value of a Series of Payments

- The previous example had a single payment. Sometimes there is a series of payments.
- Annuity: a sequence of equal cash flows, occurring at the end of each period.
- When the payments occur at the end of the period, the annuity is also known as an *ordinary annuity*.
- When the payments occur at the beginning of the period, the annuity is called an *annuity due*.

8-16

What An Annuity Looks Like

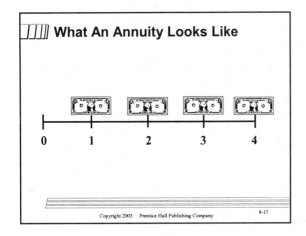

8-17

Example

- If you borrow money to buy a house or a car, you will pay a stream of equal payments.

- That's an annuity.

8-18

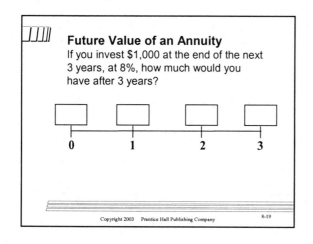

Future Value of an Annuity

If you invest $1,000 at the end of the next 3 years, at 8%, how much would you have after 3 years?

| | 0 | 1 | 2 | 3 |

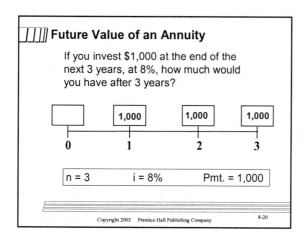

Future Value of an Annuity

If you invest $1,000 at the end of the next 3 years, at 8%, how much would you have after 3 years?

| | 1,000 | 1,000 | 1,000 |
| 0 | 1 | 2 | 3 |

| n = 3 | i = 8% | Pmt. = 1,000 |

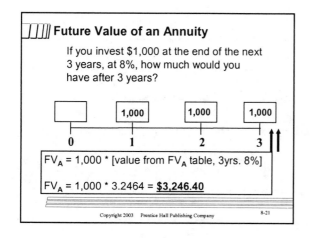

Future Value of an Annuity

If you invest $1,000 at the end of the next 3 years, at 8%, how much would you have after 3 years?

| | 1,000 | 1,000 | 1,000 |
| 0 | 1 | 2 | 3 |

$FV_A = 1,000 * [\text{value from } FV_A \text{ table, 3yrs. 8\%}]$

$FV_A = 1,000 * 3.2464 = \underline{\textbf{\$3,246.40}}$

Future Value of an Ordinary Annuity (Annuity in Arrears)

In the previous example, notice that the last payment is deposited on the last day of the last period. That means it doesn't have time to earn any interest! This type of annuity is called an ordinary annuity, or an annuity in arrears.

Future Value of an Annuity Due

- Often, when the series of payments applies to money saved, an annuity due is a better description of what happens.
- Suppose you decide to save $1,000 each year for three years, starting TODAY!

Future Value of an Annuity Due

If you invest $1,000 at the *beginning* of each of the next 3 years, at 8%, how much would you have after 3 years?   Future value

$FV_A = 1,000 * $ [value from FV_{ADue} table, 3yrs. 8%]

$FV_A = 1,000 * 3.50611 = $ **$3,506.11**

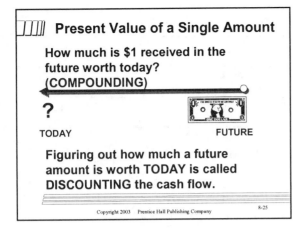

Present Value of a Single Amount

How much is $1 received in the future worth today?
(COMPOUNDING)

?

TODAY   FUTURE

Figuring out how much a future amount is worth TODAY is called DISCOUNTING the cash flow.

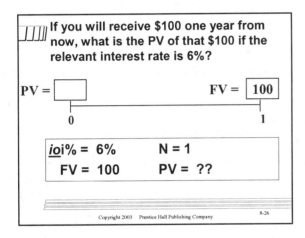

If you will receive $100 one year from now, what is the PV of that $100 if the relevant interest rate is 6%?

PV = [   ]   FV = [100]

0   1

_io_i% = 6%   N = 1
FV = 100   PV = ??

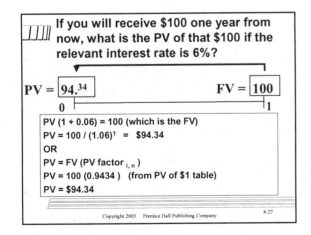

If you will receive $100 one year from now, what is the PV of that $100 if the relevant interest rate is 6%?

PV = [94.^{34}]   FV = [100]

0   1

PV (1 + 0.06) = 100 (which is the FV)
PV = $100 / (1.06)^1$ = $94.34
OR
PV = FV (PV factor $_{i, n}$)
PV = 100 (0.9434)   (from PV of $1 table)
PV = $94.34

The Value of a Series of Payments

- The previous example had a single payment. Sometimes there is a series of payments.
- Annuity: a sequence of equal cash flows, occurring at the end of each period.
- When the payments occur at the end of the period, the annuity is also known as an *ordinary annuity*.

8-28

Present Value of an Annuity

- Finding the present value of a series of cash flows is called *discounting the cash flows*.
- What is the series of future payments worth *today*?

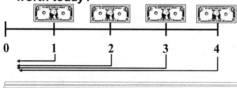

8-29

What is the PV of $1,000 at the end of each of the next 3 years, if the interest rate is 8%?

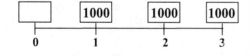

| i% = 8 | N = 3 |
| PMT = 1,000 | PV = ?? |

8-30

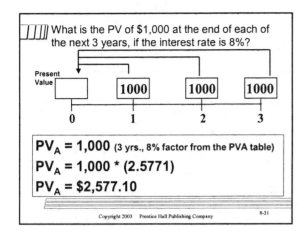

What is the PV of $1,000 at the end of each of the next 3 years, if the interest rate is 8%?

$PV_A = 1,000$ (3 yrs., 8% factor from the PVA table)

$PV_A = 1,000 * (2.5771)$

$PV_A = \$2,577.10$

8-31

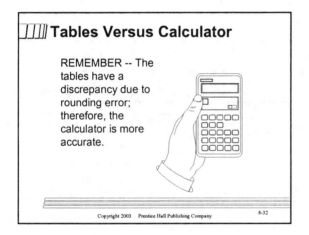

Tables Versus Calculator

REMEMBER -- The tables have a discrepancy due to rounding error; therefore, the calculator is more accurate.

8-32

Hint for Single Sum Problems

- In every single sum future value and present value problem, there are 4 variables:
- FV, PV, i, and n
- When doing problems, you will be given 3 of these variables and asked to solve for the 4th variable.
- Keeping this in mind makes "time value" problems much easier!

8-33

Hints for Annuity Problems

- In every problem, there are usually 3 amounts given:
  (1) amount of the cash flow,
  (2) interest rate (i%), and
  (3) the number of payments (n).

- First, determine if the annuity is an *ordinary annuity* (payments at the end of the period) or an *annuity due* (payments at the beginning of the period). Most calculators are programmed for ordinary annuities.

- Then, determine if you want the PRESENT value of the payments or the FUTURE value of the payments.

8-34

Characteristics of Bonds Payable

- Bonds usually involve the borrowing of a large sum of money, called principal.
- The principal is usually paid back as a lump sum at the end of the bond period.
- Individual bonds are often denominated with a par value, or face value, of $1,000.

8-35

Characteristics of Bonds Payable

- Bonds usually carry a stated rate of interest.
- Interest is normally paid semiannually.
- Interest is computed as:

Interest = Principal × Stated Rate × Time

8-36

Bonds

This is the information shown
on a bond certificate...

$1,000--principal
10%--interest rate (annual)
5yrs.--time to maturity
annual---interest payments

**The cash flows associated with the bonds are
defined by the terms on the face of the bond.**

8-37

Characteristics of Bonds Payable

- The new bondholder receives a
  bond certificate.
  - Identifies the par value, the stated
    interest rate, the interest dates, and
    the maturity date.
- The trustee makes sure the
  issuing company fulfills all of the
  provisions of the bond indenture,
  or agreement.

8-38

Bond Classifications

- Unsecured bonds (also called
  debentures) do not have pledged
  assets as a guarantee of repayment at
  maturity.
- Secured bonds include a pledge of
  specific assets as a guarantee of
  repayment at maturity.

8-39

Bond Classifications

- Ordinary bonds (also called single-payment bonds)
  - The full face amount is paid at the maturity.
- Serial bonds
  - The principal is paid in installments on a series of specified maturity dates.

8-40

Bond Classifications

- Callable bonds
  - May be retired and repaid (called) at any time at the option of the **issuer**.
- Redeemable bonds
  - May be turned in at any time for repayment at the option of the **bondholder**.
- Convertible bonds
  - May be exchanged for other securities of the issuer (usually shares of common stock) at the option of the **bondholder**.

8-41

Bond Classifications

- Registered bonds
  - Payment of interest is made by check and mailed directly to the bondholder whose name must be registered.
- Coupon bonds
  - Coupons are attached to the bond for each interest payment.
  - The bondholder "clips" each coupon and presents it for payment on the interest date.

8-42

Measuring Bonds Payable and Interest Expense

The selling price of the bond is determined by the market based on the time value of money.

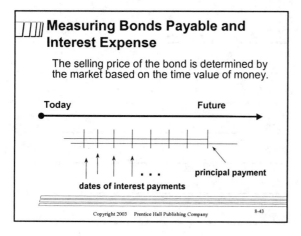

Measuring Bonds Payable and Interest Expense

- The interest rate used to compute the present value is the market interest rate.
  - Also called yield, effective rate, or true rate.
- Creditors demand a certain rate of interest to compensate them for the risks related to bonds.
- The stated rate, or coupon rate, is only used to compute the periodic interest payments.

Who Would Buy My Bond?

- $1,000, 6% stated rate.
- The market rate of interest is 8%.
- Who would buy my bond?
- Nobody---so I'll have to sell (issue) it at a *discount*.
- e.g., bondholders would give me something less for the bond.

ᒍᒌᒌᒉ Who Would Buy My Bond?

- $1,000, 6% stated rate.
- The market rate of interest is 4%.
- Who would buy these bonds?
- EVERYONE!
- So the market will bid up the price of the bond; e.g., I'll get a little **premium** for it since it has such good cash flows.
- Bondholders will pay more than the face.

Copyright 2003   Prentice Hall Publishing Company

8-46

ᒍᒌᒌᒉ Determining the Selling Price

- Bonds sell at:
  - **"Par" (100% of face value)**
  - **less than par (discount)**
  - **more than par (premium)**
- Market rate of interest vs. bond's stated rate of interest determines the selling price (market price of the bond)
- Therefore, if
  - **market % > stated %: Discount**
  - **market % < stated %: Premium**

Copyright 2003   Prentice Hall Publishing Company

8-47

ᒍᒌᒌᒉ The time value of money...

Selling price of a bond =

present value of future cash flows promised by the bonds, discounted using the market rate of interest

Copyright 2003   Prentice Hall Publishing Company

8-48

8-16

Finding The Proceeds Of A Bond Issue

- To calculate the issue price of a bond, you must find the present value of the cash flows associated with the bond.
- First, find the present value of the interest payments using the market rate of interest. Do this by finding the PV of an annuity.
- Then, find the present value of the principal payment at the end of the life of the bonds. Do this by finding the PV of a single amount.

Selling Bonds -- Example

On May 1, 1991, Clock Corp. sells $1,000,000 in bonds having a stated rate of 6% annually. The bonds mature in 10 years, and interest is paid semiannually. The market rate is 8% annually.

Determine the proceeds from this bond issue.

First, what are the cash flows associated with this bond?

- Interest payments of $60,000 (that's 6% of the $1 million face value) each year for 10 years.

AND

- A lump sum payment of $1,000,000 (the face amount of the bonds) in 10 years.

The PV of the future cash flows = issue price of the bonds

- The present value of these cash flows will be the issue price of the bonds.
- That is the amount of cash the bondholders are willing to give TODAY to receive these cash flows in the future.

Two parts to the cash flows:

INTEREST PAYMENTS	PRINCIPAL PAYMENT
PV of an ordinary annuity of $60,000 for 10 periods at an interest rate of 8%:	PV of a single amount of $1 million ten years in the future at 8%:
Use a calculator or a PV of an annuity table:	Use a calculator or a PV of a single amount table:
$60,000 (PV_{A, 8\%, 10})=$	$1,000,000 (PV_{, 8\%, 10}) =$
$60,000 (6.7101) =$	$1,000,000 (.46319)=$
402,606	463,190

Selling Bonds -- Example

- The sum of the PV of the two cash flows is $865,796.
- The bonds would be described as one that sold for "87." We'll round to a whole number just to make the example easier to follow.

What does that mean?

It means the bonds sold for 87% of their par or face value.

Selling Bonds -- Example

If the bonds sold for 87% of their face value, the proceeds would be approximately $870,000 (rounded) for $1,000,000-face bonds.

8-55

Recording Bonds Sold at a Discount

- The balance sheet would show the bonds at their face amount minus any discount.
- The discount on bonds payable is called a contra-liability, because it is deducted from the liability.
- Cash would be recorded for the difference, that is, the proceeds.

8-56

Recording Bonds Sold at a Discount

This is how the issue of the bonds would affect the accounting equation:

Assets	=	Liabilities	+	Owners' Equity
+ 870,000 cash		+1,000,000 bonds payable		
		(130,000) discount on bonds payable		

8-57

Selling Bonds -- Example

On May 1, 1991, Magic Inc. sells $1,000,000 in bonds having a stated rate of 9% annually. The bonds mature in 10 years and interest is paid semiannually. The market rate is 8% annually.

Determine the issue price of these bonds.

8-58

Selling Bonds -- Example

To figure out the proceeds from the sale, you either have to calculate the present value of the cash flows (using the market rate of interest)

OR

Be told that the bonds sold at X, a percentage of par (e.g., 104).

8-59

First, what are the cash flows associated with this bond?

- Interest payments of $90,000 (that's 9% of the $1 million face value) each year for 10 years.

AND

- A lump sum payment of $1,000,000 (the face amount of the bonds) in 10 years.

8-60

The PV of the future cash flows = issue price of the bonds

- The present value of these cash flows will be the issue price of the bonds.
- That is the amount of cash the bondholders are willing to give TODAY to receive these cash flows in the future.

8-61

Two Parts To The Cash Flows

INTEREST PAYMENTS	PRINCIPAL PAYMENT
PV of an ordinary annuity of $90,000 for 10 periods at an interest rate of 8%:	PV of a single amount of $1 million ten years in the future at 8%:
Use a calculator or a PV of an annuity table:	Use a calculator or a PV of a single amount table:
$90,000 (PV_{A,\,8\%,\,10})=$	$1,000,000 (PV_{,\,8\%,\,10}) =$
$90,000 (6.7101) =$	$1,000,000 (.46319) =$
$ 603,909	**$ 463,190**

8-62

Bonds Issued At A Premium

- The total PV of the two cash flows is $1,067,099. This is more than the face, so these bonds are being issued at a premium.
- Again, we'll round the number to make the example easier to follow. Let's say these bonds were issued at 107, or 107% of par.
- That would make the proceeds $1,070,000 (rounded).

8-63

Recording Bonds Sold at a Premium

The bonds payable will be recorded at the face value of $1 million.

The excess of the proceeds over the par value will be recorded in another liability account called premium on bonds payable. Together, these two amounts equal the book value or carrying value of the bonds.

Assets	=	Liabilities	=	Owners' Equity
$1,070,000 cash		$1,000,000 bonds payable		
		70,000 premium on bonds payable		

Measuring and Recording Interest on Bonds Issued at a Discount

- The discount must be amortized over the outstanding life of the bonds.
- The discount amortization increases the periodic interest expense for the issuer.
- Two methods are commonly used:
  - Effective-interest amortization
  - Straight-line amortization

Recall the Facts of the Problem

- Clock corp. Sold their bonds on may 1, 1991 at 87. The bonds have a 10-year maturity and $30,000 interest is paid semiannually.

- Why would the bonds sell for 87?
  - The market rate of interest was **greater** than the rate on the face on the date of issue.
  - **So clock corp. Had to offer the bonds at a "discount" to get buyers.**

Problem, Continued

- Clock Corp. sold their bonds on May 1, 1991 at 87. The bonds have a 10-year maturity and $30,000 interest is paid semiannually.
- Where did the $30,000 come from?
  - 1,000,000 x .06 x 1/2
    - The interest payments are always calculated by the terms and amounts stated on the face of the bonds.

Effective Interest Method For Amortizing A Bond Discount

If we prepared a balance sheet on the date of issue, the bond would be reported like this:

Bonds Payable	$ 1,000,000
less Discount on B/P	(130,000)
Net Bonds Payable	870,000

Effective Interest Method For Amortizing A Bond Discount

- The discount is a contra-liability (and is deducted from the face value of the bond to give the "book value.")
- In order to get the book value to equal the face value at maturity, we'll have to get rid of the balance in the discount account.
- Each time we pay interest to our bondholders, we'll amortize a little of the discount.

Effective Interest Method For Amortizing A Bond Discount

- Each time we pay interest to our bondholders, we'll amortize a little of the discount--how much?
- On the first interest date, the amount we've actually "borrowed" from the bondholders is $870,000.
- The market rate at the time we borrowed--the rate we <u>had</u> to pay to get the bondholders to buy our bonds-- was 8%.
- 870,000 x .08 x 1/2 = **34,800 (This will be the interest expense for the first 6 months.)**

8-70

Effective Interest Amortization of Bond Discount

We know the cash payment to the bondholders is $30,000:

$$1,000,000 \quad \times \quad .06 \quad \times \quad 1/2$$

par value   interest   6-month period

rate

8-71

Effective Interest Amortization of Bond Discount

The difference between the interest expense of $34,800 and the cash payment to the bondholders of $30,000 is the amount of discount amortization.

$34,800

- 30,000

$ 4,800   **This amount will be deducted from the discount.**

8-72

|||| Next Time --

- When we calculate the amount of interest expense for the second interest payment, our principal balance has changed.
- Instead of 870,000, we now have a principal balance of **874,800**. Why?
- 874,800 x .08 x 1/2 = $34,992
- This is the interest expense for the second six-month period.

|||| Effective Interest Amortization of Bond Discount

interest expense	$34,992
cash payment	30,000
discount amortization	4,992

After this payment, the new book value of the bonds will be 874,800 + 4,992 = $879,792.

|||| Effective Interest Amortization of Bond Discount

- Carrying value of bonds is defined as the par or face value of the bonds minus any unamortized discount (or plus any unamortized premium).
- In this example, the discount has now been reduced from 130,000 to 120,208. The carrying value of the bonds is the face ($1,000,000) minus the unamortized discount ($120,208) = $879,792.
- The book value of the bonds is increasing.

What's Happening?

- Each time we pay the bondholders $30,000, we are <u>not</u> paying the full amount of the true interest expense for the $870,000 loan.
- The amount we *don't* pay gets added to the carrying value of the bond. (Reducing the discount increases the carrying value of the bond.)
- So, the bond's carrying value is increasing from $870,000 to the face value of $1,000,000 over the life of the bond.

Straight-Line Amortization of Bond Discount

- The other method is not as accurate, but the calculations are easier.
- Identify the amount of the bond discount.
- Divide the bond discount by the number of interest periods.
- Include the discount amortization amount as part of the periodic interest expense entry.
- The discount will be reduced to zero by the maturity date.

Straight-Line Amortization of Bond Discount

Here's a review of the facts of the problem:

- ❖ Clock Corp. sold their bonds on May 1, 1991 at 87. The bonds have a 10-year maturity and $30,000 interest is paid semiannually.
- ❖ Why would the bonds sell for 87?
    - The market rate of interest is **greater** than the rate on the face.
- ❖ Where did the $30,000 come from?
    - 1,000,000 x .06 x 1/2

Straight-Line Amortization of Bond Discount

The discount of $130,000 is divided by 20.
(10-year bonds with interest paid twice each year)

$6,500 will be amortized from the discount every time the interest payment is made.

So, interest expense will be $36,500 every time the $30,000 payment is made.

8-79

Measuring and Recording Interest on Bonds Issued at a Premium

- The premium must be amortized over the term of the bonds.
- The premium amortization decreases the periodic interest expense for the issuer.
- Two methods are commonly used:
  - Effective-interest amortization
  - Straight-line amortization

8-80

Recall the Facts of the Problem

- Magic Inc. sold their bonds on May 1, 1991 at 107. There were $1,000,000 worth of bonds with a stated rate of 9% annually. The bonds mature in 10 years and $45,000 interest is paid semiannually. The market rate is 8% annually.
- Why would the bonds sell for 107?
  - The market rate of interest is **less** than the rate on the face.
- Where did the $45,000 come from?
  - $1,000,000 x 9% x 1/2 = 45,000

8-81

Effective Interest Method For Amortizing A Bond Premium

If we prepared a balance sheet on the date of issue, the bond would be reported like this:

Bonds Payable	$ 1,000,000
plus Premium on B/P	70,000
Net Bonds Payable	$1,070,000

8-82

Effective Interest Method For Amortizing A Bond Premium

- The premium carries a credit balance (and is added to the face value of the bond to give the "book value.")
- In order to get the book value to equal the face value at maturity, we'll have to get rid of the balance in the premium account.
- Each time we pay interest to our bondholders, we'll amortize a little of the premium.

8-83

Effective Interest Method For Amortizing A Bond Premium

- Each time we pay interest to our bondholders, we'll amortize a little of the premium--how much?
- On the first interest date, the amount we've actually "borrowed" from the bondholders is $1,070,000.
- The market rate at the time we borrowed--the rate we had to pay to get the bondholders to buy our bonds-- was 8%. The face rate is 9%
- **1,070,000 x .08 x 1/2 = 42,800 (This will be the interest expense for the first 6 months.)**

8-84

Effective Interest Method For Amortizing A Bond Premium

- If we pay the bondholders $45,000 cash and the interest expense is $42,800*, the difference will be the amount of the premium amortization.
- Notice that the interest expense is LESS than the payment to the bondholders when bonds are issued at a premium. (It is just the opposite when bonds are issued at a discount.)

*1,070,000 x .08 x 1/2=42,800

8-85

Next Time --

- When we calculate the amount of interest expense for the second interest payment, our principal balance has changed.
- Instead of 1,070,000, we now have a principal balance of 1,067,800. Why?
- Because we amortized $2,200 of the premium. Now it's only $67,800.
- 1,067,800 x .08 x 1/2 = $42,712
- This is the interest expense for the second six-month period.

8-86

Effective Interest Method For Amortizing A Bond Premium

- The payment to the bondholders is the same each time a payment is made-- $45,000.
- Interest expense for the second payment is $42,712
- The difference between the payment and the expense is the amount of amortization of the premium--$2,288.
- The new carrying value is $1,067,800 - 2,288 = $1,065,512.

8-87

Effective Interest Method For Amortizing A Bond Premium

- Carrying value is defined as the face value plus any unamortized premium.

- In this case, the premium started at 70,000 and has been reduced by 2,200 and by 2,288, for a balance of 65,512.

- The face of $1,000,000 plus the unamortized premium of 65,512 gives a carrying value of $1,065,512 after the second interest payment.

8-88

What's Happening?

- Each time we pay the bondholders $45,000, we are paying the full amount of the true interest expense for the $1,070,000 loan, plus some of the principal.
- The amount we pay in excess of the interest expense gets deducted from the carrying value of the bond. (Reducing the premium decreases the carrying value of the bond.)
- So, the bond's carrying value is decreasing from $1,070,000 to the face value of $1,000,000 over the life of the bond.

8-89

Straight-Line Amortization of Bond Premium

- Identify the amount of the bond premium.
- Divide the bond premium by the number of interest periods.
- Include the premium amortization amount as part of the periodic interest expense entry.
- The premium will be reduced to zero by the maturity date.

8-90

Straight-Line Amortization of Bond Premium

Interest payment is always $45,000.

Premium amortization is $\frac{70,000}{20} = 3,500$.

That means that the premium will be amortized by 3,500 every time a payment is made.

Interest expense will be $41,500 each time a payment is made.

8-91

Carrying Value Of BONDS PAYABLE

While the specific long-term liability *Bonds Payable* is always recorded (and kept) at face value, the *Discount* or *Premium* (*on Bonds Payable*) will be either subtracted (discount) or added (premium) to the BP amount to get the *carrying value* of the bond at any given date.

8-92

Understanding Notes to Financial Statements

- Effective-interest method of amortization is preferred by GAAP.
- Straight-line amortization may be used if it is not materially different from effective interest amortization.
- Most companies do not disclose the method used for bond interest amortization.

8-93

Trading Bonds

- When a bondholder sells a bond, there is no effect on the books of the issuing company.
- Bondholders trade among themselves in the bond market.
- Changes in the market rate of interest and the risk related to specific bonds cause the prices of bonds to change.

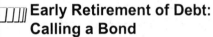

Early Retirement of Debt: Calling a Bond

- Occasionally, the issuing company will call (repay early) some or all of its bonds.
- If the bond is callable, the issuer may decided to *call* the bond (retire it before maturity).
- The liability would be removed and any *call premium* would be recorded on the income statement.

Early Retirement of Debt

- Bonds can also be retired by purchasing the bond on the open market.
- Any gains or losses incurred as a result of retiring the bonds should be reported as extraordinary items on the income statement.

Bond Sinking Funds

- A special fund to be used to retire bonds at maturity is a sinking fund.
- Normally, periodic cash contributions are made to the fund.
- Usually, it is reported on the balance sheet as a non-current asset.

8-97

Financial Analysis

- The debt-equity ratio is an important measure of the state of a company's capital structure.

Debt-Equity Ratio = Total Debt ÷ Total Equity

- When a company's debt-equity ratio is excessive, a large amount of fixed debt payments may cause problems in tight cash flow periods.

8-98

Financial Analysis

- The times-interest-earned ratio is another measure of the firm's ability to support its level of debt.

$$\frac{\text{Net income + Interest expense}}{\text{Interest expense}}$$

- A company must be earning income in excess of its interest payments!
- Like all ratios, we need a basis for comparison to give meaning to this ratio.

8-99

Chapter 9
Special Acquisitions: Financing A Business with Equity

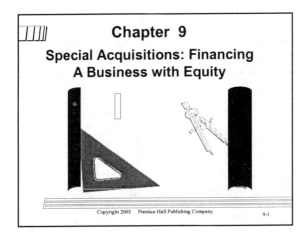

9-1

Equity in Proprietorships

➢ Contributed capital and retained earnings are combined into a single capital account:

John Doe, Capital $XXXX

➢ Distributions are called **withdrawals**.

9-2

Equity in Partnerships

➢ Each partner has her/his own separate capital account, each containing the partner's invested capital and share of retained earnings.

➢ As with proprietorships, partnerships use withdrawal accounts for the distributions made to the owners.

9-3

Equity in Corporations

The equity section for a corporation is divided into two parts:

- Contributed Capital (a.k.a. paid-in-capital)--this is the amount that owners have contributed
  - Capital Stock
  - Additional paid-in-capital
- Retained Earnings--this is what the company has earned over its whole life, less any dividends paid out

9-4

Authorized, Issued, and Outstanding Capital Stock

Authorized Shares

The maximum number of shares of capital stock that can be sold to the public is called the *authorized* number of shares.

9-5

Authorized, Issued, and Outstanding Capital Stock

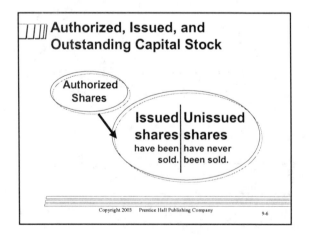

Authorized Shares

Issued shares have been sold.

Unissued shares have never been sold.

9-6

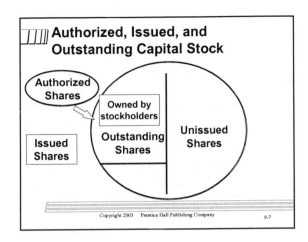

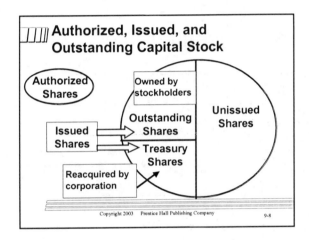

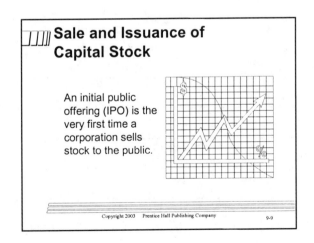

Common Stock

- ➤ Basic voting stock of the corporation
- ➤ Ranks after preferred stock for dividend and liquidation distribution.
- ➤ Dividend rates are determined by the board of directors based on the corporation's profitability.

9-10

Par Value and No-par Value Stock

- ➤ Par value
  - Is a **nominal value** per share of capital stock specified in the charter.
  - Has **no** relationship to market value.
  - Serves as the basis for **legal capital**.
- ➤ Legal capital is the amount of capital, required by the state, that must remain invested in the business.
  - It serves as a cushion for creditors.

9-11

Par Value and No-par Value Stock

- ➤ No-par value is capital stock that does not have an amount per share specified in the charter.
- ➤ When no-par stock is issued by a corporation, the amount of legal capital is defined by the state.
- ➤ Stated value is an amount per share that is specified by the corporation when it issues no-par stock.

9-12

Preferred Stock

➢ Has dividend and liquidation preference over common stock.
➢ *Cumulative preferred stock* has a preference for all past dividends over any paid to common shareholders.
➢ Generally does not have voting rights.
➢ Usually has a par or stated value.
➢ Usually has a fixed dividend rate that is stated as a percentage of the par value.

9-13

Special Features of Preferred Stock

➢ Convertible preferred stock may be exchanged for common stock.
➢ Callable preferred stock may be repurchased by the corporation at a predetermined price.

9-14

Accounting for Capital Stock Transactions

➢ Two primary sources of stockholders' equity:

- **Contributed capital**
  - Par or stated value of issued stock.
  - Additional paid-in capital in excess of par or stated value.

- **Retained earnings**
  - The cumulative net income earned by the corporation less the cumulative dividends declared by the corporation.

9-15

Accounting for the Issue of Common Stock

➢ When stock is issued, the equity account *Common Stock* is credited for the par or stated value of the stock.

➢ If the stock sold for more than par, the additional amount is credited to the equity account *Paid in Capital in Excess of Par, Common Stock*.

9-16

ABC Co. issued 300 shared of $10 par common stock for $12 per share.

Assets =   Liab. +   Cont. Cap. + Ret. Earnings

+3600 (Cash)	+3000 (Common Stock at par)
	+ 600 (PIC in excess of par)

Income Statement: No effect on Income

Statement of Changes in Equity: Increases equity

Statement of Cash Flows: Increases cash flow

9-17

Treasury Stock

➢ A corporation's own stock that had been issued but was subsequently reacquired and is still being held by that corporation.

➢ Why would a corporation reacquire its own stock?
- To reduce the shares outstanding.
- Because the market price is low.
- To increase earnings per share.
- To use in employee stock option programs.

9-18

Treasury Stock

- ➤ is considered issued stock but not outstanding stock.

- ➤ has no voting or dividend rights.

- ➤ is a contra-equity account.

- ➤ reduces **total stockholders' equity** on the Balance Sheet.

ABC Co. bought back 20 shares of its $10 par common stock for $11 per share (issued in previous transaction)

Assets =   Liab. + Cont. Cap. + Ret. Earnings

-$220 (Cash)   -$220 (Treasury Stock)

Income Statement: No effect on Income

Statement of Changes in Equity: Decreases equity

Statement of Cash Flows: Decreases cash flow

Treasury Stock Transactions

- ➤ Treasury stock is recorded at cost.
- ➤ The account, **Treasury Stock**, is contra to all of Equity and subtracted at the end of the section on the Balance Sheet.
- ➤ If the treasury stock is subsequently resold for more than the cost, another equity account, **PIC Treasury Stock**, would be credited for the excess over cost
- ➤ NO gains or losses are recorded on the purchase or on the reissue of treasury stock.

Accounting for Cash Dividends

- Dividends must be declared by the board of directors before they can be paid.
- The corporation is not legally required to declare (and subsequently pay) dividends.
- Once a dividend is declared, a liability is created.
- Cash dividends require sufficient cash and retained earnings to cover the dividend.

9-22

Dividend Dates

- Date of declaration
- Date of actual payment to shareholders

9-23

Dividends on Preferred Stock

- Current preferred dividends must be paid before paying any dividends to common stock.
- If a preferred dividend is not paid, the unpaid amount is either cumulative (a dividend in arrears) or noncumulative.
  - **Cumulative**: Unpaid dividends must be paid before common dividends.
  - **Noncumulative**: Unpaid dividends are lost.

9-24

Calculating Preferred and Common Dividends

- Suppose ABC Co. has 1000 shares of $100 par, 6% cumulative preferred stock outstanding and that NO dividends were paid in 1996.
- At the end of 1997, the Board of Directors declares a total of $20,000 worth of dividends for its preferred and common shareholders.
- How much will go to the preferred shareholders?

9-25

Preferred Shareholders Get Their Dividends First

- Cumulative means that the preferred shareholders get all the past dividends that they were not paid.
- 1000 x $100 x .06 = 6,000
- They get a total of **$12,000**: $6,000 for 1996 and $6,000 for 1997.
- Common shareholders get the remaining **$8,000**.

9-26

The Effect of Declaring the Dividends

Assets = Liabilities +   CC +   RE

+ 12,000 div/payable,   (20,000) dividends
preferred SHs
+ 8,000 div/payable
common SHs

❖ There is no effect on the income statement, but both the statement of shareholders' equity and the balance sheet will be affected by the transaction.

❖ When the cash is paid, the liability is removed and CASH is decreased. Again, there is no income statement effect.

9-27

But what if the stock is NONcumulative?

➤ Then, the past is past.

➤ Only the current year's dividends are due to the preferred shareholders.

➤ So the preferred shareholders will get $6,000 (the current year's dividend) and the common shareholders will get the rest--$14,000.

9-28

Cash Dividends

➤Needed to pay cash dividends
- retained earnings
- cash
- no restrictions from outsiders

➤Effects of cash dividends on financial statements
- decreases Assets (when they are actually paid) and Retained Earnings

9-29

ABC Co. declared the dividends of $20,000 payable to preferred ($12,000) and common ($8,000) shareholders of record as of 12/31/97.

Assets	=	Liab.	+	Cont. Cap.	+	Ret. Earnings
		+20,000				-20,000

Income Statement: No effect on Income

Statement of Changes in Equity: Decreases equity

Statement of Cash Flows: No effect on cash flow

9-30

Accounting for Stock Dividends

➢ Stock dividends are distributions to stockholders of additional shares of stock.

➢ Why issue a stock dividend?

- Low on cash.
- To decrease market price of stock.
- To increase number of stockholders (assuming some of the newly issued stock will be sold).

9-31

Accounting for Stock Dividends

➢ All stockholders receive the same percentage increase in the number of shares they own (pro rata basis).

➢ No change in total stockholders' equity.

➢ No change in par values.

➢ Effect on financial statements?

9-32

ABC Co. declared a 10% stock dividend on its 200 shares of $1 par common stock. The market value at the time of distribution is $20.

Assets=	Liab. +	Cont. Cap. +	Ret. Earnings
		+ 20 (C/S)	-400
		+ 380 (Add'l P-I-C)	

Income Statement: No effect on Income

Statement of Changes in Equity: No effect on equity

Statement of Cash Flows: No effect on cash flow

9-33

Accounting for Stock Splits

- Distributions of 100% or more of stock to stockholders.
- Decreases par value of stock.
- Increases number of outstanding shares.
- No change in total stockholders' equity.

9-34

Retained Earnings

Represents the income that has been earned less dividends that have been paid out since the first day of operations for the company.

Balance January 1, 19X3	$ 500,000
Net income	25,000
Cash dividends	(10,000)
Balance January 31, 19X3	$ 515,000

9-35

Retained Earnings

- What affects Retained Earnings?
  - net income
  - cash dividends
  - stock dividends
  - prior period adjustments
- Appropriating Retained Earnings
  - Board of Directors can restrict portions of retained earnings (a communication device)

9-36

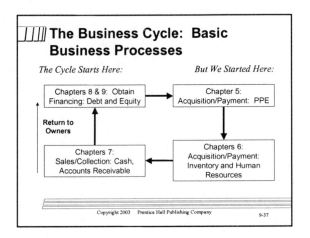

The Business Cycle: Basic Business Processes

The Cycle Starts Here: *But We Started Here:*

Chapters 8 & 9: Obtain Financing: Debt and Equity → Chapter 5: Acquisition/Payment: PPE

Return to Owners

Chapters 7: Sales/Collection: Cash, Accounts Receivable ← Chapters 6: Acquisition/Payment: Inventory and Human Resources

Copyright 2003   Prentice Hall Publishing Company

9-37

Chapter 10

Preparing a Statement of Cash Flows

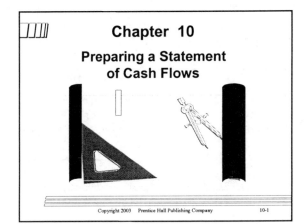

_____
_____
_____
_____
_____
_____
_____

Purpose of the Statement of Cash Flows

- To show how the business acquired its cash during the current year
- To show how the business spent its cash during the current year

> This information is crucial for decision makers predict future cash flows of the business.

_____
_____
_____
_____
_____
_____

What Is Considered "CASH" For The Statement Of Cash Flows?

- Cash includes cash and cash equivalents for purpose of the statement.

- Cash Equivalents are
  - Short-term, highly liquid investments.
  - Easily convertible into known amounts of cash.

_____
_____
_____
_____
_____
_____
_____

Categories of Cash Flows

Categories are based on
activities related to cash flows:
1. Operating the business.
2. Investing in productive assets.
3. Financing the business.

These are the sections of the
Statement of Cash Flows.

Operating Activities

- Cash inflows and outflows that are directly related to income from normal operations.
- Technically, FASB defines operating activities as those that are *not* investing or financing activities.
- There are two ways to compute net cash flow from <u>operating activities</u>:
  - Direct method
  - Indirect method

Cash Flows from Operating Activities

Cash inflows and outflows that are
directly related to income from
normal operations.

Inflows include:
- Receipts from customers.
- Interest on receivables.
- Dividends <u>received.</u>

Cash Flows from Operating Activities

Cash inflows and outflows that are directly related to income from normal operations.

Outflows include:
- Payments to suppliers.
- Interest paid on liabilities.
- Income taxes paid.
- Salary and wages payments to employees.

Cash Flows from Investing Activities

- Cash inflows and outflows that are related to the purchase and sale of productive assets.
- Inflows include proceeds from:
  - Sales of property, plant, and equipment.
  - Sales of investments in securities.
  - Collection of principal on loans made to others.

Cash Flows from Investing Activities

- Cash inflows and outflows that are related to the purchase and sale of productive assets.
- Outflows include payments for:
  - The purchase of property, plant and equipment.
  - The purchase of long-term investments.
  - Loans to others.

Cash Flows from Investing Activities

Cash inflows and outflows that are related to how cash was obtained to finance the enterprise.

Inflows include:

- Proceeds from sale of stock.
- Proceeds from sale of bonds and from borrowings.

Cash Flows from Financing Activities

Cash inflows and outflows that are related to how cash was obtained to finance the enterprise.

Outflows include:

- Payments to purchase treasury stock.
- Principal payments to retire bonds and loans.
- Dividends paid to owners.

Cash Flows from Noncash Activities

Investing and financing activities that do not involve cash, e.g.,

- Retirement of bonds by issuing stock.
- Settlement of debt by transferring assets.

Noncash activities must be disclosed separately in the financial statements.

Preparing the Statement of Cash Flows

The face of the statement includes:

Net Cash Flows from Operating Activities
+Net Cash Flows from Investing Activities
+Net Cash Flows from Financing Activities
=Net Cash Flows for the period
+ Beginning Cash Balance
=End of period Cash Balance

Two Alternative Approaches

Indirect Method
- Shows net cash inflow (outflow) from operations as an adjustment of net income.
- Used by 97% of companies.

Direct Method
- Reports the components of cash from operations as gross receipts and payments.
- Recommended by the FASB, but rarely used.

Converting Accrual Data to Cash Data

- Accounting records are kept on the accrual basis (GAAP).
- Cash data must be developed before the SCF can be prepared (especially for operating activities).
- The examples that follow demonstrate the direct method for converting accrual data to cash data.

Three Information Sources Are Used

1. The income statement for the current period.
2. Comparative beginning of period and end of period balance sheets.
3. Additional transaction details not found in the financial statements.

Direct Method

- Income statement approach
- Look at each item on the income statement to determine how to make it a "cash" number

Direct Method SCF
Converting Revenues to Cash Basis

- Accrual basis revenue includes sales that did not result in cash inflows.
- Can be computed as:

Revenue, Accrual basis	+ or - change in AR	=	Revenue, Cash basis

Example: Direct Method SCF

- The A/R balance was $45,000 on 1/1/05 and $52,000 on 12/31/05. If accrual sales revenue for 2005 was $600,000, what was cash basis revenue?
- Do you know what would make AR increase by $7,000 during the year? It must have been sales for which the customers have not yet paid.

Example: Direct Method SCF

If accrual sales revenue for 2005 was $600,000 (which we see on the income statement), what was cash basis revenue?

Because there were $7,000 more sales than cash collected, the cash must be $593,000 = $600,000 minus 7,000

Direct Method SCF

Another way to reason through this problem is:

- AR beginning balance of $45,000 is collected first. That's $45,000 cash inflow.

- Then, sales of $600,000 were made (income statement). Because the AR ending balance is $52,000, cash sales must have been [$600,000 - 52,000] or $548,000.

- The old AR collected in cash, $45,000, plus the cash sales for the period, $548,000, gives total cash collected from customers of $593,000.

Direct Method Converting Accrued Expenses to Cash

- Accrual basis expenses include expenses that have not yet been paid.
- Can be computed as:

| Expense, Accrual Basis | + or - changes in "expense" payables | Expense, Cash Basis |

Example: Direct Method SCF

Salary Expense for 2005 was $500,000. Salary Payable was $35,000 on 12/31/04 and $10,000 on 12/31/05. How much cash was paid to employees in 2005?

Example: Direct Method SCF

- First, the beginning amount of Salaries Payable was $35,000. That must have been paid in cash first during 2005.
- Salary expense for the year was $500,000, but at year end, $10,000 of that amount had not yet been paid.
- We know this because Salaries Payable on the 12/31/05 balance sheet is $10,000.

Example: Direct Method SCF

- So the total cash paid to employees during 2005:
  - $ 35,000 beginning Salaries Payable
  - + $490,000 cash paid this year
  - = $525,000 total cash paid for salaries

10-25

Example: Direct Method SCF

- Another way to reason through this problem is to start with the salary expense amount from the income statement: $500,000
- Then, adjust that for the change in Salaries Payable. Because Salaries Payable decreased by $25,000, we must have paid that amount in cash to our employees. (How else could that decrease have occurred?)
- That gives a total cash paid to employees of $525,000.

10-26

Direct Method
Converting Cost of Goods Sold to Cash Basis

- Requires analysis of two accounts: inventory and accounts payable.
- Can be computed as:

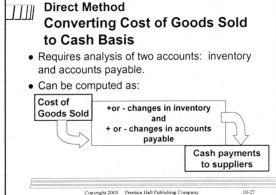

10-27

Suppose CGS was $20,000; BI was $12,000 and EI was $10,000; AP had a beginning balance of $13,000 and an ending balance of $13,600. What was cash paid to suppliers?

First, look at cost of goods sold and inventory. What happened to inventory during the period? It went down. That means that of the $20,000 of CGS, $2,000 worth came from the beginning inventory...in other words $2,000 of the cost of goods sold did not have to be purchased this year. So, only $18,000 of the cost of goods sold was this period's purchases.

Now, how much of that $18,000 of purchases was actually paid for in cash? We need to look at the change in Accounts Payable.

10-28

Suppose CGS was $20,000; BI was $12,000 and EI was $10,000; AP had a beginning balance of $13,000 and an ending balance of $13,600. What was cash paid to suppliers?

The company had to purchase $18,000 worth of inventory.

Accounts Payable went up during the year by $600. That means that, of the total purchases of $18,000, all EXCEPT $600 (the increase in A/P) was paid for in cash.

That means that cash paid to vendors was $17,400.

10-29

To Summarize This Problem

- Why is COST OF GOODS SOLD (from the income statement) not equal to cash?
- First, we might have sold some goods that we already had in the inventory or we may have had to buy all of the goods we sold PLUS some more that we put into building up the inventory.
- So, we must look at the change in inventory to see if cost of goods sold is more or less than the inventory we bought during the period.
- Here our inventory went down, from $12,000 to $10,000. That means we only had to buy $18,000 worth of the goods we sold (the other $2,000 came out of the beginning inventory).

10-30

⫞⫞⫞ To Summarize This Problem

- Now, did we actually have to pay for all $18,000 worth of those goods? (Or did we pay for those *plus* some we purchased the period before?)
- To figure that out, we have to look at Accounts Payable (A/P).
- Since A/P went UP, that means we bought some things we didn't pay for yet. How many? $600 worth—that's how much A/P went up.
- So, rather than paying for all $18,000 worth of our purchase, we only paid for $17,400 of them.

⫞⫞⫞ To Summarize:

- What kinds of accounts need to be examined to see if there is a difference between our accrual accounting records and actual cash?

versus

General Ledger

⫞⫞⫞ To Summarize:

- Accounts Receivable
- Prepaids
- Inventory
- Accounts Payable
- Other Payables

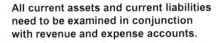

All current assets and current liabilities need to be examined in conjunction with revenue and expense accounts.

An Example:
Tom's Wear Inc.: March 2001

To use the indirect method of preparing a statement of cash flows, we'll examine each item on the income statement and make it "cash."

We'll need the income statement and beginning and ending balance sheets for the period.

Reference: The March Income Statement

Tom's Wear, Inc.
Income Statement
For the month ended March 31, 2001

Sales revenue		$2,000
Expenses		
Cost of goods sold	800	
Depreciation expense	100	
Insurance expense	50	
Interest expense	30	980
Net Income		$ 1,020

The Comparative Balance Sheets

	March 31	March 1		March 31	March 1
Cash	$3,995	$6,695	A/P	$-0-	$800
			Other	-0-	50
A/R	2,000	150	Int/Payable	30	-0-
Inventory	300	100	Notes payable	3,000	-0-
Prepaid insur.	75	125	Total liabilities	3,030	850
Machine (net of $100 accumulated depreciation)	3,900	0	Common Stock	5,000	5,000
			Retained Earnings	2,240	1,220
Total Assets	$10,270	$7,070	Total L + SHs Equtiy	$10,270	$7,070

Tom's Wear Inc.-- March 2001

We'll start on the income statement with Sales. How much CASH was collected from customers?

- Sales for March were $2,000.
- But Accounts Receivable went from a beginning balance of $150 to an ending balance of $2,000.
- Because AR increased by $1,850, we must have only collected $150 cash.

Tom's Wear Inc.-- March 2001

Cost of goods sold is $800. And inventory increased from 100 to 300. That means that $1,000 worth of inventory must have been purchased-- enough to sell $800 worth and build up the inventory by another $200.

How much cash was paid to vendors? We need to check out what happened to Accounts Payable during the month.

Tom's Wear Inc.-- March 2001

Accounts Payable started the month at $800. That means Tom's Wear owed $800 to vendors at the beginning of March.

At the end of March, the Accounts Payable balance is $0. That means Tom's Wear paid for ALL of the month's purchases ($1,000) PLUS $800 owned from February.

The total cash paid to vendors was $1,800.

Tom's Wear Inc.-- March 2001

Depreciation expense is a
non-cash expense, so we
can simply ignore it.

Tom's Wear Inc.-- March 2001

- Insurance expense for the month was $50. To figure out how much cash was actually paid for insurance, we have to look at what happened to Prepaid Insurance.
- The comparative balance sheets show that Prepaid Insurance went from $125 to $75. That means the insurance expense of $50 came totally from the Prepaid Insurance, so no cash was disbursed for insurance.

Tom's Wear Inc.-- March 2001

- Interest expense for the month was $30. To figure out how much cash was actually paid for interest, we have to look at what happened to interest payable.
- The comparative balance sheets show that interest payable went from $0 to $30. That means the interest expense of $30 has NOT been paid. So, no cash was paid for interest.

What Else?

The only other cash disbursements we have to worry about are any that were made for expenses from a prior year. That means we must look for any payables that were there at the beginning of the year, but are no longer there.

In this example, there is a $50 cash disbursement made to pay off the $50 "other" payable shown on the beginning balance sheet.

Adding up all the disbursements:

To vendors	$1,800
Insurance	$ 0
Inventory	$ 0
Other	50
Total outflow	$1,850

Tom's Wear
Statement of Cash Flows
For the month ended March 2001

Cash from operations:

Cash from customers	$ 150
Cash paid to vendors	(1,800)
Cash paid for other expenses	(50)
Net cash (outflow) from operations	$(1,700)

Indirect Method

- Net cash flows from operating activities are determined by . . .
  - Starting with **net income**, then . . .
  - Adding and subtracting items that reconcile net income to operating cash flows.
- Requires an analysis of changes in all current asset and current liability accounts, except cash.

Indirect Method

- Noncash additions to net income:
  - Depreciation, depletion, and amortization.
  - All losses.
- Noncash deductions from net income:
  - All gains.

Indirect Method

Net income

+ depreciation

+ bad debt expense

+ cash received from last year's sales
- sales made but cash not received
etc.

T-account Approach

- Make every balance sheet account balance, using the income statement accounts to calculate increases and decreases to the accounts.
- When the cash number is calculated for various increases or decreases in balance sheet accounts, put the appropriate debit or credit in the big cash T-account.

Cash from Operations—Indirect Method
Tom's Wear, Inc.
For the month end March 31, 2001

Net Income	$1,020
+depreciation expense	100
- increase in AR	(1,850)
- increase in inventory	(200)
+decrease in prepaid insurance	50
- decrease in payables	(820)
Net cash from operations	$ (1,700)

Summary of Differences Between Direct and Indirect Methods

- The direct method provides more detail about cash from operating activities.
  - Shows individual operating cash flows.
  - Shows reconciliation of operating cash flows to net income in a supplemental schedule.
- The investing and financing sections for the two methods are identical.
- Net cash flow is the same for both methods.

How Important Is The Statement Of Cash Flows?

- It is crucial to the presentation of a complete picture of the financial status of a business.
- Many businesses with great ideas and potential have failed due to their failure to manage their cash flows.
- Remember, the statement is REQUIRED by GAAP.

10-52

Chapter 11

Financial Statement Analysis

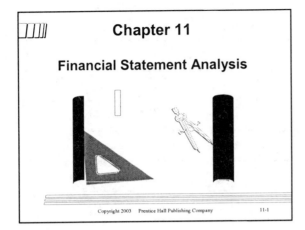

11-1

Analyzing Financial Statements

- Before we discuss financial statement analysis, let's take a closer look at some of the elements of the income statement.
- Then, we'll talk about several ways to analyze financial statements.

11-2

More About The Income Statement

- To make the information on the income statement clearer, there are several special items that are separated from the regular earnings of a business:
  - Gains and losses from discontinued operations,
  - Extraordinary items, and
  - Cumulative effect of a change in accounting principle

11-3

▌▌▌ Discontinued Operations

- If a segment or division of a business is eliminated, the gain or loss from the disposal must be shown after income from continuing operations, net of taxes.

- Any current gain or loss from the operations of that discontinued segment must also be shown separately.

11-4

▌▌▌ How Discontinued Operations Are Shown

Containers, Inc.
Income Statement
For the year ended December 31, 2003

Income before taxes		$400,000
Income tax expense		160,000
Income from continuing operations		240,000
Discontinued operations		
Income from discontinued operations net of taxes of $2,300	$ 10,100	
Gain on disposal of mailing packages segment net of taxes of $25,000	35,000	
	45,100	
Net Income		$ 285,100

11-5

▌▌▌ Extraordinary Items

- Events that are *unusual* in nature and *infrequent* in occurrence are called extraordinary items.

- The accounting rules are very strict about what types of events may be classified as extraordinary.

- Any gain or loss from these events are shown, net of taxes, after income from continuing operations and after income from discontinued operations.

11-6

Examples Of Actual Extraordinary Occurrences

- Volcano eruptions
- Take-over of foreign operations by the foreign government
- Effects of new laws or regulations that result in a one-time cost to comply

Each situation is unique and must be considered in the environment in which the business operates.

How Extraordinary Items Are Shown

Containers, Inc.
Income Statement
For the year ended December 31, 2003

Income before taxes		$400,000
Income tax expense		160,000
Income from continuing operations		240,000
Discontinued operations		
Income less taxes of $2,500	$ 10,100	
Gain on disposal less taxes of $20,000	35,000	
	45,100	
Income before extraordinary item		$ 285,100
Extraordinary item		
Expropriation of foreign operation net of tax savings of $35,000		70,000
Net Income		$215,100

Cumulative Effect
Of A Change In Accounting Principal

- The **cumulative effect** of a change in accounting principle is the amount of gain or loss from changing accounting methods.
- It must be shown separately on the income statement, net of taxes, after income from continuing operations, discontinued operations, and any extraordinary items.

Example

- Suppose the company changed from depreciating equipment using the straight-line method to depreciating the equipment using the double declining balance method.
- The equipment was purchased on January 1, 2001, at a cost of $10,000, has a useful life of 10 years, with no salvage value.

Depreciation Schedules

Method	Straight-line	Double-declining balance
Year ended:		
December 31, 2001	$1,000	$2,000
December 31, 2002	$1,000	$1,600
Total for two years	$2,000	$3,600

- The income for Containers, Inc. would have been lower by $1,600 if double-declining balance had been used from the beginning.
- A switch now means the company will have to subtract $1,600, net of any tax effect, as a cumulative effect of a change in accounting principle.

Cumulative Effect

- The income for Containers, Inc. would have been lower by $1,600 if double-declining balance had been used from the beginning.
- A switch now means the company will have to subtract $1,600, net of any tax effect, as a cumulative effect of a change in accounting principle.

How The Cumulative Effect Is Shown On The Income Statement

Containers, Inc.
Income Statement
For the year ended December 31, 2003

Income before taxes		$400,000
Income tax expense		160,000
Income from continuing operations		240,000
Discontinued operations		
Income less taxes of $2,500	$ 10,100	
Gain on disposal less taxes of $20,000	35,000	
	45,100	
Income before extraordinary item and cumulative effect of change in accounting principle		$ 285,100
Extraordinary item		
Expropriation of foreign operation net of tax saving of $35,000		70,000
Cumulative effect of a change in accounting principle		
Effect on prior years of change in depreciation method, net of $400 tax savings		1,200
Net Income		$213,900

Comprehensive Income

- The income statement shows all of the effects of revenues, expenses, gains, and losses on net income.
- Net income, in turn, affects owners' equity.
- Other items, **not** included on the income statement, may affect owners' equity.
- The total of all items that affect owners' equity, not including contributions from owners and dividends, is called **comprehensive income.**

Diagram Showing the Items that Affect Owners' Equity

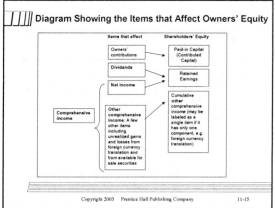

Other Comprehensive Income

- Total *comprehensive income* = *net income* plus *other comprehensive income*
- Items included in *other comprehensive income* include:
  - unrealized gains and losses from foreign currency translation
  - unrealized gains and losses on certain types of investments.

_____

_____

_____

_____

_____

_____

One More New Financial Statement Item: Investments In Securities

- A company may use some of its extra cash to invest in the debt or equity securities of another company.
- These investments must be classified as one of three types:
  - **Securities held to maturity**
  - **Trading securities**
  - **Securities available for sale**

_____

_____

_____

_____

_____

_____

Securities Held To Maturity

- Debt securities
- Intent and ability to hold to maturity
- Must not be sold in response to changes in interest rates, funding sources, etc.
- Measured at cost on the balance sheet

_____

_____

_____

_____

_____

_____

Trading Securities

- Debt and equity securities
- Readily determinable fair values
- Bought and held to sell in the near term
- Actively and frequently traded (profit!)
- Measured at fair value and classified as a current asset
- Unrealized gains and losses, included in determination of net income

Securities Available For Sale

- Debt and equity securities
- Readily determinable fair values
- Not classified as either securities held to maturity or trading securities
- Measured at fair value on balance sheet
- May be either current or noncurrent
- May have holding gains or losses, to be reported net as a separate component of owners' equity, usually as part of *other comprehensive income.*

Financial Statement Analysis

- In addition to the financial statements, annual reports contain the following:
  - Notes to the financial statements, including a summary of the accounting methods used
  - Management's discussion and analysis (MD&A) of the financial results
  - The auditor's report
  - Comparative financial data for a series of years

▱ Financial Statement Analysis

- Now that you'll be able to recognize these new items we've just discussed, you're ready to do some analysis of the financial statements.
- First, we'll talk about horizontal and vertical analysis.
- Then, we'll discuss financial ratios -- standard measures that enable analysts to compare companies of different sizes

11-22

▱ Horizontal Analysis

Horizontal analysis compares one value across several periods. First, a base year must be chosen as the basis for comparison.

	2003	2002	2001	2000
Sales	$41,500	$37,850	$36,300	$35,000

The difference between each year and the base year is expressed as a percentage of the base year.

11-23

▱ Horizontal Analysis

This shows 2000 as the base year. The base year's sales are subtracted from each year's sales. Then, this difference is expressed as a percentage of the base year's sales.

	2003	2002	2001	2000
Sales	$41,500	$37,850	$36,300	**$35,000**
				Base year
	18.6%	8.1%	3.7%	

11-24

Horizontal Analysis

For example, the sales for 2003 represent an increase of 18.6% over the base year 2000.

	2003	2002	2001	2000
Sales	$41,500	$37,850	$36,300	$35,000
	18.6%	8.1%	3.7%	Base year

Vertical Analysis

- compares each item in a financial statement to a base number set to 100%.
- Every item on the financial statement is then reported as a percentage of that base.

Vertical Analysis

	2002	%
Sales	$38,303	100.0
Cost of goods sold	19,688	51.4
Gross margin	$18,615	48.6
Total operating expenses	13,209	34.5
Operating income	$ 5,406	14.1
Other income	2,187	5.7
Income before taxes	$ 7,593	19.8
Income taxes	2,827	7.4
Net income	$ 4,766	12.4

Ratio Analysis

Ratios are standard measures that enable analysts to compare companies of different sizes.

Ratio Classification

- **Liquidity**: Can a company pay the bills as they come due?
- **Solvency**: Can the company survive over a long period of time?
- **Profitability**: Can a company earn a satisfactory rate of return?
- **Market indicators**: Is the stock a good investment?

Liquidity: Measuring Ability to Pay Current Liabilities

This ratio measures a company's ability to pay current liabilities with current assets.

Current ratio =
Total current assets ÷ Total current liabilities

Liquidity: Measuring Ability to Pay Current Liabilities

The acid-test ratio shows the company's ability to pay all current liabilities if they come due immediately.

> Acid-test ratio =
> (Cash + Short-term investments
> + Net current receivables)
> ÷ Total current liabilities

Liquidity: Measuring Ability to Pay Current Liabilities

Working capital is not a ratio, but it is often computed to evaluate a the company's ability to pay its current liabilities.

> Working capital =
> Total current assets
> _ Total current liabilities

Liquidity: Measuring Ability to Sell Inventory

This ratio measures how quickly a company is turning over its inventory. A high number indicates an ability to quickly sell inventory.

> Inventory turnover = Cost of goods sold
> ÷ Average inventory

Liquidity: Measuring Ability to Collect Receivables

This ratio measure's a company's ability to collect the cash from its credit customers.

Accounts receivable turnover =
Net credit sales
÷ Average accounts receivable

Solvency: Measuring Ability to Pay Long-term Debt

The debt to equity ratio compares the amount of debt a company has with the amount the owners have invested in the company.

Debt-to-equity ratio =
Total liabilities ÷ Total equity

Solvency: Times interest earned

This ratio compares the amount of income that has been earned in an accounting period to the interest obligation for the same period.

Times interest earned ratio =
Net income + interest expense
÷ Interest expense

Measuring Profitability: Return on assets

This ratio measures a company's success in using its assets to earn income for the persons who are financing the business.

> Return on assets =
> Net income + interest expense
> ÷ Average total assets

Measuring Profitability: Return on Equity

This ratio measures how much income is earned with the common shareholders' investment in the company.

> Rate of return on common stockholders' equity
> = (Net income – preferred dividends)
> ÷ Average common stockholders' equity

Measuring Profitability: Gross Margin Ratio

This ratio measures percentage of sales price that is gross profit. A small shift usually indicates a big change in the profitability of the company's sales.

> Gross margin ratio = Gross margin ÷ Sales

Measuring Profitability: Earnings Per Share

This ratio gives the amount of net income per share of common stock. It is one of the most widely-used measures of a company's profitability.

Earnings per share of common stock
= (Net income − Preferred dividends)
÷ Number of shares of common stock outstanding

Market Indicators: PE Ratio

Price/earning ratio is the ratio of market price per share to earnings per share. This ratio indicates the market price for $1 of earnings.

Price/Earnings Ratio =
Market price per share of common
stock ÷ Earnings per share

Market Indicators: Dividend Yield

Dividend yield gives the percentage of a stock's market value returned as dividends to stockholders each period.

Dividend per share of common
(or preferred) stock ÷ Market price per share
of common (or preferred) stock

Making Ratios Useful

- A ratio by itself does not give much information.
- To be useful, a ratio must be compared to other ratios from previous periods, compared to ratios of other companies in the industry, or compared to industry averages.

11-15